Collector's Guide to Pocket Calculators

by Guy Ball and Bruce Flamm

with additional technical information by Janice Goings-Flamm

First Edition April 1997

Library of Congress Catalog Card Number: 96-090758
ISBN: 1-888840-14-5

Published by:
Wilson/Barnett Publishing
P.O. Box 345 Tustin, CA 92781-0345
USA

Book design by Media Enterprises, Anaheim, California

Preface

If you're over forty, you probably remember your first pocket calculator fondly. It was your ticket to the future. It was an early way to embrace the brand-new, futuristic world of electronics. Man was in space and you had high technology in your hands. No longer were you tied to pen and paper, figuring out some complex arithmatic problem by hand. You could throw away the slide rules. You could leave your heavy desktop adding machine and be....free!

Well, perhaps we're getting carried away here. Yet the advent of the pocket calculator did indeed allow freedom from these "mundane" things. The use of electronics in our everyday society - a new era likened to the Industrial Revolution and the "Machine Age" - followed the growth of this new product. The skyrocketing popularity of the electronic calculator fueled the development of more powerful integrated circuits (ICs) and the refinement of their manufacturing processes. Companies worked at a feverish pace to come out with new advances at a lower price. Engineers tested the boundaries of what they knew and usually came out with better products. In many ways, this book honors the early pioneers of microelectronics - both in the business and engineering fields. Without their innovative efforts, we would not be where we are today.

The Collector's Guide to Pocket Calculators is the work of two authors who have each been collecting early pocket calculators for about 12 years. We've talked with early pioneers in the development and marketing of pocket calculators like Jack Kilby, Jerry Merryman, Joe Sugarman, Ed White -- people who played key roles in something that was very new and would impact all of our lives. We've interviewed businesspeople, engineers, and assembly-line workers who helped bring calculators to our fingertips. We've researched old newspapers and magazines and books and company archival documents. Along the way, we've created many friendships with other collectors who were doing similar things and helped us in our efforts.

In the process, we've uncovered a lot of very good information that we wanted to share with other collectors and with historians of this genre. It's taken us some four years to put it together and we think we've done it well. We realize that this is a "book-in-process" and welcome our readers' efforts to make the next edition even better.

We dedicate this book to those engineers and businessmen who said, "We can do it!"

And most importantly, we dedicate this book to our respective wives, Linda Ball and Janice Goings-Flamm, whose patience and understanding of our "obsession" is greatly appreciated. It reminds us how special they really are!

Guy Ball
Bruce Flamm

Table of Contents

Manufacturer	Page Number

Manufacturer	Page Number

Manufacturer	Page Number

Manufacturer	Page Number

Manufacturer **Page Number**

Manufacturer	Page Number

Concluded on Next Page

Novelty Calculators

Other Nostalgic Items

The History of Pocket Calculators

1960's Sowing the seeds of the calculator revolution

Early 1960's -- Mechanical calculators, slide rules, or paper and pencil are the world's main methods of calculation. As was true in the 1940's and 1950's, early 1960's calculators are complicated electric motor-assisted mechanical adding machines with no other electronic parts. They are called calculators rather than adding machines because complex gear systems allow them to perform multiplication and division by repetitive addition or subtraction. One mechanical model made by Friden is actually able to use gears and levers to extract square roots.

1963 -- Bell Punch Co. LTD and Sumlock-Comptometer LTD of England introduce the "Anita" which is claimed to be the world's first fully electronic desk-top calculator. The machine weighs 33 pounds and uses dozens of vacuum tubes (called valves in England) along with hundreds of other discrete components. Although the Anita is as large as many mechanical models, it is a major breakthrough since it is silent (no moving parts) and very fast. In the USA, the Friden 130 was released at about the same time. It used a CRT (cathode ray tube) television tube - type of display and was also one of the first fully electronic calculators in the world.

1964 -- In March, Japan's Sony Corporation claims to perfect the world's first all-transistorized (no vacuum tube) desk-top electronic calculator. Quite a hit when it was displayed at the 1964 New York World's Fair, their model MD-5 was capable of 8-digit computations and used magnetic (transistorized) switching with a Nixie tube display. Beginning from this R & D development, Sony later improved functional operations and operating systems through several later models before finally deciding several years later that their SOBAX ("solid state abacus") line of desk-top calculators was far less profitable than anticipated. Some of the SOBAX's innovative features included disappearing zeros (to left of displayed digits), floating decimal, the "rounding off" of numbers, percentage computations, and reciprocals. These would eventually become the standards used by literally all other calculators.

1964 -- Victor Business Machines contracts with General Micro-electronics (USA) to develop a metal-oxide semiconductor (MOS), integrated circuit (IC) based desk-top calculator. GMe was never able to resolve enough of their process manufacturing problems to deliver the ICs. (Victor did briefly sell some pocket and portable calculators during the early 1970's, but apparently most were made for them by other companies.)

1964-67 -- The first large electronic desk-top calculators begin to replace electro-mechanical machines. Those models, based on the newest electronic technology, use thousands of transistors, cost thousands of dollars, and weighed 30-60 pounds. Sharp's Compet CS-10A and Canon's Canola 130 are two early electronic calculators among the offerings from over thirty manufacturers in an intense international competition to offer the most advanced product. (In reference to the Sony information above, Sharp also claims to have the first all-transistorized machine.) Meanwhile, some innovators begin to dream about using this technology to build an electronic calculator that would be small enough to hold in your hand.

1965 -- Texas Instruments (USA) begins work on a hand-held calculator, code named "Cal-Tech." It was to be developed as a prototype to show the potential of TI's recently-developed integrated circuits (which were not selling as well as they had hoped). The "Cal-Tech" featured four function calculations (+, -, x, ÷) and used a thermal paper tape printout.

1967 -- North American Rockwell (USA) begins work on MOS ICs for Japan's Sharp Electronics (then named Hayakawa Electric). Sharp's plan was to reduce the electronic requirements of their desk-top calculator to 4 or 5 ICs: possibly leading to smaller and portable electronic calculators. Texas Instrument's "Cal-Tech" prototype calculator was completed in March 1967. TI would use this as a demonstration tool for their IC design and production capability.

1968 -- Hewlett-Packard releases the fully-electronic model 9100 desk-top calculator, priced at $4,900. The 9100 used a CRT (cathode ray tube) display and was about the size of a large typewriter. Bill Hewlett congratulates the development team but allegedly commented that the world needs a similar machine that would fit in a shirt pocket. Amazingly, the HP engineers would accomplish this new challenge within four years (the HP-35 in 1972)!

1969 -- The first Large Scale Integration (LSI) calculator, Sharp's QT-8, began production using IC chips made by Rockwell. The USA debut of this AC-powered, four function calculator, was at an engineering trade show in New York City in March 1970. It sold for $495 at the time. Work continues between Sharp and Rockwell to reduce the size of the calculator towards a smaller, portable unit. A later version of the QT-8 (the QT-8B from 1970) included a rechargeable battery pack in order to make it portable.

1969 -- Impressed with the "Cal-Tech" prototype and Texas Instruments' IC production capability, Canon (Japan) begins work with TI on the electronics for a small, hand-holdable calculator which would be called the "Pocketronic."

1969 -- Busicom (Japan) contracts with both Intel (USA) and Mostek (USA) to develop ICs for an electronic calculator. Intel completes the task with a single microprocessor chip, the 4004, which is used by Busicom for a desk-top electronic calculator. Intel eventually buys back the rights to the 4004 for use in other devices. The modern-day Pentium IC links back to this early calculator chip. Meanwhile, Mostek develops a complete "calculator-on-a-chip" which will be used in Busicom's first hand-held model (Handy LE-120A) later in 1971.

1970's The Pocket Calculator Revolution

1970 -- The first battery-operated "hand-held" calculators are sold. Most are too large to actually be considered "pocket calculators," but they are far smaller than anything seen before. In mid-1970, Sharp begins to sell the QT-8B for $495 which, by using rechargeable batteries, is a portable version of their desk-top QT-8. Canon's "Pocketronic" sales begin in the Fall of 1970 in Japan and February 1971 in the USA. Canon used Texas Instruments' ICs and thermal printer. Selling for just under $400, the "Pocketronic" was a four function, hand-held, printing calculator, with the only display being the printed tape running out of the side of the machine. It looks much like the "Cal-Tech" prototype (see 1965). The unit was rechargeable, used a disposable tape cartridge, and weighed 1.8 lbs. Later that year, Sharp begins to market the EL-8, a "small" hand-holdable calculator with four function calculating power, eight numeric tubes for a display, and rechargeable batteries. Redesigned from the QT-8 series, the unit is smaller and weighs 1.7 lbs. It was marketed in Japan as early as late 1970, but USA advertisements began in February 1971, pricing it at $345. An AC-only version (without the batteries) cost $299.

1970-71 -- Sanyo (Japan) markets a large, portable calculator, the ICC-0081, with four functions, rechargeable nicad batteries, and an eight digit tube display with a flip-up display cover. The unit listed for $425. Sanyo also made a smaller unit (the ICC-802D) for Dictaphone (USA) to sell as the Dictaphone 1680 (in 1970). Sanyo would also label their ICC-804D model as the Dictaphone 1681.

1971 -- In the Fall, Bowmar (USA) begins shipping their first "cigarette pack" sized calculator, the 901B. Priced initially at $240, it was the lowest priced unit on the market and was also one of the smallest. It featured the standard four math functions, an 8 digit red LED display, and rechargeable batteries. The integrated circuit (IC) and Klixon keypad were both made by TI, which was then solely a parts supplier -- not a rival calculator manufacturer. Craig (USA) and Commodore (England) also sold the Bowmar-made calculator under their own labels (as models 4501 and C110 respectively) at the same time. Bowmar, until then a LED maker, introduced this first model to potential distributors at a business trade show in May. Bowmar would go on to become the leading producer and marketer of pocket calculators in the USA before their unfortunate slide into bankruptcy in the mid-1970's. Also in 1971, Busicom (Japan) introduces the Handy LE-120A, the world's smallest hand-held calculator, to that point in time. The LE-120A was almost two-thirds the size of the Bowmar. Brother (Japan), Addo (Sweden), and a few other companies begin making portable models.

1972 -- Scores of companies rush into the pocket calculator business as demand for this amazing new product soars. Prices begin to fall as competition grows. Average price for a basic four function model is down to about $150 by the end of the year. A few models, including those by Casio (Japan), Rapid Data (Canada), and Digitrex (USA), sell for below $100. In January Hewlett Packard introduces their first pocket calculator, the HP-35, the world's first pocket calculator with scientific (transcendental) functions. In June, TI test markets their first calculator, a four function

Datamath (TI-2500), for $149.95, beginning full sales by September. In December of 1972, TI files a patent application for the hand-held calculator (based on the "Cal-Tech") with the inventors listed as Jack Kilby, Jerry Merryman, and James Van Tassel. Due to the introduction of scientific function calculators and the falling prices for calculators in general, the sales of slide rules plummet.

1973-74 -- Competition to produce cheaper pocket calculators reaches a frenzy. Many models begin to sell for under $100. Some calculator companies, unable to reduce their costs enough, are forced out of business.

1974 -- On June 25, 1974, the U.S. Patent office grants Texas Instruments the patent (3,819,921) for a "miniature electronic calculator." However, years of international debate would continue and Japan will not grant TI a similar patent until 1978.

1975 -- The pocket calculator is widely used by students as some simple four function calculators break the $20 price barrier. Controversy flares as some teachers demand that the devices be banned from classrooms for fear that students will not learn math. Almost anyone can now afford a new technology that was not available only five years earlier.

1976 -- Liquid crystal displays (similar to those used in today's pocket calculators) are finally refined and reliable enough for common usage. LCDs had some moderate use on calculators as early as 1972 (see models by Lloyds and Sharp) but manufacturing and reliability issues limited their use. LCD displays use far less current than LED or fluorescent models and allow a pocket calculator to run for months rather than hours without charging or changing batteries. LCD models from 1976-78 can usually be identified by a yellow filter over their display which helped protect them from ultraviolet light. With later improvements in the technology, the filter became unnecessary.

1977 -- The TI-30, perhaps the most common LED scientific calculator ever made is now selling for under $20. LCD models become more common.

1978 -- LCD calculators begin to capture the market with their simple, compact cases and multiple functions. Also, solar-powered calculators are becoming more available. Power-hungry non-LCD models are becoming obsolete. The pocket calculator becomes a common household item as some simple function calculators break the $10 price barrier.

1979 -- Stores begin to liquidate their remaining stock of LED and fluorescent pocket calculators. In July, HP introduces their final LED models along with their first LCD model (the HP-41C). The end of the decade symbolically marks the virtual end of the line for pocket calculators using LED and fluorescent displays.

The "Cal-Tech"

In 1965 Texas Instrument engineers embarked on a project that was the turning point for calculators. TI Lab Director Jack Kilby and two colleagues, Jerry Merryman, and James Van Tassel, began work on a hand-held calculator. Kilby had invented the integrated circuit (IC) at TI in 1958, and he and the company were very interested both in demonstrating how the devices could be used and in broadening the market for them.

The three engineers envisioned building an IC-based, battery-powered "miniature calculator" that could add, subtract, multiply, and divide, yet could fit in the palm of your hand. After two years of development, they completed the first hand-held calculator in 1967. The battery-powered device could accept six-digit numbers, perform the four basic arithmetic functions, and print results as large as 12 digits on a thermal printer. Code-named the "Cal-Tech," the calculator measured about 4.25 by 6.15 by 1.75 inches and weighed 45 ounces. Laid out in discrete components (transistors, resistors, etc.), the electronics within the device filled a large lab bench top. Thanks to TI ingenuity, most of the components were integrated into four ICs.

Shown Above: The first electronic hand-held calculator, the *Cal Tech*, invented at Texas Instruments by Jack S. Kilby, Jerry D. Merryman and James Van Tassel in 1967.

The prototype calculator was shown to a number of business machine and electronic companies. Canon (Japan) became very interested in this new technology; seeing the potential of miniaturized electronics to help fuel their growth in the business machine market.. Their Pocketronic bears a resemblance to the original "Cal-Tech" and even kept its unique, horizontal-path, thermal printing tape system.
The three engineers showed that calculator size could be reduced to fit a person's hand. As more companies saw the potential, a market was created where there was none before. Businesses and consumers loved the convenience of an electronic "personal calculating device." As the calculators shrunk in size and, very quickly, in price, the market grew to mammoth proportions.
Several samples of the "Cal-Tech" were built. One was given to the Smithsonian Institution in Washington, D.C. and another resides at the American Computer Museum in Bozeman, Montana.
(The authors wish to thank the nice folks at Texas Instruments for the Cal-Tech photos and background information.)

The Golden Age of Pocket Calculators

We consider the 1970's to be the "golden age" of pocket calculators for two reasons. First, the original type of pocket calculator (LED or fluorescent-type of display) was developed and manufactured mainly during this single decade. Second, the large number and tremendous variety of early models make them a collector's dream.
In the frenzy of the pocket calculator boom of the early 1970's over 200 companies entered the "great calculator war." By 1980 almost all these firms had either gone bankrupt or gotten out of the calculator business. Today, pocket calculators are made by the few survivors of the 1970's calculator war. Only two U.S. companies (HP and TI) along with a handful of Asian firms (Casio, Sharp, etc.) are still around and making calculators. A glance at the pocket calculator section in any modern department or discount store confirms that only a few manufacturers remain in the business. At many stores the choice is only a TI or a Casio. This was certainly not the case in 1975 when a typical display case might include models made by 10 or even 20 different companies!

The First Portable Electronic Calculators

As far as we know at this point, the calculators listed below were the first portable electronic models on the market. Among these, only the Busicom and the Bowmar could be called "pocket-sized" (and the latter only if you had a big pocket). Information about each model can be found in the main section. The following list is in chronological order of the first appearance in advertising: Sharp QT-8B (7/70), Dictaphone 1680 (10/70), Sharp EL-8 (2/71), Sanyo ICC-0081 (3/71), Canon Pocketronic (4/71), SCM Marchant 1 (4/71), Busicom Handy LE120A (9/71), Bowmar 901B / Craig 4501 / Commodore C110 (10/71), Brother 408 (12/71). Some models may have been mentioned as new products at earlier dates but did not appear in ads until the date mentioned.

Calculator Watches

Ever since the comic strip detective Dick Tracy had his wrist-radio, people have had an envious preoccupation with electronics on their wrists. And as soon as the electronics became small enough, companies rushed to satisfy that craving. In the early 1970's, electronic watches with their red LED faces hit the market. Within a few years, manufacturers went the next step and figured out a way to miniaturize a calculator to fit on your wrist.

We have listed calculator watches (and a lone wrist-calculator without a time feature) under the appropriate manufacturers. In many cases, there is no model number to note, so we simply list the calculator as "calculator watch" or "wrist calculator." The companies making these calculators include: Compu-Chron, Hewlett-Packard, Hughes Aircraft, National Semiconductor, Pulsar, Sinclair, and Uranus. They were made in small quantity because of their initial cost. By the time the prices normally would have fallen and the market would have been flooded with models, the LCD display came into favor. As a result of the limited production, LED calculator watches are difficult to find (especially in good condition) and today are usually priced in the $200-800 range.

Why collect old calculators?

Technology is changing so quickly that machines considered to be miracles one year may be obsolete the next. Hundreds of old calculators are being dumped into the trash every day. The last remaining specimens of some brands may have already vanished. With our collections we hope to preserve a segment of history.

Collecting sports cards has been popular for decades, and in the last few years, it's become a national pastime. Without detracting from those who enjoy such collections, we'd like to point out that it teaches our children to honor and revere those who throw, hit, or catch a ball. Where are the cards honoring the great scientists who made such impacts on our lives? An autographed Albert Einstein would sure be nice! Collecting calculators is one way to honor the engineers who developed this wonderful new technology. Through our hobby some of us have met the inventors of the pocket calculator, one of whom is a Nobel laureate.

In contrast to stamps, coins or baseball cards, we don't know what is yet to be discovered as we collect calculators. Previously unknown models continue to surface adding to the excitement. This hobby is still new enough that rare pocket calculators can still be found at garage sales and flea markets. And one very nice thing is that since pocket calculators are so compact, a sizable collection can be kept in a small closet.

Calculator Collecting -- the thrill of the hunt as "unknown" pocket calculators continue to appear!

This book is, by far, the most comprehensive record of early pocket calculators ever published. But you probably will still find models that are not listed! Even though the authors have a combined experience of over 25 years of calculator hunting, we continue to find previously unknown models. This "thrill of the hunt" makes calculator collecting more interesting than many other traditional and mature collectibles. For example, a collector of U.S. coins will never encounter a coin that has not been fully described in one or perhaps several different books. In contrast, unique calculator models continue to surface every day. Old coins have become so difficult to find in circulation that most collectors have to buy them from dealers. It would be virtually impossible to find a rare penny sitting in the back of your desk drawer.

But this type of thing happens all the time in calculator collecting! Since this is a relatively new collectible, it's still possible to go to a flea market or thrift store and pay a few dollars for a 1970's pocket calculator that is a real "find." For calculator collectors this is a great thrill. For flea market "pickers" with no personal interest in calculators, this is a good way to pick up some extra money.

The Pocket Calculator: An invention that changed the world!

Until 1970, there were few portable methods for accurate and rapid calculation. All of them were mechanical (Addiator, Curta, abacus, slide rule, etc.) and none was convenient for the average consumer. Early electronic calculating devices were large and expensive -- designed mainly for business.

The pocket calculator made math easy for everyone regardless of their education or occupation. In a way, a calculator collection is to this amazing revolution what the fossil record is to paleontology. By studying our collections we can see how the various electronic components evolved and witness "survival of the fittest" first hand. From the hundreds of different styles we learn about industrial design. Some models, such as those from Sinclair, earned design awards for being ahead of their time. From talking with pioneers in the calculator field we learn about innovations in science and technology taking place while a "simple" calculator was being developed. In this last case, the impact is very evident. One particular integrated circuit (the Intel 4004) was developed initially for a calculator and was the seed from which the computer generation was born. From observing the locations of manufacture we learn about international trade. From studying the staggering decline of original sales prices (and the rapid demise of dozens of companies) we learn powerful lessons about business.

Collecting calculators can be a great learning experience. It can also be great fun!

How do you know if it's a 1970's pocket calculator?

There are a few quick ways to tell what era a calculator is from.

1. Modern pocket calculators have a LCD (liquid crystal) display. The numbers on the screen look black on a silver-gray background. In contrast, 1970's models most often have displays that "light up" in some color -- such as red, green, purple, blue, or orange.

If you can't tell about the display color because you don't have batteries handy or maybe the calculator just doesn't work, the next two rules might help.

2. Check to see if it has a "socket" or hole for an AC-adapter plug. Few, if any, did after 1979 due to the use of the LCD display which requires much less power.
3. If the calculator has solar power, it generally is a modern model and too new to be of interest to collectors. Exceptions are very early models like the Royal Solar 1, Teal Photon, and TEC EC-201 which are identifiable by their very large, old style solar cell panel and yellow LCD display.

Where to find pocket calculators

Pocket calculators from the 1970's along with more modern novelty calculators can often be found at flea markets, swap meets, garage sales, boot sales (for our English readers), consignment shops, and thrift stores. Generally they are too new to be found at antique stores (though once this book is out, we wouldn't be surprised to see calculators there). Since new pocket calculators sell for a few dollars, used ones are often priced at $1 or $2. Finding an early Bowmar Brain at a second-hand store with a $2 price-tag is a wonderful feeling! And, since this is a fairly new and less-known hobby, this type of thing happens all the time.

Where to sell or trade pocket calculators

The ***International Calculator Collector***, the newsletter of the International Association of Calculator Collectors (IACC), is a wonderful place to buy, sell, or trade pocket calculators. Membership entitles you to a free classified ad in each quarterly issue. For more information on joining, see the "Other Resources" section below.

Other possible methods of selling your calculators include placing classified ads in mainstream antique newspapers like ***Antique Trader Weekly***, ***Today's Collector***, or ***Maine Antique Digest***. However with this collectible being so new, a general circulation publication may not bring the response desired. Other possibilities include ***Antique Radio Classified*** or ***Nuts and Volts***, both specialized publications to the "electronic" community.

There are a few web sites on the Internet that deal with antiques and collectibles -- some are focused on electronics and computers. Some will take ads from readers. Since their addresses change frequently, we can only list a few (see the "Other Resources" section). You may want to use one of the search engines available to locate these sites.

The authors are also interested in purchasing calculators for their collections. If you have a model you think we'd be interested in, please contact us at the addresses noted in the "Helping Us" section.

Helping Us

Even though we list about 1,500 different models, there are probably a thousand more we haven't documented yet. The authors are always looking for undiscovered models and we would appreciate your help.

We will continue to maintain a calculator database even after this book is published (possibly for a second edition or an addendum). If you find a model not listed in this book, please contact us with detailed information similar to our listings. If possible please send a photo or photo-copy of the calculator's front and back. If you are interested in selling it, please let us know that also so we understand your interest.

We're also looking for any and all historical information such as old advertisements, books, sales flyers, and even personal stories. Please contact us if you can help us with our research in this way.

For brand names beginning with the letters A-L (e.g. APF, Casio, Lloyd's, etc.) contact:

Bruce Flamm, P.O. Box 70513, Riverside, CA, 92513-0513
email: bflamm@ix.netcom.com

For brands that begin with the letters M-Z (e.g. Melcor, Radio Shack, Summit, etc.) contact:

Guy Ball, P.O. Box 345, Tustin, CA, 92781-0345
email: mrcalc@usa.net or mrcalc001@aol.com

Other Calculators

Co-author Bruce Flamm also collects mechanical calculators and large electronic calculators (except models that print on paper tape). He is looking for models with displays which are CRT (like a TV screen) or Nixie tube (large tubes with wire-numbers inside). These were made in the 1960's and early 1970's by companies like Anita, Marchant, SCM, Singer-Friden, Sharp, Sony, Victor and Wang. If you have information about or would like to sell any of these please contact Bruce at the above address.

A Note About Prices

Determining value for a pricing guide is never easy -- especially when there is such a limited secondary market of collectors who might purchase them. In addition, since many calculators are still available from flea markets and thrift stores for just a few dollars, setting a high value might raise some questions in your mind. Indeed, sellers who use the prices stated in this book need to realize that most buyers have probably purchased their last 10 calculators for just a few dollars a piece at local flea markets.

Our estimates are based on many years of experience and reflect the relative scarcity and/or desirability of individual models. We basically asked ourselves, "In a mature market, what would this model be worth?" based on its rarity and uniqueness. In many cases, these values are like "Scott Values" of the stamp collecting world -- a reference for buyers, sellers, and traders. However, in the end, prices will be determined by supply and demand. Our estimated values represent a reasonable negotiation starting point for the buyer and seller.

Condition will alter value. Our estimates are based on calculators in very good condition with no major flaws such as cracks in the case or missing parts. The most common flaw is a missing battery-compartment cover and this generally detracts about 20-30% from the value. Some collectors also want the leather or vinyl carrying case but this does not usually have much effect on pricing. Add 10% if the instruction manual is present. New-In-Box (NIB) specimens may be worth 20-50% more to some collectors.

What about working condition? Many early models have batteries which have leaked or rechargeable batteries which no longer hold a charge. The calculators may have other internal problems and no longer function. The impact on price depends on the collector. Some collectors will only buy working models and others don't care as long as the physical condition is very good.

Many "treasures" are out there just waiting to be found. The collector prices found in this book are not yet common knowledge. Thus, it is still probable that you will find many 1970's pocket calculators in flea markets and thrift stores with $2 to $5 price tags.

"Original" prices, when listed, are often from 1970's newspaper or magazine ads and thus may be retail or special sale prices. The actual introductory manufacturer's price may have been much higher. Prices fell very quickly in the 1970's. A model we list as "1974 price $39" may have actually sold for $129 in 1973 but we may not have that information. The point is not to assume that certain models were "better" than others based on our 1970's pricing data. The 1970's price information is given only as a general guide for its historical interest. Also remember that these prices are in 1970's dollars. Adjusting for inflation, a calculator costing $400 in 1972 would cost about $1,200 today!

Acknowledgments

The authors would especially like to thank Larry Gilbert, Bob King, Gregg Bunch, Janice Goings-Flamm, and Gene Wright who spent many hours reviewing an early proof of this book correcting grammatical and punctuation errors. (Any errors have to be new ones put in by the authors afterwards - these five did too good a job.) They also shared their knowledge of calculators -- advising us on pricing, variations, "missing links," and any other little details we hadn't included. Thanks also to Guy's dad, Howard Ball, who lent his editing expertise to ensure this front section made sense to a lay public (i.e., non-calculator fanatics). We appreciate everyone's help to make this an even better book.

The authors wish to express their appreciation to the following for their help in supplying information on calculators in their collection:

Thomas Brockmeier, Richard Brook, Gregg Bunch, Larry Gilbert, Kenton Green, Palmer Hanson, Fred Hatfield, Howard Hazelcorn, Bob King, Hal Layer, Philippe Leckler, Wlodek Mier-Jedrzejowicz, Peter Muckerman, Bob Otnes, Joe Pfeifer, Peter Sanhen, Robert Slade, Walt Sonnenstuhl, Sigfried Stapf, Frank Travis, Tom Welch, and Gene Wright.

We would like to thank the wonderful people at Hewlett-Packard and Texas Instruments (including Ann Westerlin and CB Wilson) for sharing archival material. Thanks also to Joe Sugarman of JS&A for copies of his calculator ads from the 1970's and the valuable historic data they provide. Our appreciation to Bill Burkett for his help on Sony's early efforts. Our gratitude to John Shea and Chris Crockett for their help with Spiegel data, as well as Len Roberts and Tony Magoulas for the Radio Shack information.

Guy would especially like to take this opportunity to thank the following who have, over the years, donated calculators to a then-fledgling collector. "I have never forgotten my promise to publicly thank you for helping me when I was starting out!

"First and foremost to my father-in-law, Robert Schefcick, who has found some of my nicest (and oddest) calculators in his regular travels to flea markets and garage sales. Also a big thanks to: Cayce and Lyn Kings, Steve Bradley, Eugene Pentecost, Rob and Vivian Richardson, Gary Tindle, Steven Ward, John Mortensen, Kurt Meyers, Emma Waxham, Marie Vu, Brian Smith, Darius Sanders, Ben Resnicoff, Eric Sprik, Joyce Taylor, Larry Teeter, Jim Leslie, Al Mann, Dave Hickman, Owen Marsh, Ron Olinger, Stephen Servin-Leete, Kevin Dodd, Jim Kern, Mike Ogan, Adele Greenwood, Paul Livio, Leo Johnson, Don Van Buskirk, Jim Temple, Jack Stafford, Souheil Abu Mrad, Ghassan Maalouli, Robert Narumi, Jose Tavares, Buzz Bester, Joseph Farb, John Richardson, Gordon Richardson, Chuck Wright, Dave Zarnow, Roger Burke, John Heisner, Kin Mar, Peter Drake, Scott Leslie, Greg Sypherd, Stu Gibson, Rich and Barbara Compeau, Maurice Yan, Terry and Barbara Sihilling, Brian Driscoll, David and Jacqui Rudge, Jack Cole, Bill Neal, Bob Chatterson, Gina Tindle, and Gary Benanti.

"During my early years of research, special background information was provided by Sally Merryman (Texas Instruments), John Campbell (Texas Instruments), Peter Behrendt (Craig), J. Michael Rockwell (Heath), Edward White (Bowmar), Lou Dubuque (Dictaphone), Ed Roberts (M.I.T.S.), and Darius Sanders. Thanks to all for their help!"

Other Resources

Internet Sites

International Association of Calculator Collectors

The IACC has two web sites featuring a variety of information relating to collecting calculators:
http://www.bath.ac.uk/~masres/calcs.html
http://www.geocities.com/SiliconValley/park/7227

Hewlett-Packard Calculator Museum

An extensive site produced by Dave Hicks which offers detailed information (including photographs) of every HP calculator made. Excellent reference source for HP collectors.
http://www.teleport.com/~dgh/hpmuseum.html

Calculating Machines

Excellent site produced by Erez Kaplan dealing with many of the earlier types of calculating machines dating back to the 1600s and up to the 1970s.
http://www.webcom.com/calc/

Commercial Dealers of Calculators

Collectric (Tom Welch)
http://www.collectric.com
D'Antiques (Dan Dotson)
http://www.dantiques.com/at10.htm

Books

A Guide to HP Handheld Calculators and Computers

by Wlodek Mier-Jedrzejowicz, Ph.D. $22.95. ISBN # 1-888840-00-5. Available through Wilson/Barnett Publishing, P.O. Box 345, Tustin, CA, 92781-0345, USA.
(Other books will be available in 1997 from Wilson/Barnett Publishing on the subject of calculators. Contact them at the address above for their latest listing.)

Organizations

International Association of Calculator Collectors (IACC).

This is the only organization in the world devoted to the collection and study of all types of calculators. Most members collect pocket electronic calculators from the

1970's but others specialize in slide rules or mechanical calculators. Yearly membership in 1997 is $16/yr. in the US, $20/yr. for other countries. For additional information, contact IACC, P.O. Box 345, Tustin, CA 92781-0345, USA. A sample issue costs $3.

Key to abbreviations:

Functions:

4-funct = 4 basic mathematical functions (addition, subtraction, multiplication, division)

sci-funct = scientific or engineering functions (logarithmic and trigonometric functions such as log, sine, and cosine and usually memory, square, pi, etc.)

mem = memory

% = percent function

exp = exponent

paren = parentheses

pi = pi value

recip = reciprocal

sgn chg = sign change

sq rt = square root

sq funct = square functions (including square and square root)

Battery Type:

button rep batt = very small, disk-shaped, replaceable batteries commonly termed button-types, used mainly in LCD models.

rep batt = replaceable batteries (such as 9V, AA, C, and N size batteries)

rep batt pack = replaceable batteries in a removable pack

sealed batt = rechargeable batteries sealed in the case

sealed batt pack = rechargeable batteries in a removable pack

Display Type:

COS-LCD = Early Liquid Crystal Display from Sharp. COS stood for Crystal-on-Substrate (also seen as Calculator-on-Substrate). This display was used as early as October 1973 but eventually was phased out by Sharp for reasons presently unknown.

fluor = fluorescent display containing all digits sealed in a single tube. The term "fluor" is generically used to denote other types of non-gray, colored displays including the orange Panaplex® used by a few calculator manufacturers.

LCD = Liquid Crystal Display, a flat, gray-type of display type that uses less power and was embraced by calculator makers by the end of the 1970's. Some calculators with early versions of this type of display (used in the early 1970s by manufacturers such as Rockwell and Sharp) are included in this guide.

LED = Light Emitting Diode display (usually red although sometimes a purple filter was used to color the display). LEDs often have small half bubble-like covers over the digits (which magnify the display).

tube or mini-tube = separate "fluorescent" tube for each digit of display.

yellow LCD = Early LCDs had a reliability problem with ultra-violet light and manufacturers used a yellow-colored filter over the normally gray display to remedy that. Refinements in later LCD designs removed the need for the filter.

Other Information:

Klixon keypad = Texas Instruments Klixon® keypad was one of the earliest key pads and used greatly by Bowmar and a few other early calculator makers. It had the four basic functions and used metal key pads about 1/2" square.

Japan (for example) = country of manufacture as stated on calculator

RPN = Reverse Polish Notation, a method of calculating and user data entry used by HP calculators. A few other manufacturers also used RPN in more limited scale.

"aka" (also known as) is used when there is another name or model variation on the calculator.

"c" (for example, c1973) is used as "circa," denoting at approximately that time.

Calculator Listing

Abatron

Brand name of Business Electronics, Ltd. of the UK. For Abatron 800 see Peripheral Magnetics.

803 4-funct red LED, 2-AA rep batt, 3.0x6.0", thin, unusual keypad, UK, value $70-85.

ACC

811A 4-funct, mem, %, sq rt, fluor, 4-AA rep batt, 3.5x5.25", interesting 2-tone case, Taiwan, c1974, value $30-$40.

Accuron

831M 4-funct, mem, 5-AA rep batt, 3.0x5.2", value $35-45.

Addo

Addo, a Swedish calculator company made electro-mechanical models in the 1960's.

9218 4-funct, %, paper-tape display, sealed batt, 4.25x6.75", almost identical models are the Facit 1140 and Radio Shack EC-3000, c1972, Sweden, value $50-75.

9364 *aka Addo-X*, 4-funct, tube display, sealed batt, 4.0x6.0", over 2" thick, a very early "hand-held" model almost identical to the ground-breaking Sharp EL-8, Japan, c1971, value $200-300.

Adler

European company connected with (possibly division of) Royal Typewriter. Many models had a unique sliding back cover made of metal, which covered the battery compartment.. Also see Triumph/Adler.

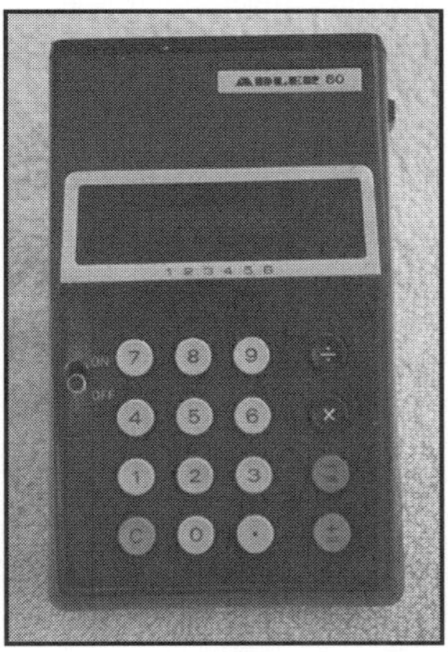

60 4-funct, 6 digit green fluor, 4-AA rep batt pack, 4.0x6.0", Japan, value $40-50.

80 *aka EC-10*, 4-funct, red LED, sealed batt, 3.75x6.0", round keys, Japan, value $35-45.

80C *aka EC21 or EC21B*, 4-funct, %, 4-AAA rep batt, 3.0x4.75", 1975 price $49.95, the EC21 version has a red LED display and a constant switch and is valued at $40-50, the EC21B version has a green fluor display and is valued at $30-40

81 *aka EC11*, 4-funct, mem, %, red LED, 3-AA rep batt, 3.0x4.75", looks like 80C, round keys, 1974 price $105, England, value $45-55.

81C *aka EC23B*, 4-funct, mem, %, sgn chg, green fluor, 4-AAA rep batt, 3.0x4.75", looks like 80C, value $35-45.

81S *aka EC24A*, 4-funct, mem, %, sq rt, sgn chg, pi, green fluor, 4-AAA rep batt, 3.0x4.75", looks like 80C, 1975 price $69, Japan, value $35-45.

82M 4-funct, metric conversions, green fluor, 4-AAA rep batt, 3.0x4.75", c1974, looks like 80C, Japan, value $45-55.

84F *aka EC27*, financial funct, mem, green fluor, 4-AAA rep batt, 3.0x4.75", looks like 80C, Japan, value $45-55.

121C *aka EC29*, 4-funct, mem, %, sq rt, 12 digit green fluor, 4-AA rep batt, 3.5x6.0", large version, looks like 80C, Japan, value $45-55.

Advanced Electronics

Advanced Electronics Corporation; Salt Lake City, Utah (USA) was a very small and little known calculator manufacturer that may only have produced one model in the 1972-73 time frame.

AEC 455 sci-funct, 12 digit red LED, 3-AA rep batt, 3.5x6.0", black color, 36 keys, key caps labeled with printed stickers, internal circuit board was handwired with multi-colored wire, c1973-74, USA, value $60-70.

Afco

Logo seen on JCE. See JCE.

Alco

Alco Marketing; Flushing, New York, USA.

888 *aka Alcor 888*, 4-funct, fluor, 3-AA rep batt, 3.0x5.5", c1973, value $35-45.

895 sci-funct, fluor, sealed batt, 3.0x5.5", c1973, value $45-55.

Mickey Math 4-funct, red LED, 4-AA rep batt, case shaped like Mickey Mouse. One of the most unusual pre-LCD calculators, Japan, value $75-100.

Alectronica

Actual company name may be different due to lack of information and translation difficulties based on the model below.

8 4-funct, %, sq rt, sgn chg, green fluor, 2-AA rep batt, 3.25x5.5", only known model with Arabic lettering - no English, possibly designed for Saudi Arabia, display reads out in Arabic characters, value $90-100.

American

USA company.

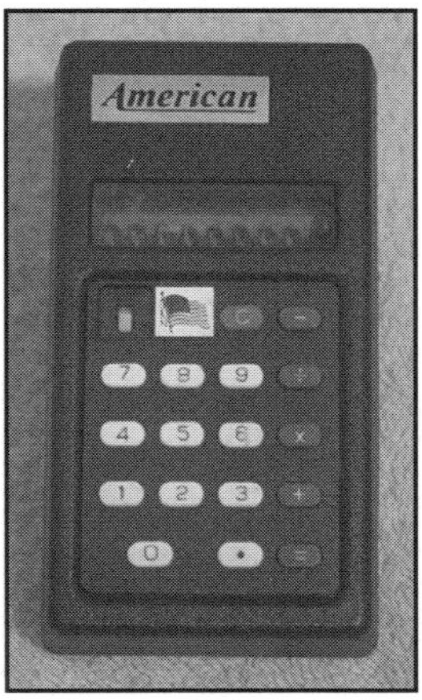

American 4-funct, red LED, sealed batt, matte black case, c1974, value $35-45.

American-1776 4-funct, red LED, sealed batt, has American flag logo, probably made for US Bicentennial, 1976 price $7.95, value $35-45.

L180 4-funct, red LED, 9V rep batt, 2.5x4.6", black case, USA, value $40-50.

M-26 4-funct, mem, %, red LED, 9V rep batt, 2.5x4.5", same case as Summit SM20, black color, USA, value $35-45.

AML

LE8C 4-funct, mem, %, fluor, 4-AA rep batt, 2.75x5.5", keyboard similar to Craig 4509B, Japan, value $60-75.

Anita

Brand name used by British-based Sumlock Comptometer, Ltd. for their calculator line.

811 *version 1,* 4-funct, mem, %, red LED, 3-AAA rep batt, 2.75x4.75", has a metal back cover which slides up, similar to Adler models, unique round keys, very stylish, England, value $60-70.

811 *version 2,* 4-funct, mem, red LED, 2 button rep batt, 2.5x4.5", similar functions to version 1 but case is thinner and keys are rectangular.

APF

APF Electronics Inc. New York, NY (USA). Most of their models were made in the Orient. Most APF models used fluorescent displays; a few had red LEDs (and are thus more sought after). Their model numbering system is a collector's dream. Models were given consecutive integer numbers. Models up to 10 were listed in Roman numerals and then Arabic numerals were used. Each number is preceded by the word, "Mark." Model numbers below 20 are the least common.

Mark V 4-funct, fluor, 4-C rep batt, 4.75x7.5", flip-up cover over display, battery meter, separate slide switches for constant and decimal place, folding handle, a true classic, 1973 price $100, Japan, value $60-75.

Mark VI 4-funct, mem, %, fluor, 4-AA rep batt, 4.5x6.0", 1973 price $89.95, Japan, value $45-55.

Mark 10 4-funct, mem, %, fluor, 4-AA rep batt, 4.5x6.75", like Mark VI but with display tilted toward viewer, 1974 price $79, Japan, value $45-55.

Mark 14 4-funct, mem, %, red LED, 6-AA rep batt, 3.25x5.25", boxy case, similar to early Bowmar, has "D" button to restore display, 1974 price $69.95, one of few APF's made in USA, value $75-85.

Mark 15 4-funct, %, red LED, 9V rep batt, 3.0x5.5", like Mark 14 it was one of few APF's actually made in USA, c1974, value $45-55.

Mark 21 4-funct, mem, %, fluor, sealed batt, 3.0x6.25", Japan, value $20-30.

Mark 22 sci-funct, fluor, sealed batt, 3.0x6.25", same case as Mark 21, 1977 price $24.95, looks like Mark 21, Japan, value $20-30.

Mark 23 4-funct, sq rt, mem, fluor, sealed batt, 3.0x6.25", same case as Mark 21, c1974, looks like Mark 21, Japan, value $20-30.

Mark 24 4-funct, mem, %, sgn chg, red LED, 9V rep batt, 3.0x6.0", Japan, value $20-30.

In 1970-72, most of the first calculator companies built their models in their own factories. As time when on and prices became very competitive, companies moved production lines to Asian countries with lower priced labor.

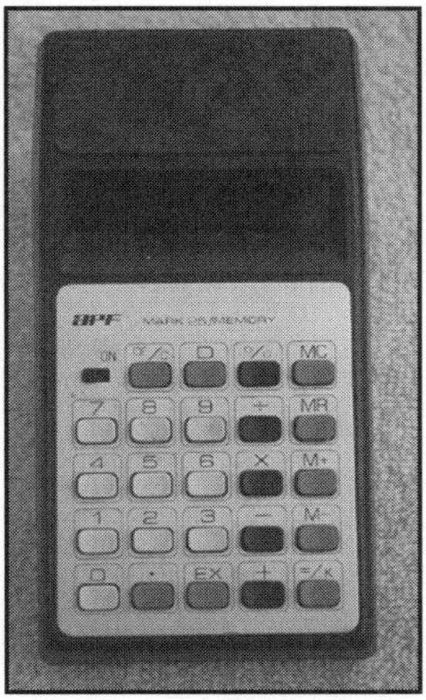

Mark 25 4-funct, %, mem, fluor, 9V rep batt, 3.0x5.5", fake burl-wood, 1975 price $29.95, Japan, value $20-30.

Mark 26 4-funct, %, mem, red LED, 9V rep batt, 2.5x4.5", 1975 price $22.85, Japan, value $20-30.

Mark 27 4-funct, %, mem, fluor, 9V rep batt, 3.0x5.0", unusual white plastic case, c1973, Japan, value $20-30.

Mark 28 4-funct, %, mem, fluor, 9V rep batt, 2.5x4.5", c1973, looks like Mark 26 but not LED, Japan, value $20-30.

Mark 30 4-funct, %, mem, fluor, 9V rep batt, 3.0x5.5", fake burl-wood, 1975 price $39.95, looks like Mark 25, Japan, value $25-35.

Mark 31 4-funct, sq rt, mem, fluor, 9V rep batt, 3.0x5.5", 1976 price $24.95, looks like Mark 25, Japan, value $25-30.

When a 1970's era price is given, multiply it by 3. That will give you the approximate cost in today's prices.

Mark 32 4-funct, sq rt, mem, red LED, 9V rep batt, 3.0x5.0", c1973, looks like Mark 27, Japan, value $25-35.

Mark 34 4-funct, sq rt, mem, fluor, 9V rep batt, 2.75x5.5", 1978 price $15.95, Japan, value $25-35.

Mark 40 4-funct, %, red LED, 9V rep batt, 2.5x4.5", same as Mark 26 but no mem, 1975 price $16.85, looks like Mark 26, Japan, value $20-30.

Mark 41 4-funct, %, sq rt, red LED, 9V rep batt, 2.5x4.5", looks like Mark 26, Hong Kong, value $20-30.

Mark 42 4-funct, %, sq rt, red LED, 9V rep batt, 2.5x5.0", Hong Kong, value $30-40.

Mark 43 4-funct, %, red LED, 9V rep

batt, 2.5x4.5", similar to Mark 40 but strange keypad, looks like Mark 26, Japan, value $20-30.

Mark 50 sci-funct, mem, fluor, 9V rep batt, 3.0x5.5", 1975 price $29.99, looks like Mark 21, Japan, value $20-30.

Mark 51 sci-funct, mem, fluor, 9V rep batt, 3.0x5.5", looks like Mark 21, Japan, value $25-35.

Mark 55 sci-funct, conversions, red LED, sealed batt, 3.0x6.25", 1977 price $59.85, looks like Mark 21, Japan, value $20-30.

Mark 56 sci-funct, red LED, sealed batt, 3.0x6.0", 1977 price $59.85, looks like Mark 21, Japan, value $25-35.

Mark 60 4-funct, %, red LED, 9V rep batt, 2.5x4.5", Japan, value $20-30.

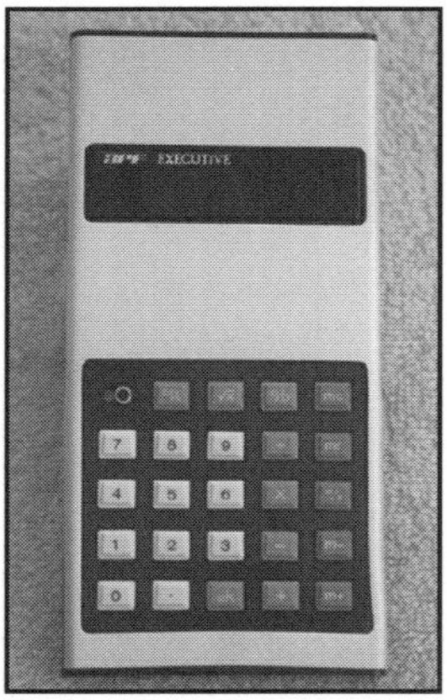

Mark 61 *aka Executive*, 4-funct, sq rt, mem, fluor, sealed batt, 2.75x5.5", thinnest known APF (0.5"), aluminum case with natural color, 1977 price $19.85, Japan, value $25-35.

Mark 61S *aka Executive*, 4-funct, sq rt, mem, fluor, sealed batt, 2.75x5.5", same as Mark 61 except in black color, Japan, value $35-45.

Mark 62 4-funct, sq rt, %, red LED, 9V rep batt, 2.5x5.0", Hong Kong, value $35-40.

Mark 64 4-funct, sq rt, mem, red LED, 9V rep batt, 2.5x5.0", looks like Mark 62, at least two keypad variations exist, Hong Kong, value $35-40.

Mark 65 4-funct, mem, %, sq rt, fluor, 3-AAA rep batt, 2.75x5.0", 1977 price $13.85, value $35-45.

Mark 65R 4-funct, mem, %, sq rt, fluor, sealed batt, 2.75x5.0", same as Mark 65 except the 65R has a sealed batt, 1977 price $18.95, looks like Mark 65, Japan or Hong Kong, value $25-35.

Mark 66R 4-funct, mem, %, sq funct, recip, paren, fluor, sealed batt, 2.75x5.0", Sears catalog 1977 price $21.85, looks like Mark 65, Hong Kong, value $35-45.

Mark 68R sci-funct, fluor, sealed batt, 2.75x5.0", Sears catalog 1977 price $26.85, looks like Mark 65, value $40-50.

Mark 70 4-funct, %, mem, fluor, 9V rep batt, 3.0x5.0", c1974, looks like Mark 27, Japan, value $35-45.

Mark 72 4-funct, sq rt, mem, red LED, 9V rep batt, 2.75x5.5", looks like Mark 34, Hong Kong, value $25-35.

Mark 73 *aka B-5000M*, 4-funct, mem, %, red LED, 9V rep batt, 3.0x5.0", Hong Kong, value $20-30.

Mark 74 4-funct, mem, %, sgn chg, red LED, 9V rep batt, 3.0x5.5", looks like Mark 34, Hong Kong, value $30-40.

Mark 82 4-funct, %, red LED, 9V rep batt, 2.5x5.25" Japan, value $25-35.

Mark 84 4-funct, mem, %, red LED, 9V rep batt, 2.5x5.25", 1977 price $11.85, Japan, value $25-35.

Mark 85 4-funct, mem, fluor, 3-AAA rep batt, 2.75x5.0", looks like Mark 65, Japan, value $25-35.

Mark 86 4-funct, sq rt, mem, fluor, 3-AAA rep batt, 2.75x5.0", 1976 price $19.85, looks like Mark 65, Japan, value $25-35.

Mark 88 sci-funct, mem, fluor, 3-AAA rep batt, 2.75x5.0", 1976 price $24.85, looks like Mark 65, Japan, value $25-40.

Mark 90 sci-funct, red LED, sealed batt, 3.0x6.0", 1977 price $79.95, Japan, value $45-55.

RS-1 *aka Kel-Co*, 4-funct, %, horse race handicapping calculator, red LED, 9V rep batt, 2.75x5.5", very similar to Cannella RS1, Hong Kong, value $30-40.

RS-2 *aka Trotting/pacing computer and Kel-co by APF*, 4-funct, horse race handicapping calculator, red LED, 9V rep batt, looks like Mark 34, Hong Kong, value $35-45.

Apollo

Apollo; Des Plaines, Illinois USA.

ARC-8200NC 4-funct, red LED, 9V rep batt, 3.0x5.5", unusual case style, c1972, USA, value $70-85.

Argyle

Apparently a brand name for calculators made for and sold by Spiegel, a catalog marketing company out of Chicago, Illinois (USA).

Mark III 4-funct, red LED, sealed batt, 3.25x5.25", c1972, thick, boxy, early style, Japan, value $60-80.

Aries

Aries; Peabody, Massachusetts (USA). Made calculator kits for home hobbyists.

AR-420 4-funct, red LED, sealed batt, 3.0x4.75", membrane type keypad, available as kit, 1973 price $99, USA, value $50-60.

Aristo

West German drafting and engineering equipment company with very unique styles. Aristo also made slide rules. Their models sold mainly in Europe.

M27 4-funct, red LED, 2.5x3.5", c1973, West Germany, value $85-95.

M36 4-funct, mem, %, red LED, 3-AA rep batt, 2.5x3.5", c1973-74, West Germany, value $85-95.

M64 4-funct, mem, %, sq rt, red LED, 3-AA rep batt, 2.5x6.0", c1973, West Germany, value $75-95.

M65 4-funct, mem, %, sq funct, sgn chg, recip, red LED, 3-AA rep batt, 2.5x3.5", c1973-74, West Germany, value $85-95.

M75 sci-funct, red LED, 3-AA rep batt, 2.5x6.0", c1974, West Germany, value $70-90.

M80 sci-funct, red LED, 3-AA rep batt, 2.5x6.0", c1973-74, West Germany, value $85-95.

M85 sci-funct, red LED, 3-AA rep batt, 3.0x6.0", wider than others, c1973-74, West Germany, value $95-110.

Atlas

European brand which may have been made by MBO.

> ***The battle of whether or not to allow pocket calculators in the class room raged-on well into the 1980's. Many math teachers felt that children would learn only how to press buttons.***

R300A 4-funct, mem, %, sq funct, pi, paren, sgn chg, green fluor, 2-AA rep batt, 3.25x5.5", value $45-55.

Atlas Rand

Atlas-Rand brand calculators were made by Keystone Electronics (USA). See the Keystone listing for further information. Case styles similar to Keystone and Berkey

240 4-funct, %, fluor, 4-AA rep batt, 3.25x5.25", same case as 260 except uses rep batt, USA, value $20-30.

260 4-funct, %, fluor, sealed batt, 3.25x5.25", same case as 240 except uses sealed batt, USA value $35-45.

Aurora

DC10 4-funct, mem, %, 10 digit fluor, 2-D rep batt, 6.5x6.75", Taiwan, value $30-40.

Bashaw

Bashaw Industries; Fairfield, New Jersey, (USA).

101 *aka Mathematician*, 4-funct, mem, %, red LED, 2-AA rep batt, 3.0x5.0", c1973, USA, value $45-55.

Berkey

Keystone Electronics (USA) made calculators under the Berkey nameplates. See Keystone for additional information. Model 100 notes "Berkey/Omega" - the Omega significance is unknown.

100 4-funct, %, fluor, 4-AA rep batt, 3.25x5.25", USA, value $45-55.

350 4-funct, orange fluor, 4-AA rep

batt, 3.25x5.25", 1974 price $95, USA, value $35-45.

4030 sci-funct, fluor, 4-AA rep batt, 3.5x6.75", unusual styling, USA, value $45-55.

Binatone

Super-thin 4-funct, mem, sq rt, green fluor, sealed batt, 2.75x4.75", all-metal case, apparently sold in England, identical to Concept Super-thin, value $55-65.

Bohn

The Bohn Rex-Rotary Company originally made rotary mechanical calculators. In the early 1970's they produced a few electronic calculators that were small enough to fit in a coat pocket.

Instant 4-funct, green-tube display, 5-AA rep batt, 4.0x6.5", blue case, c1972, Taiwan, value $25-35.

Omnitrex 4-funct, %, green-tube display, 5-AA rep batt, 4.0x6.5", 1973 price $100, two-tone case, Taiwan, value $35-40.

Omnitrex M 4-funct, mem, green-tube display, 5-AA rep batt, 4.0x6.5", two-tone case, 1974 price $79.95, Taiwan, value $35-40.

Omnitrex SR1 4-funct, mem, %, sq funct, recip, green-tube display, sealed batt, 4.0x6.5", case similar to Omnitrex M, 1974 price $99.95, Taiwan, value $40-50.

Bohsei

Marketer of very inexpensive calculators.

DT10 4-funct, mem, %, green fluor, 2-D rep batt, 6.25x6.75", similar to Aurora DC-10 and others, Taiwan, value $15-25.

In the late 1960's Sharp introduced its CS line of "portable" Nixie®-tube display calculators. Although they required a 110V power source, they featured a fold out handle and were about the size of a small typewriter. In 1971, Sharp introduced the EL-8, one of the first hand-held calculators.

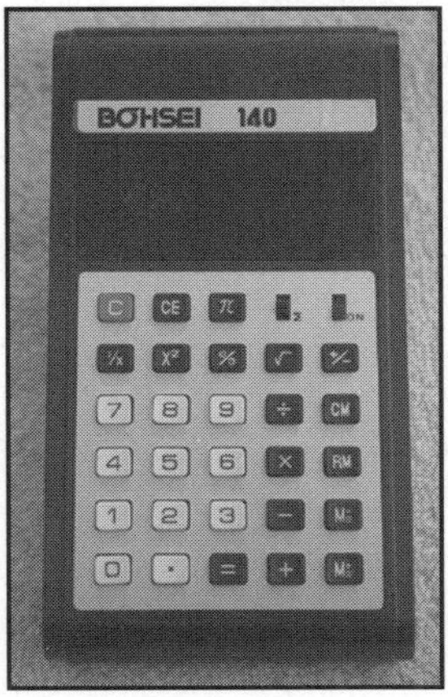

140 4-funct, mem, %, sq funct, recip, sgn chg, pi, green fluor, 2-AA rep batt, 3.25x6.0", Japan, value $35-45.

1000 4-funct, mem, %, sq rt, recip, green fluor, 2-AA rep batt, 3.0x5.25", 1978 price $7.99, Hong Kong, value $10-15.

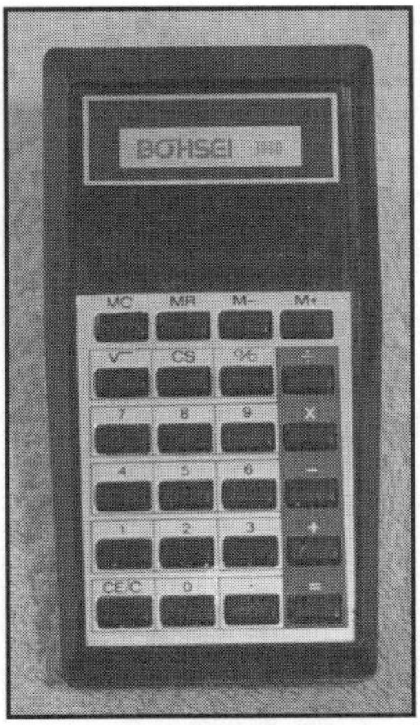

3000 4-funct, mem, %, red LED, 9V rep batt, 2.75x5.25", cheap little model, same case as Nobility 3000, Tronica 3000 and Janon 3000, 1978 price $7.99, Hong Kong, value $5-10.

Boots

English brand sold through a drug store/department store chain of the same name.

425 *aka 425 Scientific*, sci-funct, fluor, 2-AA rep batt, 3.25x5.5", on back of unit the labeling indicates model was a Casio FX31, Japan value $45-55.

Bowmar

To many, the "Bowmar Brain" is synonymous with the early pocket electronic calculator. Originally an LED manufacturer, Bowmar/Ali, Inc., found they could not sell components to Japanese electronic calculator makers. In early 1971 they began plans to manufacture portable calculators for sale by other marketing companies. In September 1971 they modified their plans and began shipping a hand-held model under their nameplate. By 1972 they were reputed to be the world's largest producer. Their early models were also produced for other companies (Craig, Sears, Radio Shack, etc.) For example, the Craig 4501 is a Bowmar 901B with a Craig label on it. These early models are the most desirable. While early Bowmar models were made in the USA, some later production runs were made both in the USA and in Mexico.

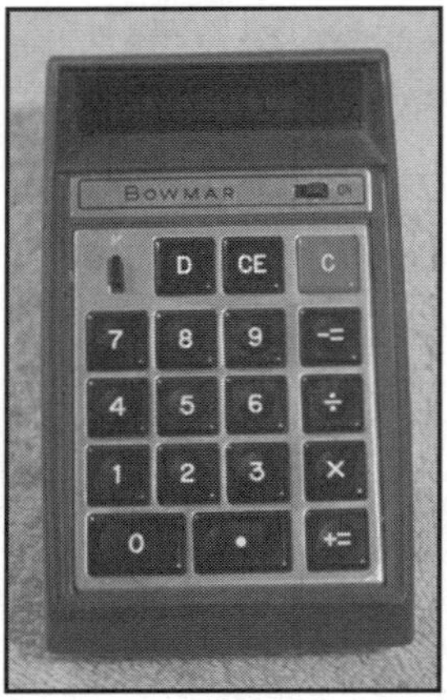

901B 4-funct, red LED, sealed batt, 3.0x5.0", the original Bowmar "pocket" calculator, Klixon keypad, fall 1971 price $240, USA, value $55-65.

901D *aka Bowmar 10*, 4-funct, 10 digit red LED, sealed batt, 3.0x5.0", same case as 901B except for white and black colors, 1972 price $150, USA, value $80-100.

The first scientific calculator, the HP-35, was made in 1972 by test equipment maker Hewlett-Packard, after co-founder Bill Hewlett decided he wanted a "small computer" that could fit in your shirt pocket.

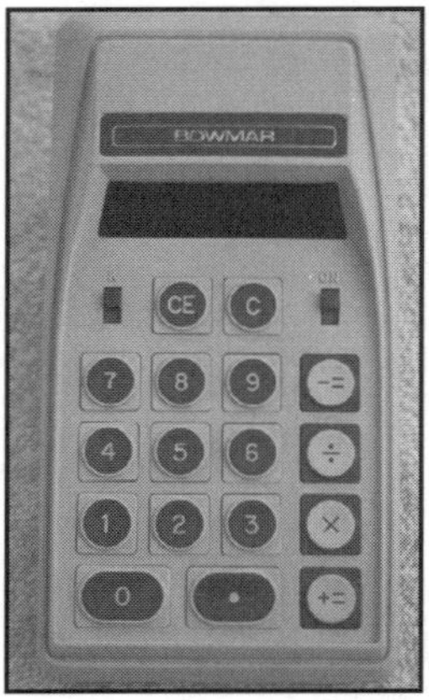

905 4-funct, red LED, sealed batt, 3.0x6.0", sloped case, tan color, 1972 price $99.95, USA, value $40-50.
90112 see MX8.

90506 4-funct, %, red LED, sealed batt, 3.0x6.0", slope case like 905, variations: one example has Klixon keypad - one does not, c1972, USA, value $55-65

90512 4-funct, red LED, sealed batt, 3.0x6.0", sloped case like 905 but black, c1972, one example of the 90512 has a "Century Mark IV" logo on the front, USA, value $45-55.

90911 4-funct, red LED, 3-AA rep

batt, 2.75x6.0", fold-back cover, c1972, Mexico, value $35-45.

91801 *see MX40.*

91802 *see MX40.*

MX8 *aka 90112*, 4-funct, red LED, sealed batt, 3.0x5.0", same case as 901B, differences unknown, possibly just a new number series for the 901B, c1973, value $55-65.

MX10 *aka 90150*, 4-funct, 10 digit red LED, sealed batt, 3.0x5.0", same white case as 901D, differences unknown, possibly just a new number series for the 901D, c 1973, value $65-75.

MX20 *aka 90901 or Brainchild*, 4-funct, red LED, 3-AA rep batt, 2.75x6.0", same black case as 90911, fold-back cover, 1973 price $59.95, value $45-55.

MX25 4-funct, %, red LED, 3-AA rep batt, 2.75x6.0", same black case as 90911, fold-back cover, 1975 price $35, Mexico, value $45-55.

MX40 aka 91801 and 91802, 4-funct, red LED, sealed batt, 3.0x6.0", 2 color variations - 91801 was red and 91802 was yellow, although there appears to be an all-red case and a red and black case both numbered 91801 in addition to yellow and yellow and black case both numbered 91802, sloped case like 905, Klixon keypad, 1973 price $79.95, USA or Mexico, value $35-45.

MX50 *aka 90505*, 4-funct, %, red LED, sealed batt, 3.0x6.0", sloped case similar to 905 but has chrome edge, 1973 price $99, USA, value $35-45.

MX55 4-funct, %, red LED, sealed batt, 3.0x6.0", sloped case like 905, one example of the MX55 has a "Century Mark IV" logo on the front, 1974 price $69, USA or Mexico, value $35-45.

MX60 4-funct, %, red LED, 3-AA rep batt, 3.0x6.0", sloped case like 905, Klixon keypad, 1973 price $89.95, USA, value $40-50.

MX61 *aka 90601*, 4-funct, %, red LED, 3-AA rep batt, 3.0x6.0", sloped case like 905, Klixon keypad, silver case, USA, value $45-55.

MX70 *aka 90701*, 4-funct, mem, red LED, sealed batt, 3.0x5.25", boxy shape reminiscent of 901B, 1973 price $129.95, USA, value $35-45.

MX75 *aka 90705*, 4-funct, mem, red LED, sealed batt, 3.0x5.25", Klixon keypad, looks like MX70, USA, 1974 price $99.95, value $35-45.

MX80 *aka 90152*, 4-funct, mem, 10 digit red LED, sealed batt, 3.0x5.25", Klixon keypad, looks like MX70, 1973 price $119.95, USA, value $35-45.

MX90 4-funct, mem, %, sq rt, recip, sgn chg, red LED, sealed batt, 3.0x5.25", 1974 price $80, looks like MX70, USA, value $45-55.

MX100 *aka 92001 or MX100-2*, sci-funct, mem, red LED, sealed batt, 3.0x5.25", looks like MX70, 1974 price $179, USA, value $35-45.

MX120 *aka Super Brain*, sci-funct, red LED, 3-AA rep batt, 3.0x6.0", same black case as 90911, fold-back cover, value $50-60.

By 1975, pocket calculators with scientific functions were hot items on college campuses but few high school students could afford them. The TI-30 introduced in 1976 at about $25. changed that. It became the world's best-selling scientific LED calculator.

MX140 sci-funct, mem, red LED, sealed batt, 3.0x5.25", has 2 separate function keys, 1974 price $160, looks like MX70, USA or Mexico, value $45-55.

Century Mark IV *see MX55 and 90512.*

Count 4-funct, mem, %, sgn chg, sq rt, blue fluor, sealed batt, 3.0x5.5", thin metal case, looks like Rockwell 24MS, only known non-standard Bowmar design, possibly a final model produced after company was in bankruptcy or receivership, Taiwan, value $50-60.

Math Mate 1 4-funct, %, red LED, approx. 3.0x6.0", blue keys, labeled "math mate" on front - model number not available, value $50-60.

Math Mate 2 4-funct, mem, %, red LED, approx. 3.0x6.0", brown keys, labeled "math mate" on front - model number not available, value $50-60.

Bradford

Information about Bradford is minimal. The brand may have been the "house-brand" for a now-defunct USA department store - W.T. Grants, which used the Bradford name on their house-brand items.

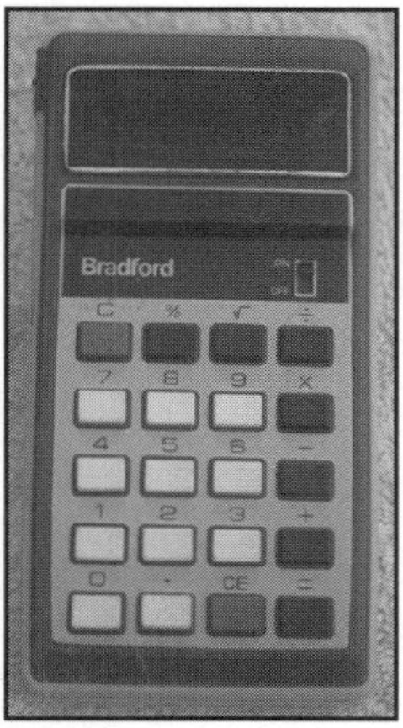

8DPS 4-funct, %, sq rt, green fluor, 2-AA rep batt, 3.0x5.5", same case as Craig 4521, Japan, value $40-50.

Braun

German conglomerate and electronics company.

ET-23 4-funct, mem, %, sq rt, sgn chg, fluor, sealed batt, 3.0x5.75", black, very stylish, Germany, value $75-100.

Brother

Well-known in the 1970's for their sewing machines and electric typewriters. For a short time, Brother International Corp. also made some interesting electronic calculators. Some of the first Brother models have the word "Pro-Cal" in front of the model number. Although modern pocket calculators are mass-produced and cost only a few dollars, in the early 1970's these machines were the epitome of expensive state-of-the-art technology. This is reflected in the fact that many Brother labels state, "Your new Brother calculator is of the finest precision construction, manufactured under rigid quality control in some of the world's most modern factories."

408 4-funct, 9-tube display, 7.2v sealed batt, 4.25x7.0", large rocker-type power switch, massive (over 2" thick), spring-recoil keys, first sold in 1971, probably Brother's first model, 1972 price $300, Japan, value $45-55.

408AX 4-funct, green fluor, 5-AA rep batt, 3.75x6.0", separate overflow and neg. display, c1972, Japan, value $45-55.

Slide rules were still the main method of calculation in college class rooms in the early 1970's. Although the first pocket calculators were sold in about 1970, for several years they would be far too expensive for most students.

408AY 4-funct, green fluor, 4-AA rep batt, 4.0x6.0", interesting round spring-recoil keys, c1973, Japan, value $45-55.

408C 4-funct, mini-tube, sealed batt, 4.0x6.75", similar to 408, c1972, Japan, value $50-60.

508A 4-funct, 9-tube display, 5-AA rep batt, 4.25x7.0", like 408 but has rep batt and decimal slide switch, c1972, Japan, value $45-55.

508S sci-funct, mem, green fluor, 6v sealed batt, 4.0x6.0", same case as 408AY, a very early scientific model, c1973, Japan, value $45-55.

508AD 4-funct, sq rt, mem, green fluor, 2-AA rep batt, 3.0x5.5", interesting brushed-metal front, Japan, value $35-45.

512SR sci-funct, green fluor, 4-AA rep batt, 3.5x6.25", c1975, Japan, value $35-45.

807 4-funct, sq rt, %, red LED, 4-AA rep batt, 3.0x5.0", 800-series have interesting red-plastic cover over displays, 1974 price $30, Hong Kong, value $20-30.

827A 4-funct, mem, %, red LED, 4-AA rep batt, 3.0x5.0", looks like 807, Hong Kong, value $20-30.

827R 4-funct, mem, %, red LED, 4-AA rep batt, 3.0x5.0", looks like 807, Hong Kong, value $20-30.

861 4-funct, mem, %, fluor, sealed batt, 3.0x5.25", Korea, value $35-45.

862 4-funct, sq rt, mem, %, fluor, sealed batt, 3.25x5.75", 1975 price $59.95, Korea, value $25-35.

863 sci-funct, mem, fluor, sealed batt, 3.25x5.75", case like 862 but has sci-functions, 1975 price $79.95, Korea, value $25-35.

Busicom

Busicom was the brand name used for calculators made by Nippon Calculating Machine Corporation of Japan, one of the first companies to enter the pocket calculator market. This company also made desktop electronic models and funded the effort by Intel to develop their first microprocessor chip. Busicom's early models, which are difficult to find, were designed by the company itself. Later models seemed to use designs employed by other manufacturers indicating that Busicom became simply a general marketer of calculators.

60DA 4-funct, tube, 2-AA rep batt, 4.0x7.0", 1973 price $70, Japan, value $60-70.

80A *aka Handy LE-80A*, 4-funct, red LED, rep batt, 2.5x3.5", c1972, Japan, value $60-70.

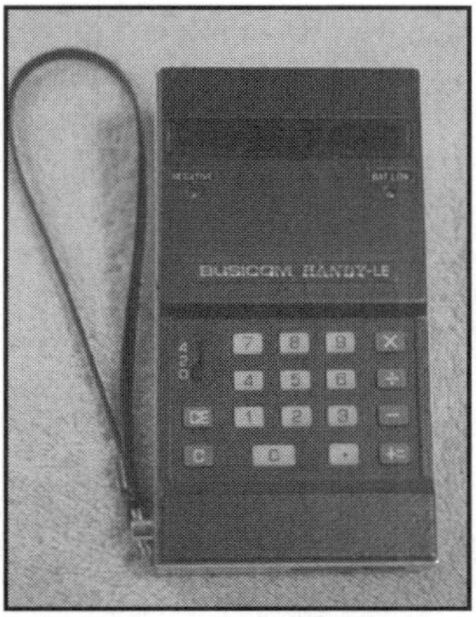

120A *aka Handy LE-120A*, 4-funct, red LED, 4-AA rep batt, 2.5x4.75", may also have been termed the "120" without the "A" in sales materials, incredibly small considering it was one of the world's first pocket models, used what is termed the first "one-chip calculator" IC built by Mostek, a near identical model was made by Nippon for NCR, first sold in 1971 for $395, 1972 ad listed gold-plated model for $1,000 and gold over silver model for $3,000! Japan, value $200-300.

120DC *aka Executive*, 4-funct., 12 mini tubes, 4-C rep batt, 5.5x8.25", large portable, c1972, Japan, value $70-90.

120S *aka Handy LE-120S*, 4-funct, 10 digit red LED, 4-AA rep batt, 2.5x5.0", 1972 price $295, Japan, value $90-130.

801DD 4-funct, %, sq rt, green fluor, 2-AA rep batt, 3.0x6.0", Japan, value $40-50.

801DD 4-funct, %, rq rt, green fluor, 2-AA rep batt, 3.0x6.0", Japan, value $40-50.

PA-80S 4-funct, %, LED, rep batt, 2.25x3.25", looks like Vista Z48P, more "modern" style, Japan, value $45-50.

Calculated Industries

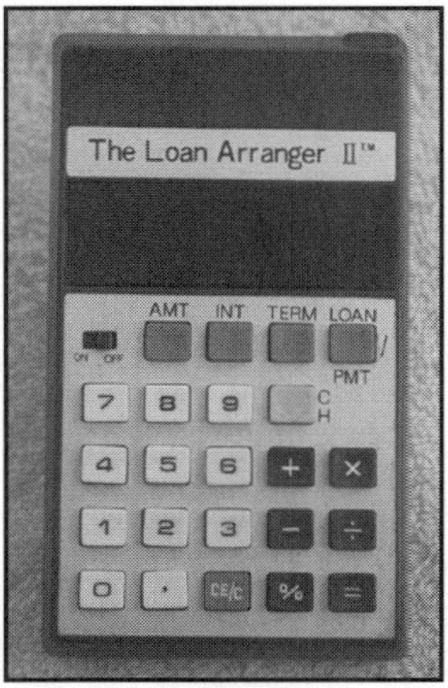

Loan Arranger II 4-funct, %, loan calculating functions, fluor, 9V rep batt, Taiwan, value $20-30.

Calcumatic

Distributed by Leisurecraft Products Ltd, USA. Little is known about this company.

840 4-funct, red LED, 4-AA rep batt, 3.25x6.25", chrome faceplate with green, blue, and white keys, unusual plastic slip case, made by General Instruments of Canada, 1974 price $49.95, Canada, value $65-75.

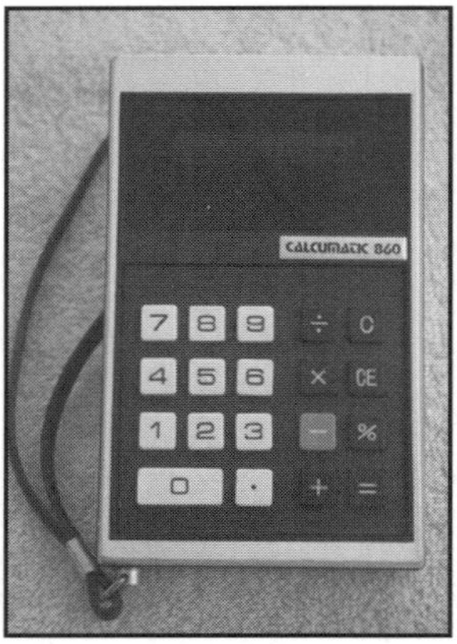

860 4-funct, %, green fluor, 4-AA rep batt, 3.0x5.0", 1975 price $24.95, Japan, value $35-45.

870 4-funct, sq rt, green fluor, 4-AA rep batt, 3.0x5.0", Japan, 1975 price $39.95, value $45-55.

Calcu-pen

The actual manufacturer is unknown, but a LCD version of the "Calcu-pen" was made in 1981 by Satolex. There may be a connection. One early ad shows the LED version of the "Calcu-Pen" sold by Phenix International of Wayne, New Jersey (USA).

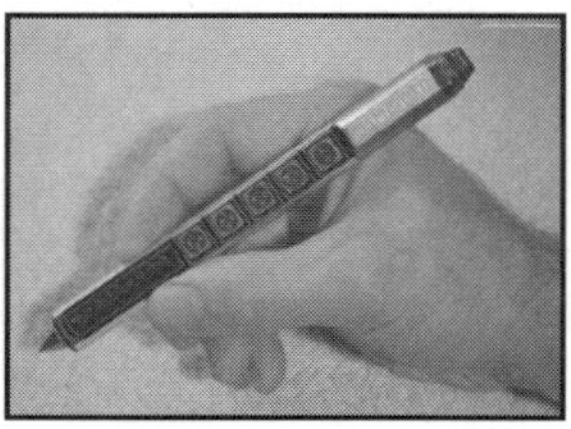

Calcu-pen 4-funct, red LED, 2-N rep batt, 6.3" long, 0.6" in diameter, penwith a built-in calculator, uses square 4-position "Quadraplane" rocker switches on barrel, one of the most interesting calculators ever made, 1975 price $79.95, Japan, value $100-200.

Calfax

This company sold a few interesting pocket calculators in the early 1970's. At least one known model says, "manufactured by American Import Merchants Corporation, Calfax Division."

800-CD 4-funct, red LED, 9V rep batt, 3.25x5.0", an impressive-looking model encircled by a thin brushed aluminum band, Hong Kong, value $65-75.

820 CD 4-funct, red LED, 9V rep batt, 3.0x5.5", Hong Kong, value $40-50.

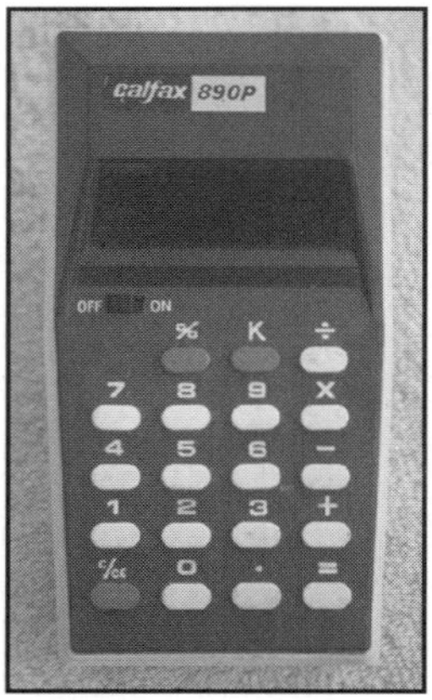

890P 4-funct, %, red LED, 9V rep batt, 3.0x5.5", interesting wedge-shape and colorful keypad, the "P" in the model name probably means percent (an exciting feature in that era), the most common Calfax, c1975, Hong Kong, value $25-30.

899S sci-funct, red LED, 9V rep batt, 3.0x5.5", Hong Kong, value $45-55.

Calfax 4-funct, mem, %, red LED, 9V rep batt, 3.0x5.5", no model number/name other than "Calfax," Hong Kong, value $35-45.

Data Brain II 4-funct, %, mem, red LED, 3.0x5.25", interesting two-tone case, if a Data Brain I was made it must be quite uncommon, c1974, Hong Kong, value $35-45.

Calstar

DT-10 4-funct, mem, %, 10 digit fluor, 2-D rep batt, 6.5x7.0" Taiwan, value $25-35.

Caltek

European-market company.

830D 4-funct, %, sq funct, recip, sgn chg, pi, fluor, 1-AA rep batt, 3.0x4.75", on back label is a note saying "manufactured by Detron Co.," looks like Olympia 816MS, Korea, value $35-45.

The collecting of calculators is as varied as the people collecting them. Some collect only models with scientific functions. Some collect only those by certain companies (such as Hewlett-Packard). Most people collect all brands and models. Many collectors focus only on portable or pocket calculators with LED or tube-type display. Some also collect models with early LCD displays and a growing number are collecting some of the non-portable, AC power models of the late 1960s.

Caltronic

606 4-funct, red LED, 9V rep batt, 3.25x6.0", 6 digit display, 12 digit capability, value $45-55.

812 4-funct, red LED, 9V rep batt, 3.0x5.75", has Klixon keypad yet uses a 9V batt generally not found in early models, 1972 price $77.77, Hong Kong, value $75-85.

Candle

Only a few models from this company are known. Candle apparently also made other electronic products including transistor radios and portable televisions. On the 801M, there is a company listing on the bottom of the back label -- "Hatzlachh Supply, Inc." -- with no other information. This might be the name of the parent company.

800N 4-funct, %, sq rt, sgn chg, green fluor, 2-AA rep batt, 3.0x5.5", Korea, value $45-55.

801M 4-funct, mem, %, sgn chg, red LED, sealed batt, 3.0x5.0", slide switch for decimal place selection, c1973, Korea, value $50-60.

808E 4-funct, mem, sq rt, green fluor, 4-AA rep batt, 3.0x5.5", the case is reminiscent of the original Texas Instrument's Datamath, c1973, Korea, value $75-85.

Cannella

RS-1 *aka Kel-Co Class Computer*, 4-funct, %, horse race handicapping calculator, red LED, 9V rep batt, 2.75x5.5", same as APF RS1, c1979, Hong Kong, value $30-40.

Canon

Canon Corp. was a major player in the development of early portable electronic calculators. In the late 1960's the company worked with Texas Instruments to develop a "hand-held" calculator. The project, based on TI's "Cal-Tech" prototype, culminated in 1970 with the introduction of the "Pocketronic" in Japan. The Pocketronic was first sold in the USA in February of 1971 and marked a major change in calculator history. The Pocketronic used 3 TI MOS devices containing "the equivalent of 4.000 radio vacuum tubes and other 'pre-integrated circuit-type' components." Although the name "Pocketronic" was a bit of an exaggeration (it would only fit in a huge coat pocket) it was remarkably small for 1971. Before the Pocketronic and early portables, calculators had thousands of individual electronic components and were about the size of a small suitcase! In late 1972, even though most calculators were half the size of the Pocketronic, its popularity continued because it kept a record of its results on a small paper ribbon. Many people did not trust these tiny new electronic calculators and wanted printed results so they could check the answers!

Palmtronic 8 mini 4-funct, %, fluor, 2-AA rep batt, 2.5x3.6", very small and cute, 1976 price $8.95, Japan, value $40-50.

Until 1970, slide rule makers like Post and K&E flourished. But within five years pocket calculators swept their market, making them obsolete.

Pocketronic 4-funct, paper-tape display, sealed batt, 4.0x8.0", used a 0.25" wide paper tape fed horizontally from a special flat tape cartridge, boxy shape, at 1.8 pounds it would fill a big pocket! 1971 price $395, Japan, value $100-$150.

Pocketronic 2 4-funct, %, paper tape display, sealed batt, 4.0x8.0", very similar to Pocketronic but with a more stylish design, used same tape cartridge as Pocketronic and weighed about as much, 1974 price $160, USA ("of Japanese and US components"), value $130-170.

8-T *aka Sexagesimal Calculator*, 4-funct, mem, unknown dating functions, fluor, 2-AA rep batt, 3.0x5.75", brown color, Japan, value $45-55.

F-5 *aka Palmtronic F-5*, sci-funct, red LED, used sealed batt pack or 4-AA rep batt pack, 3.0x5.5", Japan, value $40-50.

FC-80 4-funct, sq rt, full metric conversions, red LED, 4-AA rep batt, 3.0x5.5", weird slide-out batt compartment like LE-81M, 1974 price $130, Japan, value $45-55.

L812 *aka Canola L812*, 4-funct, mem, %, sgn chg, fluor, 4-AA rep batt, 6.25x5.25", small desk-top style, Japan, value $25-35.

L813 4-funct, mem, %, fluor, 4-AA rep batt, 6.25x5.25", small desk-top style, similar case to L812, Japan, value $25-35.

L1011 *aka Canola 1011*, 4-funct, mem, %, 10 digit fluor display, 4-AA rep batt, 6.25x5.25", small desk-top style, Japan, value $25-35.

LD-8M2 4-funct, %, sq rt, mem, green fluor, 2-AA rep batt, 2.75x5.0", similar to LD-81 but has mem, Japan, value $35-55.

LD-8M3 *aka Palmtronic 8M*, 4-funct, mem, %, sq rt, fluor, 2-AA rep batt, 3.0x5.5", Japan, value $35-55.

LD-8MS 4-funct, %, sq rt, mem, fluor, 2-AAA rep batt, 2.75x5.0", same as LD-8S but taller and has mem, Japan, value $20-25.

LD-8RS 4-funct, %, green fluor, 2-AAA rep batt, 2.75x4.5", thin, similar to LD-8S, Japan, value $25-35.

LD-8S 4-funct, %, sq rt, green fluor, 2-AAA rep batt, 2.75x4.5", impressive brushed metal front, Japan, value $20-25.

LD-80 4-funct, %, green fluor, 4-AA rep batt, 3.5x5.75", interesting shape similar to early Panasonics, c1975, Japan, value $35-55.

LD-81 4-funct, %, sq rt, green fluor, 2-AA rep batt, 2.75x5.0", made in fairly large numbers, Japan, value $15-25.

LD-84 *aka Palmtronic*-8, 4-funct, %, sq rt, green fluor, 2-AA rep batt, 2.75x5.0", value $25-35.

LD-84M *aka Palmtronic-8M*, 4-funct, %, sq rt, mem, green fluor, 2-AA rep batt, 2.75x5.5", similar case to LD-84 but taller, Japan, value $15-25.

LE-10 4-funct, 10 digit red LED, 3.0x5.75", used sealed batt pack or 4-AA rep batt pack, battery power meter, boxy case, 1972 price $259, Japan, value $45-55.

Even though Texas Instruments developed the first portable calculator in 1967 (the "Cal-Tech"), they didn't become interested in making and selling their own calculators until late 1971 when they saw the business and consumer markets starting to grow. The "Cal-Tech" had actually been developed just to sell their new integrated circuit products.

LE-80R 4-funct, sq, red LED, 4-AA rep batt, 3.25x5.75", a very interesting model with batt meter, slide out batt tray, carrying strap, slide switch for constant funct, 1974 price $119.95, Japan, value $55-75.

LE-81M 4-funct, %, sq rt, red LED, 4-AA rep batt, 3.0x5.5", unusual slide out batt tray (also see LE-10 and LE-82), 1974 price $79.95, Japan, value $35-55.

LE-82 4-funct, %, red LED, 4-AA rep batt, 3.25x5.75", a very interesting model with batt meter, looks like LE80R, 1974 price $119.95, Japan, value $55-75.

LE-83 4-funct, red LED, 4-AA rep

batt, 2.75x6.0", unusual batt compartment accessed through front of calculator (as in LE 84 and LE 85), 1974 price $44.95, Japan, value $25-45.

LE-84 4-funct, red LED, 4-AA rep batt, 2.75x6.0", similar to LE-83 but more common, 1975 price $24.95, Japan, value $15-25.

LE-85 4-funct, %, sq rt, red LED, 4-AA rep batt, 2.75x6.0", similar to LE-83 but has % and sq rt, Japan, 1975 price $39.95, value $25-35.

MD-8 *aka Multi-8*, 4-funct, mem, %, sq rt, green fluor, 3.0x6.25", has bizarre 2-lines of display, 1977 price $29.95, Japan, value $50-75.

Casio

In the early 1970's Casio Computer Company, LTD, of Japan made a wide variety of fluorescent display pocket calculators. Casio (along with TI and HP) survived the intense competition which long ago forced most companies out of the calculator business. Unlike other brands, many Casio models are "horizontal" meaning that the data entry keys are to the side of the display rather than below it. This creates an unusual shape that interests many collectors. A few of the early horizontal models even had a carrying strap designed to fit around the users wrist. The early Casio models were called "mini" although they were quite large by today's standards. The smaller Casio "personal" and "pocket" models are about 3x5" while the tiny "pocket-mini" models are about 2.5x4". This was impressive miniaturization for the 1970's.

Be aware that Casio model numbers are quite confusing. At times there is one model number on the calculator's front side and a totally different one on the back! In such cases, we use "aka" (also known as) to help avoid confusion. In addition, many of the early models (e.g. the Mini, the Personal and Pocket) were made with the first version having no additional model number. Others in the series will have a model number and usually differ from the first in case style or features.

8U 4-funct, green fluor, 5-AA rep batt, 4.75x7.0", decimal slide switch, 1974 price $89.50, Japan, value $15-20.

101MR 4-funct, mem, %, sq rt, sgn chg, green fluor, 4-AA rep batt, 4.5x6.5", decimal slide switch, 1974 price $99.50, Japan, value $20-30.

121MR 4-funct, mem, %, sq rt, green

fluor, 4-AA rep batt, 4.74x6.75", decimal slide switch, 1975 price $49.95, Japan, value $20-30.

803MR 4-funct, mem, %, sq rt, green fluor, 4-AA rep batt, 4.0x6.25", decimal slide switch, Japan, value $25-30.

805MR 4-funct, mem, %, sq rt, green fluor, 4-AA rep batt, 4.0x6.25", almost identical to 803MR, Japan, value $20-30.

AL-8 statistical-funct, mem, %, fluor, 2-AA rep batt, 3.25x5.5", one of the first calculators to directly accept fractions such as 1/2, 1976 price $24.95, Japan, value $25-45.

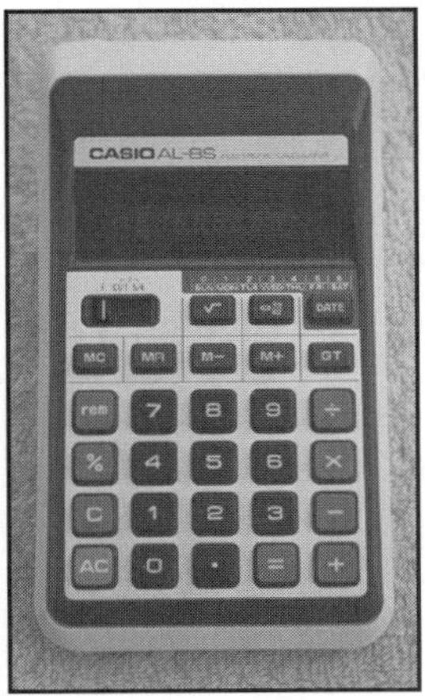

AL-8S 4-funct, mem, date function, fluor, 2-AA rep batt, 3.25x5.5", 1977 price $24.95, Japan, value $25-45.

AL-10 4-funct, %, fluor, 2-AA rep batt, 3.25x5.5", one of the first calculators to directly accept fractions such as 1/2, Japan, value $40.50.

CD-813 *see Memory-8A.*

CM-601 *see Mini.*

CM-602 *see Mini.*

CM-604 *see Mini.*

CM-605 *see Mini.*

CM-607 *see Personal Mini.*

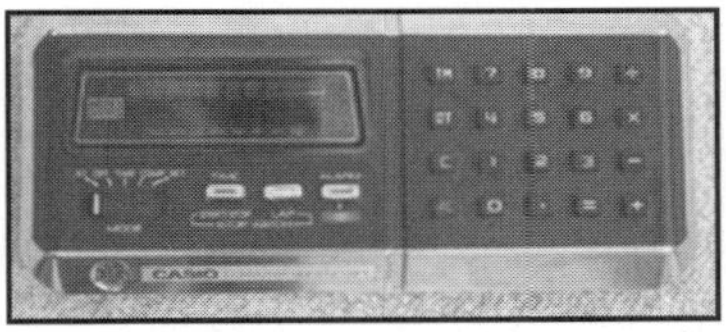

CQ-1 *aka Computer Quartz CQ-1*, 4-funct, green fluor, 1-AA and 2 button rep batt, horizontal 2.5x5.5", unusual calculator with clock & alarm, c1975-77, 1977 price $60, Japan, value $45-65.

CQ-2 *aka Computer Quartz CQ-2*, 4-funct, green fluor, 1-AA and 2 button rep batt, horizontal 2.75x5.75", slightly larger than CQ-1 with same clock and alarm functions, even stranger looking, c1976-77, 1977 price $50, Japan, value $45-65.

F-2 4-funct, mem, %, sq rt, sgn chg, 2-D rep batt, 7.5x9.5", desktop sized portable, Japan, value $25-35.

FX10 sci-funct, green fluor, 4-AA rep batt, 3.75x5.75", probably Casio's first scientific model, 1974 price $99.95, Japan, value $35-45.

FX11 sci-funct, green fluor, 4-AA rep batt, 3.75x5.75", similar to FX10 1975 price $50, Japan, value $20-30.

FX-15 sci-funct, blue fluor, 4-AA rep batt, 3.5x5.75", Japan, value $35-45.

FX20 sci-funct, green fluor, 2-AA rep batt, 3.0x5.0", Japan, value $25-35.

FX21 sci-funct, green fluor, 2-AA rep batt, 3.25x5.5", 1977 price $19.95, Japan, value $25-35.

FX31 sci-funct, green fluor, 2-AA rep batt, 3.25x5.5", similar to FX21 but has statistical functions, Japan, value $25-35.

H-1 4-funct, sq rt, %, mem, 2-AA rep batt, 3.0x5.25", decimal slide-switch, unusual style for a Casio, Japan, value $25-35.

H-801 *see Biolator.*

H-802 *see Personal I.*

H-810 *see Pocket Mini.*

H-811 *see Memory-8S.*

H-812 *see Memory-8F.*

H-813B *see Personal-M1.*

H-814 *see Memory A-1.*

H-816 *see Memory B-1.*

> ***A 1973 Popular Science article featured the Sound Design 8300 portable 4-function calculator. It used 4 "D" cell batteries and weighed several pounds. 20 years later, a laptop computer would fit in the same size case.***

J3 *aka J-1211*, 4-funct, mem, %, sq rt, sgn chg, unusual 13-digit fluor display, 2-AA rep batt, 4.0x6.25", two decimal slide switches, Japan, value $30-40.

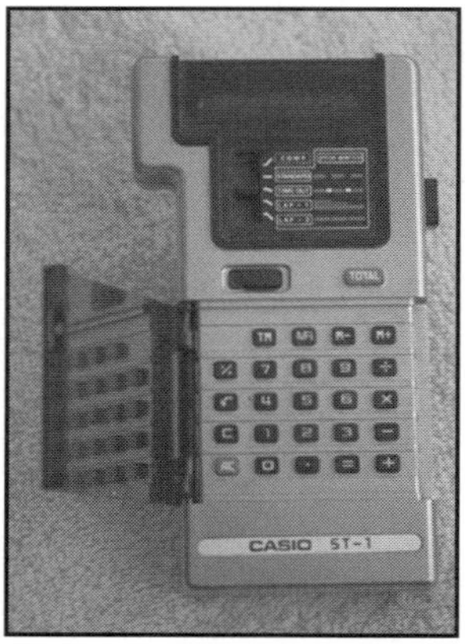

ST-1 4-funct, mem, %, sq rt, fluor, 1-AA rep batt, 2.75x5.0", stop watch functions, very unique case design, with smoked plastic cover over the keypad (for use when you were using it as a stopwatch), Japan, value $55-65.

Y-811 *see Memory 8-R.*

Biolator aka H-801, 4-funct, fluor, 2-AA rep batt, supposedly calculates "biorhythms", c1976-77, 1977 price $30, Japan, value $20-30.

Memory-8A *aka CD-813*, 4-funct,

mem, sq rt, %, green fluor, 2-AA rep batt, 3.0x5.25", c1974, Japan, value $15-25.

Memory-8F *aka H-812*, 4-funct, mem, sq rt, green fluor, 2-AA rep batt, 3.0x5.25", c1974, Japan, value $10-20.

Memory 8-R aka Y-811, 4-funct, mem, %, green fluor, horizontal 5.75x2.75", c1973, Japan, value $15-20.

Memory-8S *aka H-811*, 4-funct, mem, sq rt, green fluor, 2-AA rep batt, 2.75x5.0", c1974, Japan, value $10-20.

Memory A-1 *aka H-814*, 4-funct, mem, sq rt, green fluor, 1-AA rep batt, 2.75x4.5", c1974, Japan, value $15-25.

Memory B-1 aka H-816, 4-funct, mem, %, sq rt, fluor, 2-AA rep batt, 3.0x5.0", c1974, Japan, value $10-20.

Micro-Mini 4-funct, yellow LCD, button rep batt, 1.75x2.5", metal case, early LCD from c1976, 1977 price $30, Japan, value $35-45,

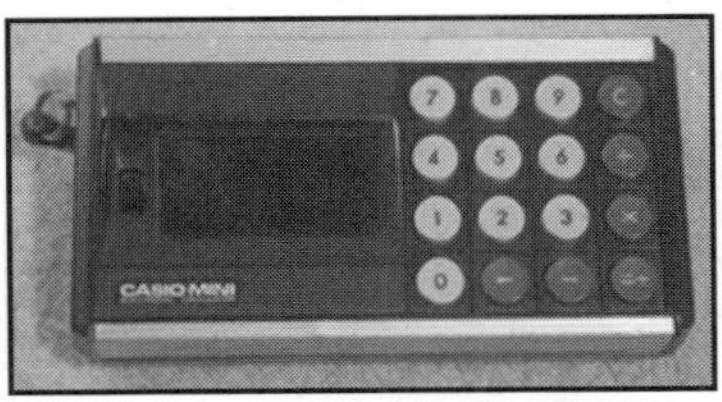

Mini 4-funct, 6-digit tube display, 4-AA rep batt, horizontal 6x3", similar to CM-601 style but with early tube display, round keys, one of the first models to sell for under $100, c1972, Japan, value $45-55.

Mini *aka CM-601*, 4-funct, 6-digit fluor, 4-AA rep batt, horizontal 6x3", wrist strap, one of the first Casio models, c1972, Japan, value $35-50.

Mini *aka CM-602*, 4-funct, 6-digit fluor, 4-AA rep batt, horizontal 6x3", wrist strap, similar to CM-601 but has square keys and decimal point slide switch. 1973 price $59.95, Japan, value $35-50.

Mini *aka CM-604*, 4-funct, 6-digit fluor, 4-AA rep batt, horizontal, 6x3", wrist strap, similar to CM-602 but has modern plastic case, 1974 price $39.95, Japan, value $15-25.

Mini *aka CM-605*, 4-funct, 6-digit fluor, 4-AA rep batt, horizontal, 5.75x2.75", similar to CM-604 but smaller and no wrist strap, c1975, Japan, value $15-25.

Mini Memory 4-funct, 8-digit fluor, 4-AA rep batt, horizontal 6x3", no wrist strap, similar to CM-604 but has memory, Japan, value $15-25.

Mini-Printer 4-funct, mem, sq rt, red

LED and horizontal paper printer, sealed batt, 4.25x7.75", 1975 price $129.95, Japan, value $50-65.

Personal I *aka H802*, 4-funct, sq rt, %, blue fluor, 2-AA rep batt, 3.0x5.0", 1976 price $9.95, Japan, value $15-25.

Personal M-1 *aka H813B*, 4-funct, mem, sq rt, %, blue fluor, 2-AA rep batt, 3.0x5.0", Japan, value $15-25.

Personal-Mini 4-funct, 6-digit fluor, 2-AA rep batt, horizontal 5.5x2.75", similar to CM-605 but even smaller, Japan, value $20-30.

Personal-Mini *aka CM-607*, 4-funct, 6-digit fluor, 2-AA rep batt, horizontal 5.5x2.75", same case as Personal-Mini above, but with blue colored top-half of case, Japan, value $40-50.

Pocket-8 4-funct, sq rt, fluor, 2-AA rep batt, 3.0x5.0", 1975 price $34.95, Japan, value $20-25.

Pocket-Mini 4-funct, sq rt, red LED, 2-AA rep batt, 2.5x4.0", note that most known pre-LCD Casio's have blue or green fluorescent display not red LED. Also, round keys rather than square as in other mini's. Japan, value $45-65.

Pocket-Mini *aka P810*, 4-funct, mem, %, fluor, 2-AA rep batt, 2.5x4.0", Japan, value $25-35.

Pocket-Mini *aka P811*, 4-funct, mem, %, fluor, 2-AA rep batt, 2.5x4.25", like P810 but with modern-looking plastic case, Japan, value $25-35.

Pocket-Mini *aka CP801B*, 4-funct, sq rt, %, fluor, 2-AA rep batt, 2.5x4.0", Japan, value $25-35.

Pocket-Mini *aka CP801C*, 4-funct, %, fluor, 2-AA rep batt, 2.5x4.0", Japan, value $25-35.

Root-8 4-funct, sq rt, blue fluor, 4-AA rep batt, 7.0x3.25", horizontal, similar to Mini case designs, Japan, value $50-60.

CBM

See Commodore.

Century

Centurion 4-funct, red LED, sealed batt, 3.0x5.25", brown case with black and red keys, assembled in Mexico from

USA parts, value $55-75.

Mark IV 4-funct, red LED, 9V rep batt, 3.25x5.5", one of the few early pocket calculators made in Canada, c1974, value $55-75.

Chason

Chason Electronics

JE-408 4-funct, mem, %, purple LED, 9V rep batt, 2.75x4.25" small, black color, Taiwan, value $40-50.

Checkmate

See the Checkmate models made by Litronix.

Citizen

Citizen Business Machines (Japan). Most Citizen calculators appear to be sold mainly in Europe and Asia. The Cimatron company name has been seen in conjunction with Citizen and may be a division or a partner at some point.

800D 4-funct, %, sq rt, sgn chg, pi, green fluor, 4-AA rep batt, 3.25x5.5", c1973-74, Japan, value $35-45.

800R 4-funct, %, green fluor, sealed batt, 3.5x6.0", c1973-74, Japan, value $40-50.

800XL 4-funct, fluor, sealed batt, 4.0x6.25", metal case, very futuristic looking, Japan, value $100-125.

810R 4-funct, mem, %, green fluor, sealed batt, 3.5x6.0", similar case to 800R, Japan, value $35-45.

820R 4-funct, mem, %, sq rt, green fluor, 4-AA rep batt, 3.5x6.0", similar to 800R and 810R styles, Japan, value $35-45.

Carry M6 4-funct, mem, %, green fluor, sealed batt, 3.0x5.25", value $35-45.

C Itoh

Japanese company which sold models mainly in the Asian and European markets.

Pocket 8 4-funct, %, sq rt, green fluor, 2-AA rep batt, 3.5x5.5", Brazil, value $45-55.

Colex

811-A 4-funct, mem, %, green fluor, 4-AA rep batt, 3.75x6.0", case similar to ESR-70, 1974 price $79.95, Hong Kong, value $35-45.

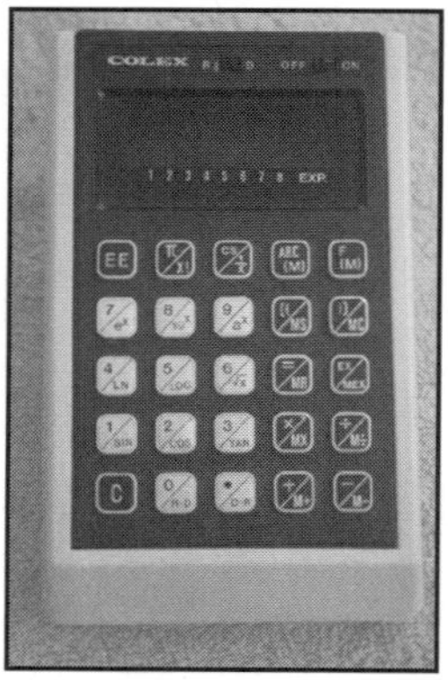

ESR-70 sci-funct, green fluor, 4-AA rep batt, 3.75x6.0", white case, Hong Kong, value $40-50.

Columbia

Columbia Scientific of Santa Monica California (USA) sold a few very interesting pocket calculators in the early 1970's. Although some models were assembled outside of the USA, the label boasts, "MOS/LSI, LED, key board, power switch, and diodes made in the USA."

Columbia 4-funct, red LED, 6-AA rep batt, 3.0x5.25", almost 1.5" thick, boxy, uses TI Klixon keypad, Korea, 1972 price $100, value $65-85.

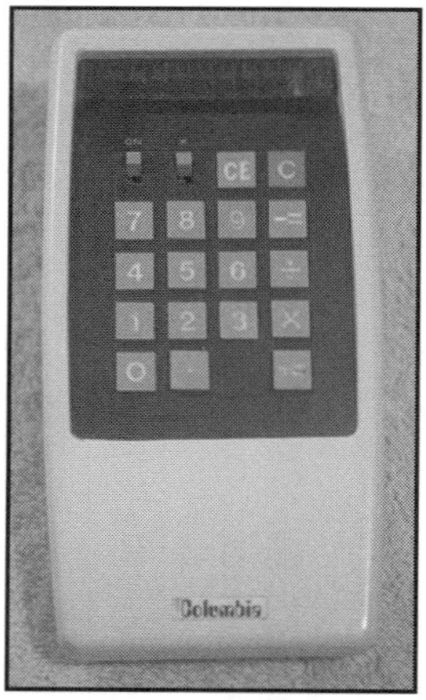

Columbia-2 4-funct, red LED, sealed batt, 3.0x5.5", very unusual curvy white case, 1974 price $74.95, USA, value $75-85.

Columbia-3 aka ML-8, 4-funct, %, sgn chg, red LED, sealed batt, 3.0x5.25", thin, similar case to Columbia-3M, white, Korea, value $45-55.

Columbia-3M *aka 803M*, 4-funct, %, sgn chg, red LED, sealed batt, 3.0x5.25", thin, 1974 price $99.95, Korea, value $45-55.

Scientific 4-funct, %, sq funct, recip, red LED, sealed batt, 3.0x5.5", 1974 price $119.95, USA, value $45-60.

Commodore

Commodore Business Machines (CBM) was one of the earliest companies to manufacture pocket calculators. The colorful Commodore data-entry keys are of interest to many collectors. Their first model, the C110, was made by Bowmar. In 1972 the Minuteman 1, their first original design and a unique one at that, appeared in the February issue of Popular Science. The US and MM (Minuteman) series were their first pocket calculators, followed by the "green line" and "custom green line" series denoted by a "GL" before the model number. The SR (slide rule) series had scientific functions and were among the last pre-LCD calculators made by Commodore. Apparently, Commodore had an English division that made models primarily for the European market. Often these English versions used the "CBM" logo instead of or in addition to the Commodore name. Commodore would later become well-known in the early 1980's for their innovative line of personal computers.

9D-31 4-funct, mem, %, sq funct, recip, sgn chg, pi, paren, green fluor, 2-AA rep batt, 3.0x5.5", Japan, value $35-45.

9R-23 4-funct, mem, %, sealed batt, green fluor, 3.0x5.5", Japan, value $25-35.

9R-31 4-funct, mem, %, sq funct, recip, sgn chg, pi, paren, green fluor, sealed batt, 3.0x5.5", Japan, value $35-45.

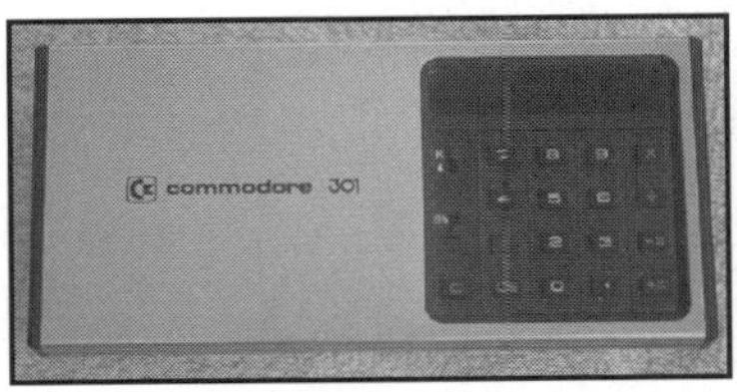

301 4-funct, red LED, sealed batt, 6.0x2.75", horizontal, very thin, aluminum case, Japan, value $45-55.

> *"The calculator that started my collecting interest was the Panasonic 850. Its white curvy case and blue mini-tube display caught my eye in a Salvation Army thrift store. At the time, I was looking for antique cameras, but from that seed grew my love for collecting early calculators."*
> *--Guy Ball*

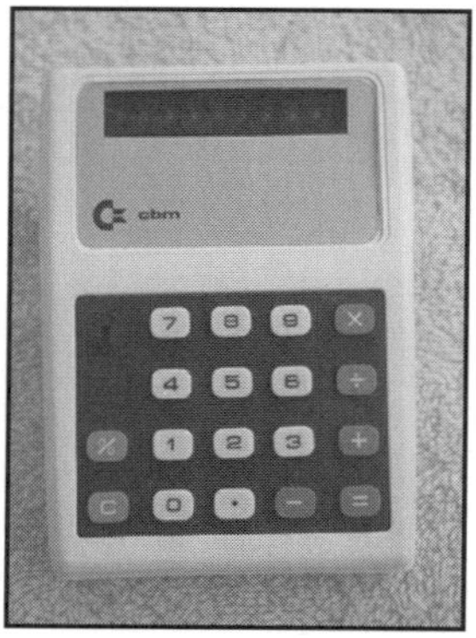

385R 4-funct, %, red LED, sealed batt, 3.0x4.0", same white color and case style as MM3 series, CBM logo, England, value $45-55.

774D 4-funct, red LED, 9V rep batt, 2.5x5.5", c1973, USA, value $25-35.

776M 4-funct, mem, %, red LED, 9V rep batt, 2.5x5.5", c1974, USA, value $35-45.

796M 4-funct, mem, red LED, 9V rep batt, 2.5x5.5", c1973, England, value $25-35.

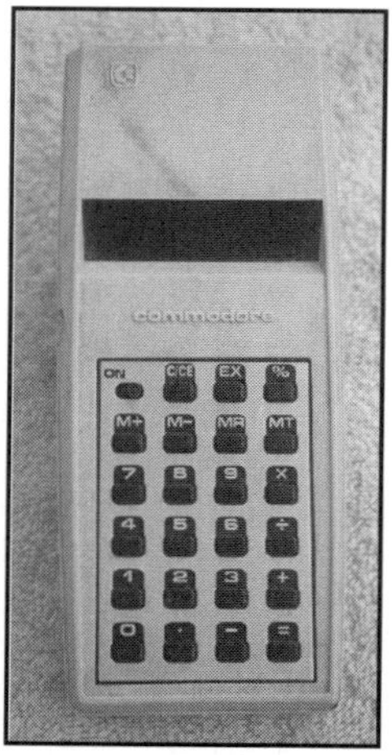

797D 4-funct, mem, %, red LED, 9V rep batt, 2.5x6.25", slim-line case, Japan, value $40-50.

797M 4-funct, mem, %, red LED, 9V rep batt, 2.5x5.5", Hong Kong, value $40-50.

798A 4-funct, mem, %, sq rt, red LED, 9V rep batt, 2.5x6.25", slim-line case, Hong Kong, value $40-50.

884D 4-funct, red LED, 9V rep batt, 3.0x5.5", c1974, USA, value $25-35.

886D 4-funct, %, red LED, 9V rep batt, 3.0x5.5", 1975 price $21.88, USA, value $25-35.

887D 4-funct, mem, %, red LED, 9V rep batt, 3.0x5.5", USA, value $25-35.

897D 4-funct, mem, %, red LED, 9V rep batt, 3.0x5.75", USA, value $30-40.

899A 4-funct, mem, %, sq funct, recip, sgn chg, pi, paren, red LED, 9V rep batt, similar case to 899D, England, value $35-45.

899D 4-funct, mem, %, sq funct, recip, sgn chg, pi, paren, red LED, 9V rep batt, similar case to 899A, Japan, value $35-45.

979D *aka GL979D*, 4-funct, mem, %, recip, sq rt, green fluor, 2-AA rep batt, 3.0x5.5", Japan, value $30-40.

986R *aka GL986R*, 4-funct, green fluor, sealed batt, 3.0x5.5", Japan, value $30-40.

987R *aka GL987R*, 4-funct, mem, %, green fluor, sealed batt, 3.0x5.5", same case as GL-997R, models made in Japan and USA, value $35-45.

989R *aka GL989*R, 4-funct, mem, %, sq funct, recip, green fluor, sealed batt, 3.0x5.5", atypical keypad for Commodore, Japan, value $40-50.

996R *aka GL996R*, 4-funct, sealed batt, green fluor, 3.0x5.5", Japan, value $25-35.

997R *aka GL997R*, 4-funct, mem, %, green fluor, sealed batt, 3.0x5.5", models made in Japan and UK, value $30-40.

997RF *aka GL997RF*, 4-funct, mem, %, green fluor, sealed batt, 3.0x5.5", Japan, value $35-45.

4902 *see F4902*

7923 4-funct, mem, %, fluor, 9V rep batt, 3.0x6.0", value $40-50.

C110 4-funct, red LED, sealed batt, 3.0x5.25", same as Bowmar 901B and Craig 4501, probably made by Bowmar, c1971-72, USA, value $80-120.

F4146R financial funct, red LED, sealed batt, 3.0x5.0", USA, value $35-45.

F4902 financial funct, 49 keys, red LED, 9V rep batt, 3.0x6.0", Hong Kong, value $30-40.

M55 *aka Mathematician*, sci-funct, 14 digit green fluor, sealed batt, 4.0x6.0", 55 keys!, additional functions for Gaussian distributions and Legendre polynomials plus Bessel and other uncommon functions, similar style to N60 and S61, 1976 price $99.95, value $65-85.

MM1 *aka Minuteman* 1, 4-funct, decimal slide switch, red LED, sealed batt, TI Klixon keypad, one of Commodore's earliest models, 1972 price $118, 3.5x6.0", USA, value $65-75.

MM2 *aka Minuteman 2*, 4-funct, decimal slide switch, red LED, sealed batt, 3.5x6.0", two versions were made - one with a TI Klixon keypad with metal keys and the on/off and constant switches in different locations - the other version has similar square keys made of plastic and the two switches are close together, 1972 price $179, USA, value $55-65.

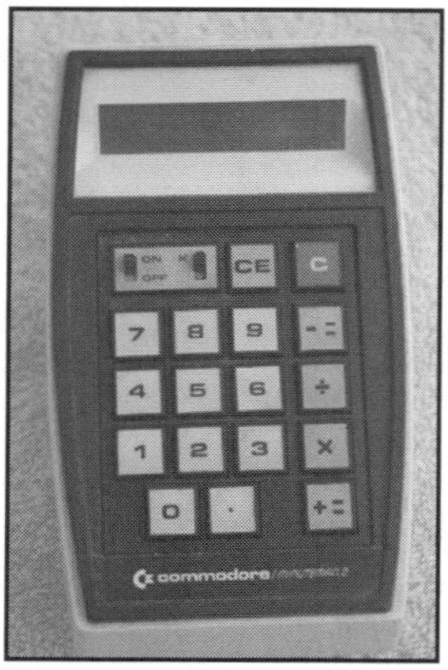

MM2PM *aka Minuteman 2PM*, 4-funct, mem, red LED, sealed batt, 3.5x6.0", c1972, USA, value $55-65.

MM2SR *aka, Minuteman 2SR,* 4-funct mem, %, sq funct, recip, red LED, sealed batt, 3.5x6.0", similar case to MM2 but with smaller keys (not Klixon), USA, value $55-65.

MM3 *aka Minuteman* 3, 4-funct, red LED, AA rep batt, 3.0x4.0", all of the MM3 series have a small and unusual white case, 1973 price $39.95, Japan, value $25-35.

MM3B *aka Minuteman 3B*, 4-funct, red LED, AA rep batt, 3.0x4.0", Japan, value $35-45.

MM3M *aka Minuteman 3M*, 4-funct, mem, red LED, sealed batt, 3.0x4.0", 1974 price $69.95, USA, value $30-40.

MM3MT *aka Minuteman 3MT*, 4-funct, mem, red LED, sealed batt, 3.0x4.0", England, value $35-45.

MM3PM *aka Minuteman 3PM*, 4-funct, mem, %, red LED, AA rep batt, 3.0x4.0", Japan, value $35-45.

MM3PR *aka Minuteman 3PR*, 4-funct, %, red LED, sealed batt, 3.0x4.0", c1973, Japan, value $40-50.

MM3R *aka Minuteman* 3R, 4-funct, red LED, sealed batt, 3.0x4.0", USA, value $30-40.

MM3S *aka Minuteman 3S*, 4-funct, sq rt, red LED, sealed batt, 3.0x4.0", 1974 price $59, USA, value $25-35.

MM6 *aka Minuteman 6*, 4-funct, red LED, 9V rep batt, 2.5x3.5", very unusual wedge-shape with metal faceplate, 1974 price $30, USA, value $30-40.

N60 *aka Navigator*, navigational-funct, 14 digit green fluor, sealed batt, 4.0x6.0", 60 keys!, similar to S61 below, 1976 price $99.95, England, value $45-75.

P50 sci-funct, programmable, red LED, 9V rep batt, 3.25x6.0", c1975, USA, value $45-60.

PR100 sci-funct, programmable, red LED, sealed batt, 45 keys, 3.0x6.0", 1977 price $59.95, England, value $35-45.

S61 *aka Statistician*, sci & statistical-funct, 14 digit green fluor, sealed batt, 4.0x6.0", Sixty colorful keys most with two functions!, 1977 price $99.95, models made in Japan and England, value $45-75.

SR1400 *aka electronic slide rule 1400*, sci-funct, red LED, sealed batt, 3.0x6.0", atypical keypad for Commodore, USA, 1974 price $100, value $45-55.

SR1800 sci-funct, green fluor, AA rep or rechargeable batt, 3.0x6.0", 1976 price $39.95, Japan, value $35-45.

SR4120D sci-funct, red LED, 9V rep batt, 3.0x6.0", 48 keys, England, value $40-50.

SR4146R financial funct, mem, %, red LED, sealed batt, 3.0x6.0", USA, value $45-55.

In 1963, the ANITA, perhaps the world's first fully electronic calculator, was made in England. It was the size of a suitcase and used thousands of transistors - even vacuum tubes! Only 7 years later, the first hand-held models appeared.

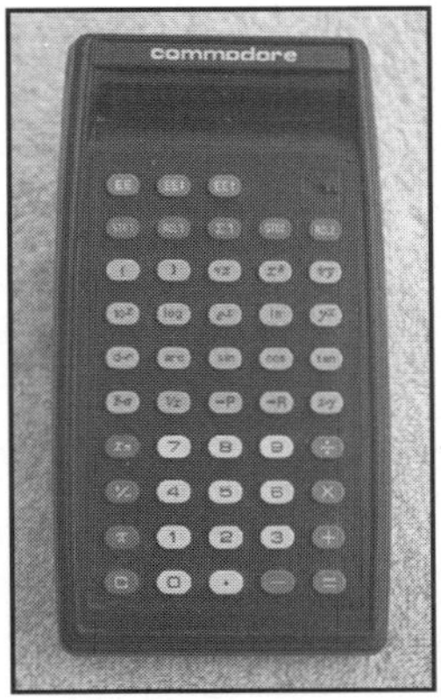

SR4148R sci-funct, 14 digit red LED, sealed batt, 3.2x6.0", USA or England, value $45-60.

SR4190R sci-funct, 14 digit red LED, sealed batt, 3.2x6.0", 1977 price $59.90, value $45-60

SR5190R sci-funct, metric conversions, red LED, sealed batt, 3.0x6.25", USA, value $45-60.

SR6120R sci-funct, red LED, sealed batt, 3.0x6.0", England, value $45-60.

SR6140R sci-funct, red LED, sealed batt, 3.2x5.9", England, value $45-60.

SR7919 sci-funct, red LED, 9V rep batt, 2.5x5.5", small case, USA, value $40-50.

SR9190R sci and conversion funct, red LED, sealed batt, 3.0x6.0", England, value $45-55.

US3 4-funct, 8 digit tube display, 2 additional tubes used to indicate errors and low power, C-cell rep batt, 5.25x6.25" size, 1972 price $139, USA, value $55-95.

US4 4-funct, mem, 8 digit tube display, AA rep batt, 3.25x5.5", 1972 price $149, Japan, value $55-75.

Compex

AK-10 4-funct, mem, %, sq rt, sgn chg, green fluor, 2-AA rep batt, 3.25x5.25", label says "Cal-comp Electronics," Taiwan, value $45-55.

EC-1000W 4-funct, mem, %, 10 digit blue fluor, 2-D rep batt, 6x6.5", same case as Royal D-120 and Unisonic 1000M, Taiwan, value $20-30.

SR-10 4-funct, mem, %, sq rt, sgn chg, green fluor, 2-AA rep batt, 3.25x5.25", Taiwan, value $45-55.

CompuChron

Calculator Watch 4-funct, %, red LED, 4-button rep batt, 1.5x1.75", internal module made by Hughes Aircraft Company, similar to Hughes model except for hard-edged case, value $100-200.

Compucorp

Compucorp series 300 calculators are in a class by themselves. At four pounds they can not really be called "pocket" calculators! But they can be hand-held and they are battery-operated using internal rechargeable batteries. The Compucorp calculators are also called "micro-computers" and this may be a fair claim. Introduced in 1973 they were probably more functional than the first mass-marketed personal computer (MITS Altair 8800) which were not sold until 1975. Most of the Compucorps were programmable, a feature which was rare in a hand-held calculator in 1973.

These remarkable machines were ahead of their time and priced accordingly. Desk-top Compucorps which preceded the 300-series portables cost over $2,500 in 1971. Adjusted for inflation, this is about $9,000 in today's dollars! Some Compucorp hand-held (series 300) models were sold under the Monroe logo.

320-G *aka Scientist*, sci-funct, exp, fluor, sealed batt, 5.5x9.0", 1973 price $595, 1973 price $595, USA, value $100-150.

322-G *aka Scientist*, sci-funct, exp, fluor, sealed batt, 5.5x9.0", 1973 price $795, USA, value $100-150.

324-G sci-funct, exp, programmable, fluor, sealed batt, 5.5x9.0", 1974 price $795, USA, value $100-150.

326 sci-funct, exp, programmable, fluor, sealed batt, 5.5x9.0", c1974, USA, value $100-150.

340 *aka Statistician*, statistical functions, fluor, sealed batt, 5.5x9.0", USA, value $100-150.

360 *aka Bond Trader*, bond trading functions, fluor, sealed batt, 5.5x9.0", USA, value $100-150.

Computech

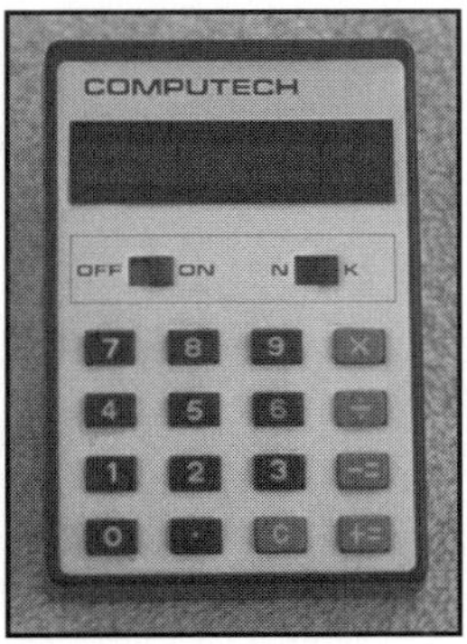

M-801 4-funct, red LED, 4-N rep batt, 2.12x3.12", very small, Eiko Business Machine name on back label, Japan, value $60-70.

Concept

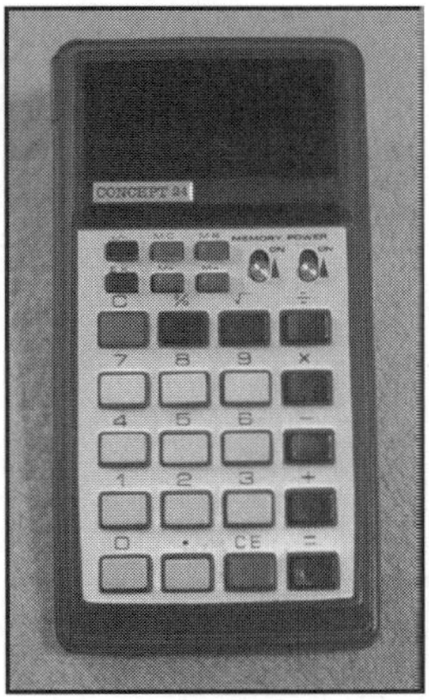

24 4-funct, mem, sq rt, green fluor, 2-AA sealed batt, 3.0x5.75", Japan, value $30-40.

Compact *aka super-thin*, 4-funct, mem, sq rt, green fluor, sealed batt, 2.75x4.75", all metal case, identical to Binatone Super Thin, all-metal case, value $45-55.

Conic

750 4-funct, %, red LED, 9V rep batt, 2.5x5.0", Hong Kong, value $50-75.

Corvus

Corvus Corp. Dallas Texas. The consumer division of IC maker Mostek. Many of their models used RPN, similar to the HPs.

312 4-funct, %, sq rt, red LED, sealed batt, 3.0x6.0", interesting white case, 1974 price $69.95, USA, value $30-45.

322 4-funct, mem, %, red LED, sealed batt, 3.0x6.0", interesting brown case, harder to find than 312 model, 1974 price $79.95, USA, value $45-55.

400 4-funct, %, red LED, 4-N-cell rep batt, 3.0x4.75", unusual shape and bright white color, more scarce than larger Corvus models, c1974, USA, value $45-65.

411 4-funct, mem, sq rt, exp, red LED, sealed batt, 3.0x6.0", early model with sci. notation, 1975 price $49.95, USA, value $30-40.

415 4-funct, mem, %, red LED, sealed batt, 3.0x6.0", 1974 price $89.95, USA, value $30-45.

500 sci and conversion funct, red LED, sealed batt, 3.0x5.75", unusual style for a Corvus. c1975, Hong Kong, value $50-60.

625 4-funct, mem, %, sq rt, red LED, sealed batt, 2.75x5.5", similar case to 500, Hong Kong, value $50-60.

Checkmaster dedicated functions to keep track of your check book including "check," "deposit," and "balance," red LED, 6-AA rep batt, 6.75x3.5", horizontal format, ivory colored, would retain your balance even when shut off, 1975 price $29.95, USA, value $40-50.

Craig

Craig Electronics of Compton, California (USA) was a major distributor of stereo equipment and other consumer electronics in the 1960's. Craig's automobile 8-track tape players were very popular. Some early Craig calculators were actually made by Bowmar.

For example, the original Craig 4501 is really a Bowmar 901B with a Craig label. These early models are the most desirable. One of the authors (BF) purchased a 4-function Craig 4501 pocket calculator in 1972 for about $200. This was about $600 in inflation-adjusted dollars and just about depleted his entire bank account! It has remained with its original owner for over twenty-four years and still functions perfectly.

4501 4-funct, red LED, sealed batt, 3.0x5.0", made for Craig by Bowmar, same as Bowmar 901B, 1971 price $239.95, USA, value $45-55.

4501A 4-funct, red LED, sealed batt, 3.0x5.0", made for Craig by Bowmar, same apparent unit as 4501, 1972 price $210, USA, value $55-65.

4502 4-funct, decimal slide switch, 4C-rep batt, tube display, massive 4.5x8.5", battery meter, 1972 price $119.95, Japan, value $50-75.

4503 4-funct, decimal slide switch, 4C-rep batt, tube display, massive 4.5x8.5", similar to 4502 case but without battery meter, 1972 price $119.95, Japan, value $50-75.

4504 4-funct, purple LED, 6-AA rep batt, 2.5x5.5", carrying strap, 2 variations with minor keypad and case changes, 1973 price $129.95, Japan, value $35-45.

4505 4-funct, mem, %, fluor, 4-AA rep batt, 6.0x2.75", horizontal, 1974 price $109.95, Japan, value $45-55.

4506 4-funct, mem, %, green fluor, AA rep batt, green fluor, 3.25x5.5", 1974 price $99.95 Japan, value $45-65.

4507 4-funct, %, red LED, 3-AA rep batt, 2.75x5.5", 2 types are known (different case shapes) - one is same as Bowmar 90506, 1974 price $69.95, USA, value $25-35.

4508 4-funct, %, red LED, sealed batt, 3.0x5.0", made for Craig by Bowmar, same case as 4501 except 4508 has a % key instead of a "D", 1974 price $99.95, USA, value $45-55.

4509 4-funct, AA rep batt, purple cover LED, 2.75x5.5", 1974 price $59.95, Japan, value $40-50.

4509B 4-funct, %, purple cover LED, 4-AA rep batt, 2.75x5.5", 1975 price $40, Japan, value $35-45.

4511 4-funct, 9V rep batt, red LED, 2.0x4.0", small and unusual Craig, c1974, Japan, value $45-55.

4511A 4-funct, 9V rep batt, red LED, 2.0x4.0", small and unusual Craig, same as 4511 but has % key, 1974 price $39, Japan, value $50-65.

4512 sci-funct, mem, blue fluor, 4-AA rep batt, 6.0x2.75", horizontal, 1975 price $100, Japan, value $45-65.

4512A *aka Engineering Calculator*, sci-funct, mem, blue fluor, 4-AA rep batt, 6.0x2.75", similar case to 4512, horizontal, 1975 price $100, Japan, value $55-70.

4513 4-funct, mem, sq funct, %, recip, sgn chg, blue fluor, 4-AA rep batt, 6.0x2.75", horizontal, 1975 price $59.95, Japan, value $45-70.

4514 4-funct, mem, %, blue fluor, 4-AA rep batt, 6.0x2.75", horizontal, similar to 4505 and 4512, 1975 price $50, Japan, value $40-50.

4515 4-funct, red LED, 4-AA rep batt, 3.25x5.0, tan plastic body with burgundy metal faceplate, Japan, value $35-45.

4516 4-funct, mem, %, sgn chg, green fluor, AA rep batt, 3.5x5.75", Japan, value $35-45.

4517 4-funct, sq rt, %, blue fluor, 4-AA rep batt, 6x2.75", horizontal, Japan, value $45-75.

4518 4-funct, mem, %, purple LED, 9V rep batt, 2.5x4.5", value $55-75.

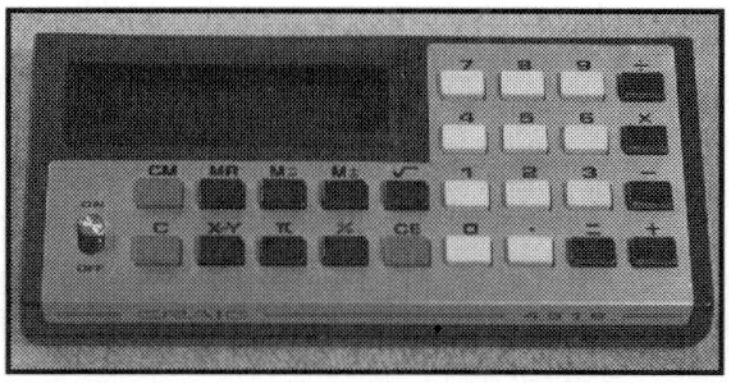

4519 4-funct, mem, sq rt, %, blue fluor, 4-AA rep batt, 6.0x2.75", horizontal, similar to 4513 but has pi function, Japan, value $45-75.

4521 4-funct, %, sq rt, green fluor, 2-AA rep batt, 2.75x5.5", similar case to 4522 and 4523, 1976 price $22.95, Japan, value $20-30.

4522 4-funct, mem, %, green fluor, AA rep batt, 2.75x5.5", 1976 price $26.95, Japan, value $20-30.

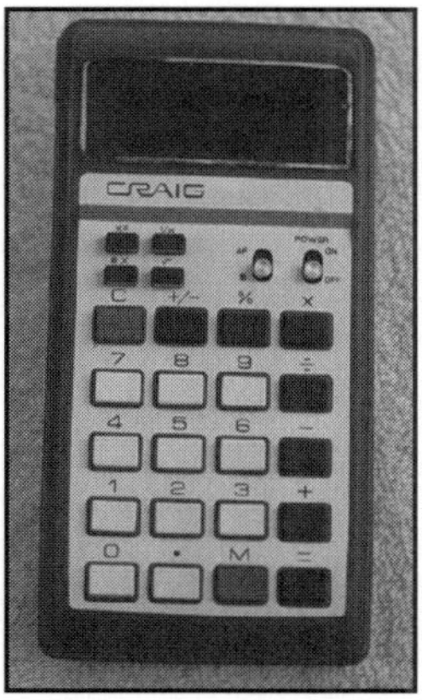

4523 4-funct, mem, %, sq funct, recip, sgn chg, green fluor, 2-AA rep batt, 2.75x5.5", unusual 4-key cluster on top of calculator, 1976 price $26.95, Japan, value $25-35.

M100 *aka Translator*, 4-funct, AA rep batt, blue fluor, 6.5x3.5", also a language translator, USA, value $15-25.

Crown Radio

A maker of transistor pocket radios in the 1960's, Crown produced only a few early hand-held calculators.

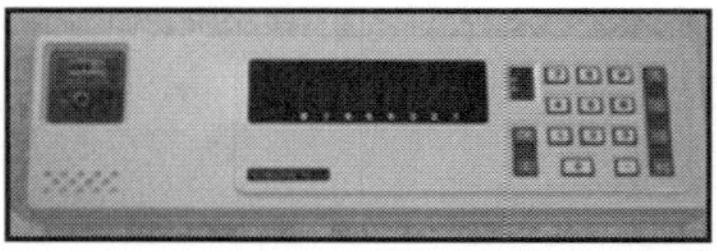

CL-130 4-funct, mini-tube display, 2.75x9.75", a very interesting early electronic calculator complete with battery indicator, c1972, Japan, value $125-200.

Cybernet

6PD 4-funct, mem, %, green fluor and paper printer, sealed batt, 3.25x6.75", Japan, value $35-45.

Daltone

Daltone made several calculator kits for consumer construction.

80 *aka Daltone 80*, 4-funct, %, red LED, 9V rep batt, 2.5x4.5", sold as kit, 1975 price $24.50, value S65-75.

Opti-Cal 1 4-funct, mem, %, fluor, 4-AA rep batt, 3.5x5.75", unusual case shape, black with silver top, c1973-74, value $70-90.

Dataking

LC-800 4-funct, mem, %, early LCD, 2-9V rep batt, 3.5x6.0", early LCD display with see-through panel at top of calculator to help light LCD, same as Ibico 086 and Lloyd's 40, 1974 price $59.95, Mexico (of US parts), value $40-50.

Decimo

This company mainly sold pocket calculators in England in the 1970's. The Cambridge University Science Museum has over 30 different models. Decimo calculators tend to have interesting names. The Cambridge Museum has models called the Spy, the Super Spy, and the Counter Spy! Some names include the term Vatman, relating to the calculator's ability to calculate the country's Value Added Tax.

DaVinci 4-funct, %, sgn chg, green fluor, 4-AA rep batt, 3.25x5.5", Japan, value $50-60.

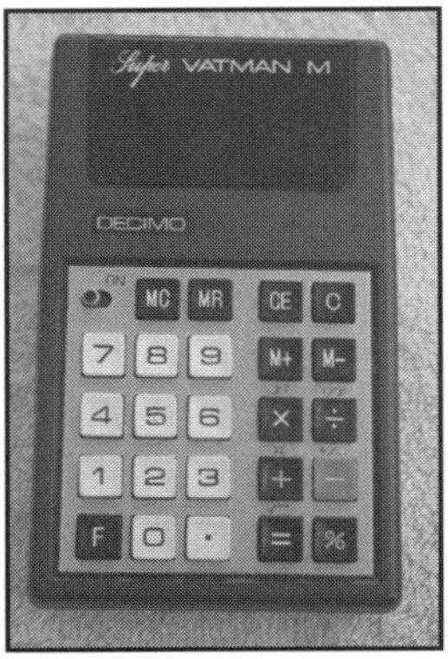

Super Vatman-M 4-funct, mem, %, sq funct, recip, pi, sgn chg, green fluor, 4-AA rep batt, 3.25x5.0", c1975, Japan, value $45-55.

Vatman 4-funct, % (or VAT %), sq rt, green fluor, 4-AA rep batt, 3.25x5.0", two slight style variations with placement of sq rt key and different % key wording, c1975, Japan, value $45-55.

"I paid about $200 for my first pocket calculator, a Craig 4501. It wiped out my savings account, but it was worth it. Of course, I still needed my slide rule since the Craig had no log or trig functions. I proudly wore the 4501 on my belt for many years and it still works fine after two and a half decades. I'll never sell it."
--Bruce Flamm

Vatman Executive 4-funct, sq rt, green fluor, 4-AA rep batt, 3.25x5.0", c1975, Japan, value $45-55.

Vatman Vantage 4-funct, %, sq rt, green fluor, 4-AA rep batt, 3.25x5.0", case similar to Super Vatman-M, Japan, value $45-55.

Detron

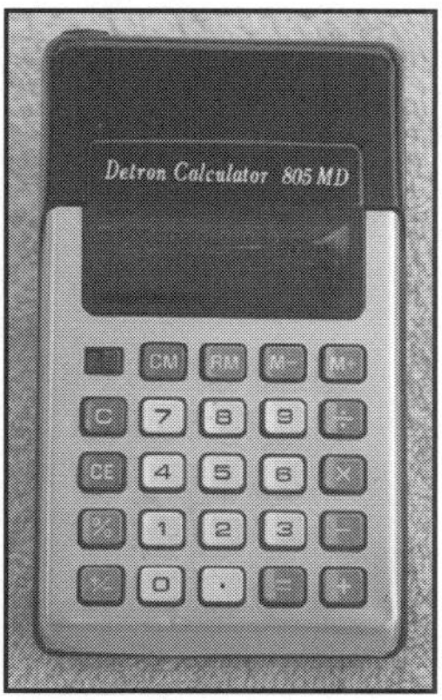

805MD 4-funct, mem, %, sgn chg, blue fluor, 2-AA rep batt, 3.0x5.0", Korea, value $40-50.

Detson

British marketing company.

E406 4-funct, %, sgn chg, fluor, 4-AA rep batt, 3.5x5.5", case similar to Lloyd's 408 and 419 models, c1975-76, Japan, value $35-45.

E420 4-funct, mem, %, sq rt, recip, sgn chg, blue fluor, 2-AA rep batt, 3.0x5.0", Korea, value $40-50.

Dictaphone

Large American company known for their dictating office machines. They sold two Sanyo manufactured models in the very early 1970's before they discontinued their calculator line.

1680 4-funct, 8 digit tube with 16 digit calculating and display capability, sealed batt, 5.5x8.25", battery strength meter, flip top cover for the display, same model as Sanyo ICC-82D, 1971

price $495, Japan, value $100-120.

1681 4-funct, 8 digit tube with 16 digit calculating and display capability, sealed batt, 5.5x8.75", battery strength meter, probably made by Sanyo, 1972 price $325, Japan, value $100-120.

Digical

Mark V 4-funct, fluor, 4-C rep batt, 4.75x7.5", large keys, battery meter, "on" switch flips up little door in top the covers display, Japan, value $70-80.

Digi-matic

See Sears.

Digitrex

MCK-8 4-funct, red LED, sealed batt, 2.25x3.0", TI Klixon keypad, 1972 price $98.88, value $50-60.

Digita-Victor

VIC-52 4-funct, mem, red LED, 4-AA rep batt, 3.0x5.5", may be a Mexican division of Victor, label is in Spanish, interesting slide-switch for memory, Mexico, value $50-75.

Dixon

See Prinztronic.

Eiko

See Unitrex.

Eldorado

Eldorado Electrodata Corp., of Concord, California (USA) was originally an electronic instrumentation company that branched out very briefly into electronic calculators. They produced a few AC-only, desk-top models and even fewer "portable" versions.

8KB 4-funct, fluor, sealed batt, 5.75x9.0", large portable desk-top, mustard color, 1972 price $199.95, USA, value $50-60.

Mathmagic 4-funct, fluor, sealed batt, 1973 price $120, USA, value $50-60.

Touchmagic B 4-funct, orange fluor display, AC only model, 3.75x6.25", small portable-like, but used AC-line cord, c1972, blue case, USA, value $45-55.

Electronic Readout Systems

1660 *aka Super Slim Slide Rule,* 4-funct, mem, %, sq funct, fluor, sealed batt, 3.0x6.0", Hong Kong, value $30-40.

Elektronika

Ministry of Electronics,(USSR). The various model lines of the Elektronika series were produced by state-run companies. The B3- line was built by a company in Zelenograd (a suburb of Moscow), and the C3- line was built by the Svetlana company in St. Petersburg. After the Ministry of Electronics was organized about 1979, all calculators in the USSR soon fell under the "MK" model line naming convention.

B3-04 4-funct, LCD, sealed batt, 3x4.5", first Russian-made hand-held calculator and first Russian LCD, similar to Sharp EL-805M model, 1974, USSR, value $85-120.

B3-09M 4-funct, %, recip, fluor, sealed batt, c1975, first Russian fluorescent, USSR, value $80-95.

B3-14M 4-funct, recip, sq rt, fluor, sealed batt, 3.25x6.0", similar to Corvus model 312, c1975, USSR, value $55-75.

B3-23 4-funct, %, LED, sealed batt, 2.25x6.0", first Russian LED, USSR, value $85-100.

B3-24G 4-funct, mem, LED, sealed batt, 2.25x6.0", USSR, value $55-75.

B3-25A 4-funct, fluor, sealed batt, 2.25x6.0", USSR, value $55-75.

B3-18 *aka B3-18A*, sci-funct, fluor, sealed batt, 3.5x6.25", similar to Rockwell 61R, first Russian scientific, c1976, USSR, value $85-110.

B3-19 *aka B3-19M*, sci-funct, LED, sealed batt, 3.5x6.5", RPN entry, c1976, USSR, value $50-70.

B3-21 sci-funct, programmable, fluor, 3.5x7.0", RPN entry, first Russian programmable, c1977, USSR, value $50-70.

B3-26 4-funct, mem, %, sq rt, sgn chg, fluor, c1976, USSR, value $50-70.

B3-30 4-funct, %, sq rt, LCD, sealed batt, 2.5x4.25", a return to LCD technology, very short-lived model, c1978, USSR, value $50-70.

B3-32 sci-funct, green fluor, 3-AA rep batt, 3.0x4.75", found determinants and roots of quadratic equations, c1980, USSR, value $45-60.

B3-34 sci-funct, programmable, fluor, sealed batt, 3.5x7.0", RPN entry, c1979, USSR, value $45-60.

B3-36 sci-funct, factorial, LED, sealed batt, 3.0x5.75", c1980, USSR, value $45-60.

B3-37 sci-funct, LED, rep batt, 3.0x6.0", c1976, USSR, value $50-70.

C3-15 sci-funct, red LED, 4-AA rep batt, 3.5x6.75", unique magnitude function, c1977, USSR, value $45-60.

C3-27 4-funct, fluor, rep batt, 3.0x6.5", c1975, USSR, value $55-75.

C3-33 4-funct, mem, %, recip, sgn chg, LED, 2-AA rep batt, 3.5x6.25", similar to Radofin style, c1976, USSR, value $60-70.

MK-52 sci-funct, green fluor, 4-AA rep batt, 8.25x3.0", RPN entry, probably last USSR-built calc, ROM cartridges available, c1986, USSR, value $55-75.

MK-54 sci-funct, programmable, green fluor, 3-AA rep batt, 3x6.5", RPN entry, start of MK line, c1980, USSR, value $45-60.

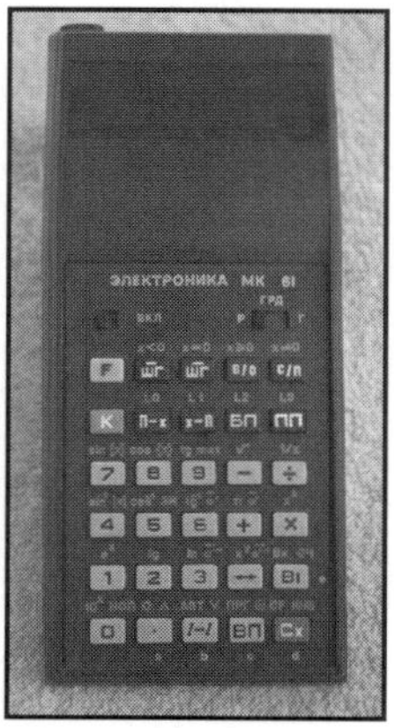

MK-61 sci-funct, green fluor, 3-AA rep batt, 3.25x6.5", RPN entry, c1983 - 1989, USSR, value $45-60.

Elite

European brand distributed through Kaufhof, a large German marketing company.

4000M 4-funct, mem, %, green fluor, 4-AA rep batt, 3.5x6.0", value $40-50.

4003 4-funct, mem, %, sq funct, recip, green fluor, 2-AA rep batt, 3.25x5.5", value $40-50.

5000TM sci-funct, green fluor, 4-AA rep batt, 3.5x5.5", value $50-60.

7004 SR sci-funct, green fluor, 4-AA rep batt, value $50-60.

S2003 4-funct, mem, %, sq funct, recip, green fluor, 4-AA rep batt, value $40-50.

Elka

Bulgarian calculator company.

732 4-funct, red LED, 4-AA rep batt, 2.75x5.25", bright yellow plastic case, IC chips made by Rockwell and Texas Instruments, c1975, Bulgaria, value $50-65.

Eltex

Eltex Electronic Company, West Germany.

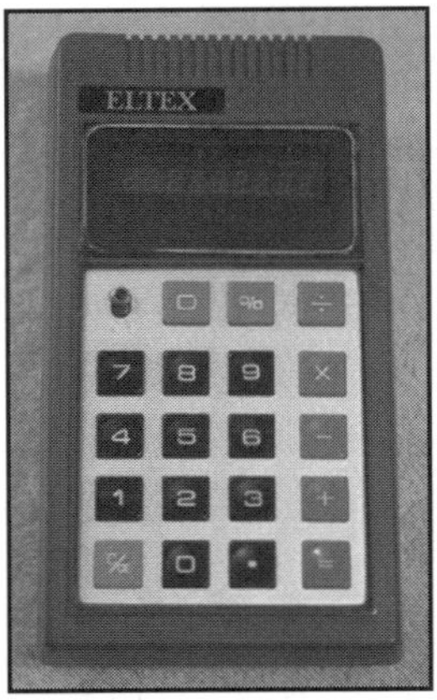

2000 4-funct, %, fluor, 4-AA rep batt, 3.0x5.75", Singapore, value $50-60.

Emerson

SX-4500 4-funct, mem, %, LED, 4-AA rep batt, 7.5x4.5", has built-in mini-tape recorder, Japan, value $100-130.

Enterprex

As was true of many companies in the early 1970's Enterprex imported pocket calculators under their logo but did not actually manufacture them. As of the mid-1990's Enterprex is still in business and continues to import calculators from the Orient.

100M 4-funct, mem, fluor, 2-D rep batt, 6.75x6.75", ivory case, similar to Royal D-120, value $25-35.

406 4-funct, red LED, 9V rep batt, 2.75x5.0", a basic 4-function machine,

Hong Kong, value $35-40.

605 4-funct, %, red LED, 2-AA rep batt, 3.0x5.0", value $35-45.

616 4-funct, mem, %, red LED, 2-AA rep batt, 3.0x5.0", similar case to 605, Hong Kong, value $30-40.

BJ21 4-funct, sq rt, fluor, 3-AAA rep batt, 3.0x5.5", this 1970's calculator had a slide switch which converts the math functions to game functions. An almost identical model was imported by Radio Shack (EC-21) and a very similar model was sold by Unisonic. All have metal cases and were made in Taiwan, value $45-55.

M-90 4-funct, mem, sq rt, fluor, 2-AA rep batt, 2.75x5.0", looks like a Commodore model, Taiwan, value $35-45.

R-90 4-funct, mem, sq rt, 2-AA rep batt, 3.0x4.75", unusual Enterprex with numerals on faceplate - not on keys, Taiwan, value $35-45.

In the mid-1960's, electronic (transistor) desktop calculators were so expensive that electro-mechanical calculators and adding machines still outsold them. Yet by 1970, electro-mechanical machines were essentially obsolete.

SR-55 *aka Jr. Sliderule and Electric Slide Rule*, 4-funct, mem, %, sq funct, recip, sgn chg, green fluor, 2-AA rep batt, 3.0x5.75", Taiwan, value $45-55.

ST-100 4-funct, mem, %, sq rt, sgn chg, green fluor, sealed batt, 3.0x5.25", thin, metal case, Taiwan, value $35-45.

Z-50 4-funct, mem, %, red LED, 9V rep batt, 2.75x5.0", attractive 2-tone case, at least 2 style variations are known, Taiwan, value $25-30.

Z-90 4-funct, mem, %, sq rt, sgn chg, fluor, 2-AA rep batt, 3.0x5.25", 1978 price $10.47, Taiwan, value $30-40.

Exactra

See the Exactra models by Texas Instruments.

Faber-Castell

West German drafting and engineering equipment. They also made slide rules. Their models sold mainly in Europe.

TR 3 sci-funct, red LED, sealed batt pack, 6.75x2.25", horizontal unit with a slide rule on the back, very stylish, very unique, West Germany, value $175-250.

Facit

European company.

1140 4-funct, %, paper tape display, sealed batt, 4.25x6.75", unusual rounded plastic shape, same as Addo 9218, c1976, Sweden, value $45-55.

Falcon

F600 4-funct, mem, %, sq rt, green fluor, 2-AA rep batt, 3.0x5.0", black case, value $40-50.

Friden

See Singer.

General Instrument

Integrated circuit maker. One of the few known companies in Canada that produced calculators in the early 1970's. Interestingly, the operating instructions were actually molded into the plastic on the back of their calculators.

EZ-2000 4-funct, red LED, sealed batt, 3.0x6.5", Canada, c1973, value $45-55.

EZ-3000 4-funct, red LED, sealed batt, 3.0x6.0", compact version of EZ-2000, Canada, c1973, value $45-55.

EZ-3100 4-funct, %, red LED, sealed batt, 3.0x6.0", similar to EZ-3000 but less common, Canada, value $50-60.

Gillette

The razor-making giant apparently decided to enter the calculator business in a very limited way. Only one model is known to have been produced.

PC-1 4-funct, red LED, 9V rep batt,

3.0x6.25", same style as Sinclair's Oxford series, made by Sinclair for Gillette, England, value $65-75.

Hapco

Hapco of Boulder, Colorado (USA).

Mark II 4-funct, red LED, sealed batt, 3.0x4.0", USA, value $50-60.

Hanimex

British company which made calculators in addition to other consumer items like photographic equipment. Some Hanimex calculator labels state "Hanimex group of companies" and list eight or ten nations. However, most if not all models appear to have been actually made in Hong Kong.

202 4-funct, %, red LED, 9V rep batt, 2.5x4.0", similar case to Casio Pocket Mini, Hong Kong, value $30-40.

Today, calculators that originally sold for several hundred dollars can be obtained for just a few dollars (or less) at thrift stores, flea markets, and garage sales. This will change as the collectibility grows and becomes more popular. Finding older calculators cheaply will become more difficult as demand increases and more people recognize their value.

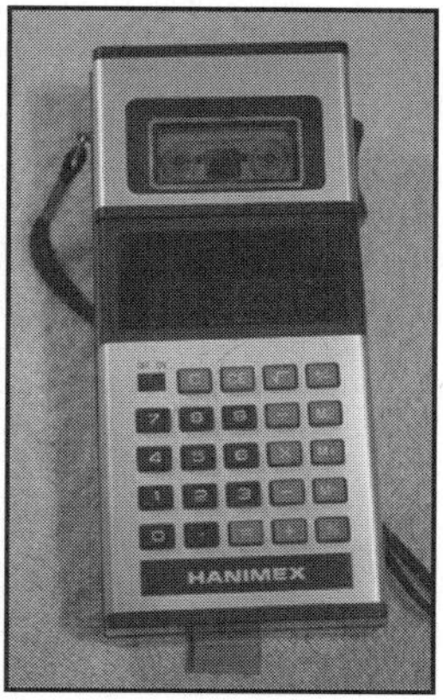

205 *aka calculator-recorder*, 4-funct, mem, sq rt, green fluor, 3-AA rep batt, 2.75x6.25", Hong Kong, this very unusual model has a built in micro-cassette tape recorder, value $200-250.

305 4-funct, %, red LED, 9V rep batt, 3.0x6.0", stylish black case, c1975, Hong Kong, value $60-70.

807 4-funct, mem, %, sq rt, red LED, 2-AA rep batt, 3.0x5.0", c1975, Hong Kong, value $40-50.

811 4-funct, mem, sq rt, red LED, 2-AA rep batt, 3.0x5.0", Hong Kong, value $40-50.

1640 4-funct, mem, %, sq rt, red LED,

9V rep batt, 2.6x5.2", Hong Kong, value $40-50.

2170 4-funct, mem, %, sq funct, recip, sgn chg, green fluor, 2-AA rep batt, 3.5x5.5", Hong Kong, value $40-50.

BC-900B 4-funct, %, fluor, 4-AA rep batt, appears to be an early model, two-tone case, c1975, Hong Kong, value $60-70.

BCM-19V 4-funct, mem, %, red LED, 9V rep batt, 2.5x4.0", perhaps the smallest Hanimex ever made, Hong Kong, value $30-40.

BCM-30 4-funct, mem, %, red LED, 9V rep batt, 2.75x5.0", Hong Kong, value $25-30.

BCM-803 4-funct, mem, %, red LED, 2-AA rep batt, 3.0x4.75", c1975, Hong Kong, value $40-50.

BCM-817 4-funct, mem, green fluor, unusual off-white case, 3.0x5.5", c1975, Hong Kong, value $35-45.

BCM-818 4-funct, mem, %, sq rt, sgn chg, green fluor, 4-AAA rep batt, value $40-50.

CM-401 4-funct, mem, %, fluor and paper printer, 5-AA rechargeable batt, 4.0x7.5", Hong Kong, value $35-45.

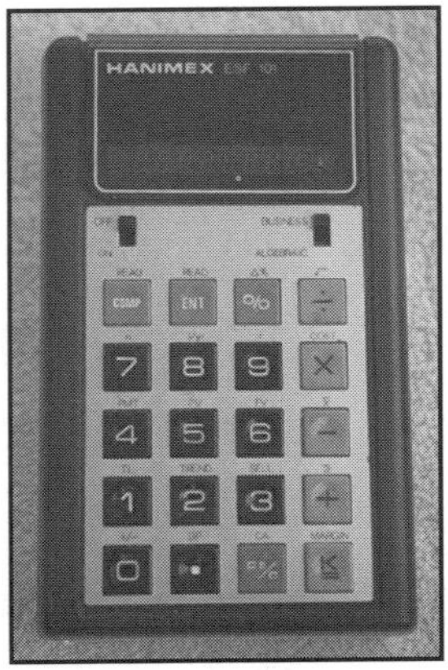

ESF-101 financial funct, sgn chg, sq rt, fluor, 4-AA rep batt, 3.5x5.5", Hong Kong, value $45-55.

TP750 4-funct, mem, %, sgn chg, paper tape display only, 4-C rep batt, 5.75x9.0", Hong Kong, value $30-40.

Heathkit

USA company known for their electronic hobbyist kits. They only sold a few electronic calculator kits - portable and desk-top styles.

IC-2006 4-funct, red LED, 9V rep batt, 3.2x5.5", available as a kit, 1973 price $69.95, USA, value $70-90.

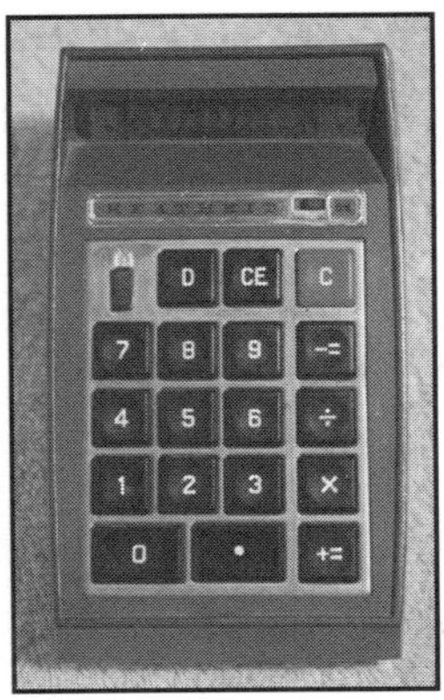

IC-2009 4-funct, red LED, sealed batt,

3.2x5.5", similar to Bowmar 901 case style using the TI keypad, 1973 price 92.50, USA, value $60-75.

Hermes

Administrator 4-funct, mem, %, 4-button rep batt, 2.5x4.5", value $45-55.

Hewlett-Packard

HPs are perhaps the most sought after of all pocket calculators. There are hundreds of loyal HP fans who collect only this brand. Perhaps this is because so many engineers and scientists have used these wonderful machines throughout their careers. Additional details of HP models can be found in the excellent ***A Guide to HP Handheld Calculators and Computers*** *(see the "Resource" section of book for ordering information). Between 1972 and 1979 HP made some 28 different LED-display pocket calculators and the HP-01 LED calculator watch. Avid HP collectors strive to obtain all LED models. The "classic" family (HP 35, 45, 55, 65, 67, 70 and 80) are larger than the series 30 models. The series 20 are even smaller. HP model numbers are a bit confusing. Unlike many other brands, the earliest models do not have the lowest model numbers. For example, the HP-35 was made years before the HP-25. Although literally dozens of US companies made calculators during the 1970's only HP and TI survived the intense market competition. These are the only two US companies that continue to produce pocket calculators today, but they no longer actually manufacture any models in the United States.*
Originally, HP calculators were manufactured in the USA with some made also in Singapore and a few made in Brazil.

01 4-funct, red LED, 3-button rep batt, 2.0x1.5", with the possible exception of the Sinclair "wrist calculator" the HP-01 calculator-watch is the smallest known LED-display calculator. Price when introduced in 1977 was $650 for the steel case and $850 for the gold-tone version making the HP-01 one of the most expensive calculators ever sold, USA, value: steel-case $500-800; gold-tone $600-900.

10 4-funct, mem, red LED, sealed batt pack, 3.5x6.5", has mini-printer like HP-19C, unlike most early HPs the HP-10 uses algebraic data entry not RPN, 1977 price $175, USA, value $100-150.

19C sci-funct, programmable, red LED, sealed batt pack, 3.5x6.5", this is like the 29C but with a built-in mini-printer, 1977 price $345, USA, value $100-150.

21 sci-funct, red LED, sealed batt pack, 2.75x5.0", 1975 price $125, USA, value $35-55.

22 business functions, red LED, sealed batt pack, 2.75x5.0", 1975 price $165, USA, value $100-125.

25 sci-funct, 49-step programmable, red LED, sealed batt pack, 2.75x5.0", 1975 price $195, USA, value $40-60.

25C same as 25 but with continuous memory which holds data when calculator is turned off, 1976 price $200, USA, value $60-80.

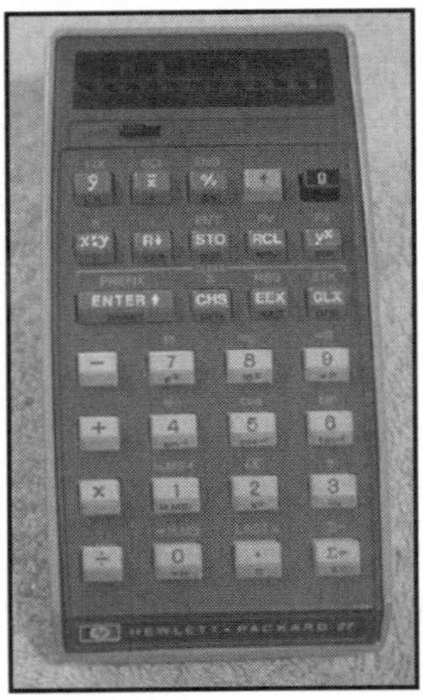

27 financial and sci-funct, red LED, sealed batt pack, 2.75x5.0", an upgraded HP 22, 1976 price $200, USA, value $100-125.

29C sci-funct, 98-step programmable, red LED, sealed batt pack, 2.75x5.0", an improved HP-25, 1977 price $195, USA, value $90-110.

31E sci-funct, red LED, sealed batt pack, 3.0x5.5", replaced the HP-21, 1978 price $60, USA, value $75-95.

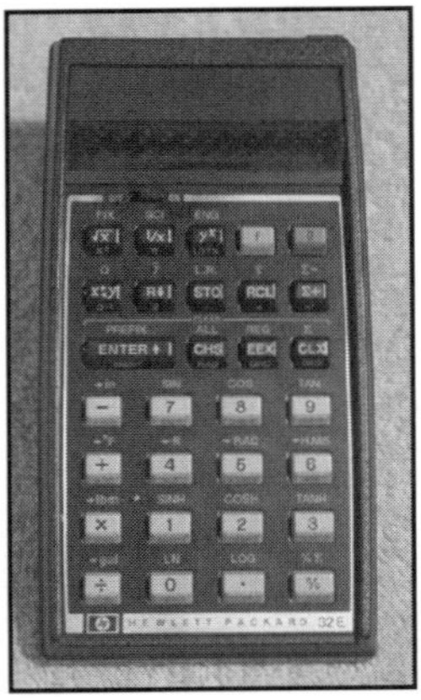

32E sci-funct, red LED, sealed batt pack, 3.0x5.5", like 31E but adds statistical funct, 1978 price $80, USA, value $30-50.

33C Same as 33E but has continuous memory, 1979 price $120, USA, value $50-70.

33E sci-funct, 49-step programmable, red LED, sealed batt pack, 3.0x5.5", replaced the HP-25, 1978 price $100, USA, value $40-50.

34C sci-funct, 210-step programmable, red LED, sealed batt pack, 3.0x5.5", 1979 price $150, USA, value $50-70.

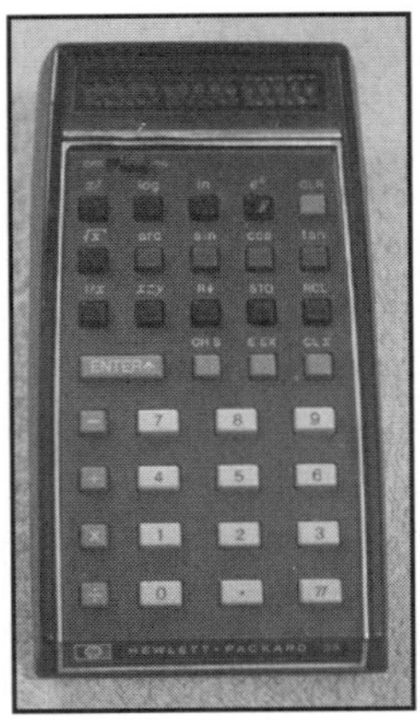

35 sci-funct, red LED, sealed batt

pack, 3.0x5.75", HP's first pocket calculator and probably the world's first hand-held scientific calculator, first sold in January 1972, several slightly different versions exist, 1972 price $395, USA, value $80-130.

37E financial funct, red LED, sealed batt pack, 3.0x5.5", 1979 price $75, USA, value $25-45.

38C business funct, programmable, red LED, sealed batt pack, 3.0x5.5", 1979 price $150, USA, value $50-75.

38E business funct, programmable, red LED, sealed batt pack, 3.0x5.5", 1978 price $120, USA, value $25-45.

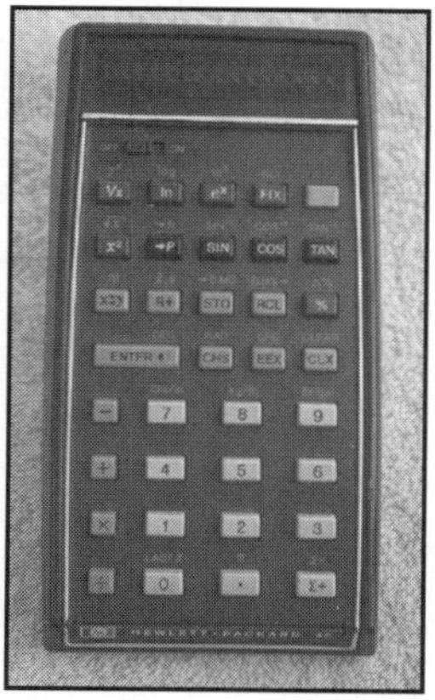

45 sci-funct, red LED, sealed batt pack, 3.0x5.75", the third model made by HP (after the 35 and 80), 1973 price $395, USA, value $75-100.

55 sci-funct, programmable, red LED, sealed batt pack, 3.0x5.75", a cheaper alternative to the HP-65 but lacking the card reader, 1975 price $395, USA, value $90-110.

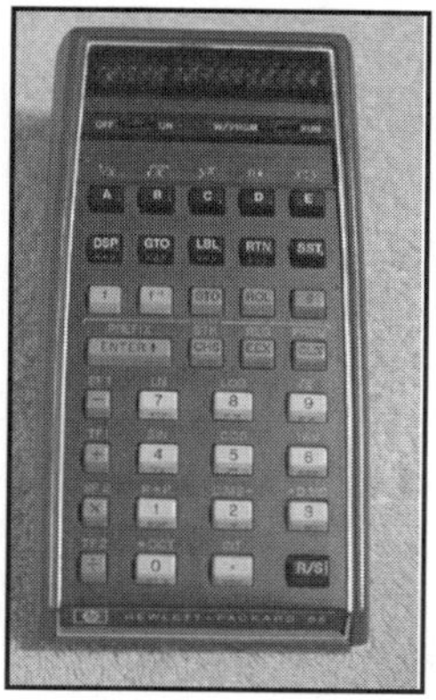

65 sci-funct, programmable, red LED, sealed batt pack, 3.0x5.75", perhaps the world's first programmable pocket calculator, also introduced a build in card reader for saving programs (but not data), the HP-65 came out over a year before the first widely-available personal computer (MITS-Altair) yet was in many ways more advanced. One of the most expensive (non-printing) pocket calculators ever sold (and many feel well worth the price), 1974 price $795, USA, value $200-250.

67 sci-funct, programmable, red LED, sealed batt pack, 3.0x5.75", an improved and more economical version of the HP-65, 1976 price $450, USA, value $60-80.

70 business funct, red LED, sealed batt

pack, 3.0x5.75", a lower-priced version of the HP-80, was withdrawn after only one year and hence is rare, 1974 price $275, USA, value $200-300.

80 business functions, red LED, sealed batt pack, 3.0x5.75", HP's second pocket calculator and their first business model, 1973 price $395, USA, value $60-100.

91 sci-funct, red LED, sealed batt pack, 8.0x9.0", one of the first portable calculators to include a built-in printer, 1976 price $500, USA, value $150-250.

92 business functions, red LED, sealed batt pack, 8.0x9.0", built-in printer, ahead of its time, 1977 price $500, USA, value $200-300.

97 sci-funct, programmable, red LED, sealed batt pack, 8.0x9.0", the printing version of the HP-67, built-in card reader, 1976 price $750, USA, value $60-100.

97S sci-funct, programmable, red LED, sealed batt pack, 8.0x9.0", a special version of the HP-97 with input/output feature to communicate with other devices, 1977 price $1375, USA, value $120-220.

Homeland

Appears to have been available only in England. On the 8006, there is a company listing on the bottom of the back label -- "Toshiba Business Machine" -- with no other information. This may be the parent company or just the manufacturer.

In 1964, the US made Friden 130 was the state-of-the-art calculator. It was the size of a TV, used a CRT (television tube) display and cost thousands of dollars. Less than 10 years later, Friden introduced its 1008 pocket model for about $300.

8006 4-funct, %, sq rt, fluor, 1-AA rep batt, 3.25x4.75", Japan, value $35-45.
8010 4-funct, %, sq rt, green fluor, 2-AA rep batt, 3.0x5.25", Japan, value $35-45.

Hughes Aircraft

Hughes Aircraft Company (USA) is a manufacturer of advanced electronic systems for the military and space programs. Their semiconductor division in Newport Beach, California made LED watches for other companies to sell during the 1970's. They made one calculator watch which may never have been widely sold under their own name.

Calculator Watch 4-funct, %, red LED, 4-button rep batt, 1.5x1.75" similar looking to CompuChron model except with round-edged case, available in gold or silver tone, value $150-300.

Iain Jones

Iain Jones International LTD, Great Neck, New York (USA), was one of the first companies to enter the pocket calculator business but apparently didn't survive very long. Made only a few models during 1972-1973. Possibly a British company based in the USA.

Mini 4-funct, red LED, 9V rep batt, 3.1x5.75", 1973 price $99.95, value $80-90.

Phoenix 4-funct, red LED, sealed batt, 3.0x5.25", decimal slide switch, looks like the original Bowmar 901B but more difficult to find, 1973 price $129, USA, value $120-150.

Ibico

Calculators sold primarily in Europe and Japan.

076 4-funct, mem, %, sq funct, recip, fluor, 4-AAA rep batt, 3.0x5.0", Japan, value $30-40.

083 4-funct, %, green fluor, 4-AA rep batt, 3.5x5.0", c1974, Japan, value $30-40.

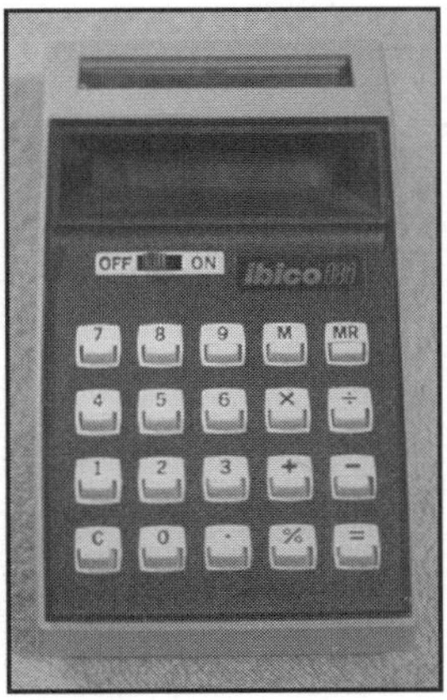

086 4-funct, mem, %, early LCD, 2-9V rep batt, 3.5x6.0", early LCD display with see-through panel at top of calculator to help light LCD, same as Dataking LC-800 and Lloyd's 40, Mexico (of US parts), value $40-50.

088 4-funct, mem, %, sq funct, recip, fluor, 4-AAA rep batt, 3.25x5.25", Japan, value $30-40.

ICP

ICP is the abbreviation for International Consumer Products, Ltd., a subsidiary of Arlen Realty and Development Corp, a very large US shopping center developer who diversified into calculators briefly.

504 4-funct, 6 digit red LED with 12 digit display and calculating ability, 9V rep batt, 3.25x5.75", unusual silver and black colored case, Taiwan, value $60-70.

530 4-funct, mem, %, sgn chg, red LED, 4-AA rep batt, 3.0x5.75", 1974 price $79.95, value $40-50.

537 sci-funct, mem, red LED, 4-AA rep batt, 3.0x5.75", looks like Qualitron models, 1974 price $159, value $45-55.

Imperial

Imperial Typewriter and Business Machines, Ltd.; Leicester, England. Appears to be a division of Adler/Royal due to the similarity of the design.

90K 4-funct, %, green fluor, 4.75x2.8", 4-AA, Japan, value $40-50.

Interton

Interton Electronics. Apparently available mainly in Europe.

PC-2010 4-funct, 4-AA rep batt, 3.0x5.25", value $35-45.

PC-4010 4-funct, %, sq funct, recip, sgn chg, green fluor, 9V, 3.0x5.75", value $35-45.

Invicta

Invicta Plastics, Ltd, Leicester, England.

Electronic Master Mind Master Mind game, fluor, 2-AA rep batt, 3.0x5.0" c1977, Hong Kong, value $15-25.

ITT

International conglomerate ITT is not known to have made or sold calculators except for these apparently designed for the European market.

S-Trainer 4-funct, educational calculator, red LED, 9V rep batt, 3.0x6.0", similar to Novus case styles, has a data connector on side, Hong Kong, value $30-40.

JCE

John Colling Enterprises; Palo Alto, California (USA).

Mark II 4-funct, red LED, 5-AA rep batt, 3.25x5.5", beige case, Klixon keypad, switch on end for decimal position, c1972, USA, value $35-45.

Percent 4-funct, %, red large digit LED, 5-AA rep or rechargeable batt, 3.25x5.5", black case, Klixon keypad, switch on end for decimal position, looks like Mark II, c1972, USA, value $55-65.

Super "D" 4-funct, red large digit LED, 5-AA rep batt, 3.25x5.5", black case, Klixon keypad, switch on end for decimal position, looks like Mark II, c1972, USA, value $55-65.

J.C. Penney

American department store chain which also sold calculators through a general merchandise catalog.

2300 4-funct, sq rt, mem, fluor, sealed batt, 3.0x6.25", same case as APF Mark 23, Japan, value $40-50.

2310 4-funct, %, red LED, 4-N rep batt, 3.0x4.75", similar to Corvus 400, tan colored case and cinnamon colored keys, USA, value $40-50.

5000 4-funct, mem, green fluor, sealed batt, 3.5x6.0", similar to Royal Award MGT, Japan, value $45-55.

GL-986R 4-funct, mem, %, green fluor, sealed batt, 3.0x5.5", same as Commodore GL-986R, USA, value $30-40.

GL-996R 4-funct, %, green fluor, sealed batt, 3.0x5.5", Japan, value $35-45.

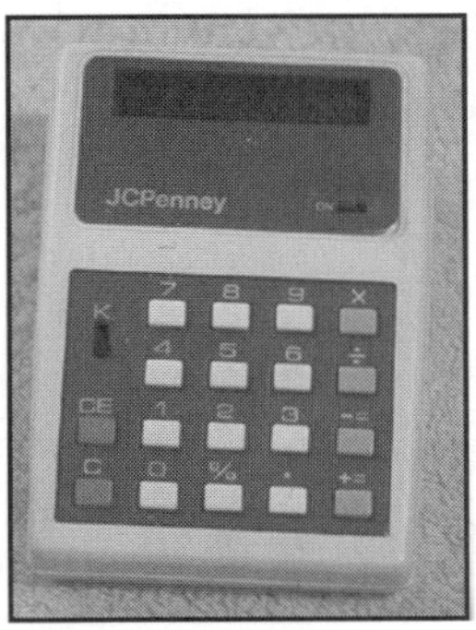

MM3R 4-funct, %, red LED, sealed

batt, 3.0x4.0", similar to Commodore MM3R, USA, value $35-45.

Karstadt

Karstadt, West Germany.

MR40 4-funct, mem, %, sq rt, sgn chg, green fluor, 4-AA rep batt, 3.5x5.5", similar case to Unimark 805T and Prinztronic 88P, Japan, value $45-55.

Keystone

Most, if not all, Keystone models were made in the USA in the early 1970's. The company, located in Paramus New Jersey, apparently did not survive the wild price drops of the mid-1970's which decimated profit margins. A few Keystone models also say "Berkey" or "Berkey-Keystone" on the case. (See Berkey calculators.) Some models with sealed, rechargeable batteries have a tiny charge indicator just above the keypad. Displays appear to be mainly Panaplex®, a display type made by Burroughs.

88 4-funct, %, orange fluor, 4-AA rep batt, 3.2x5.25", c1974-75, USA, value $50-60.

98 4-funct, mem, %, fluor, sealed batt, 3.2x5.25", looks like 88, c1974-75, USA, value $50-60.

108 4-funct, mem, sq rt, fluor, sealed batt, 3.2x5.25", looks like 88, USA, value $50-$60.

370 4-funct, %, fluor, sealed batt, 3.2x5.25", looks like 88, USA, value $50-60.

390 4-funct, mem, %, fluor, sealed batt, 3.2x5.25", looks like 88, 1973 price $159.95, USA, value $50-60.

395 4-funct, mem, %, sq rt, fluor, sealed batt, 3.2x5.25", looks like 88, 1974 price $140, USA, value $55-65.

2010 4-funct, %, sgn chg, 2-AA rep

batt, 3.2x5.5", USA, value $45-55.

2030 4-funct, mem, %, fluor, sealed batt, 3.2x6.0", looks like 2010, 1975 price $65, USA, value $40-50.

2040 4-funct, mem, %, sq rt, fluor, sealed batt, 3.2x6.0", looks like 2010, c1975, USA, value $40-50.

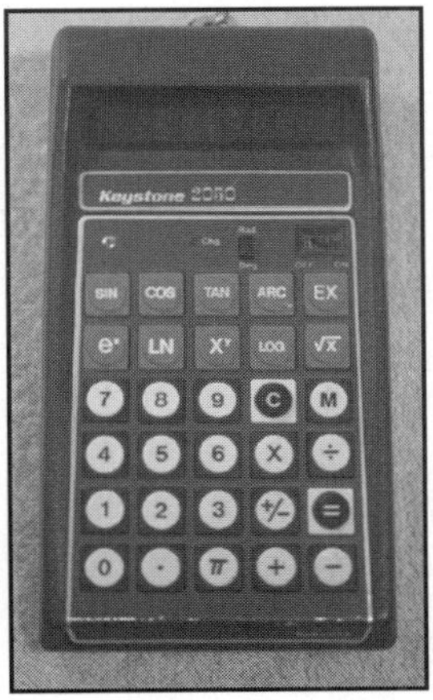

2050 sci-funct, fluor, sealed batt, 3.6x6.75", looks like 2010, 1975 price $120, USA, value $45-55.

SC 650 4-funct, %, sgn chg, fluor, 2-AA rep batt, 3.2x5.5", looks like 2010, USA, value $50-60.

SC 652 4-funct, mem, %, sgn chg, fluor, sealed batt, 3.2x6.0", looks like 2010, USA, value $50-60.

SC 654 4-funct, mem, %, sq rt, sgn chg, fluor, sealed batt, 3.2x6.0", USA, value $50-60.

SC 656 sci-funct, 3.2x6.0", sealed batt, USA, value $50-60.

Kings Point

Early Kings Point models (8000 and SPM series) used tube displays and often had several interesting display lights such as low-battery indicators. These fascinating models also had metal face-plates and a unique spring-loaded battery compartment door. They use the prefix "SC" to indicate scientific calculator.

8412 *aka Micro Memory*, 4-funct, mem, %, tube display, 4-AA rep batt, 3.25x6.0", Japan, value $40-50.

8413 *aka Micro Algebra*, 4-funct, sq rt, tube display, 4-AA rep batt, 3.25x6.0", Japan, value $45-55.

8414 *aka Micro Executive*, 4-funct, %, tube display, 4-AA rep batt, 3.25x6.0", Japan, value $45-55.

9202 4-funct, mem, %, blue fluor, 4-C batt, 4.5x7.5", similar case to Soundesign 8300, Japan, value $40-50.

FN-85 *aka financial computer*, financial funct, fluor, sealed batt, 3.5x6.5", case similar to SC series, does not use LED display, 1976 price $99.95, Hong Kong, value $55-60.

KP-200 *aka Slide Rule*, 4-funct, %, sq funct, recip, 10 digit fluor, 3-AA rep batt, 3.25x6.75", Hong Kong, value $45-55.

KP-450 4-funct, mem, %, blue fluor, 3-AA rep batt, 3.3x6.6", Hong Kong, value $50-60.

PC-2 4-funct, %, LED, 9V rep batt, 2.75x5.6", Japan, value $50-60.

SC-11 sci-funct, red LED, 9V rep batt, 2.5x5.5", the smallest known Kings Point model, Korea, value $40-50.

SC-20 sci-funct, mem, exp, red LED, sealed batt, 3.5x6.5", Hong Kong, value $40-50.

SC-33 sci-funct, mem, exp, red LED, sealed batt, 3.5x6.5", Hong Kong, value $45-55.

SC-40 sci-funct, mem, exp, red LED, sealed batt, 3.5x6.5", 1974 price $139, Japan, value $50-55.

SC-44 sci-funct, mem, exp, red LED, sealed batt, 3.5x6.5", c1974, Hong Kong, value $55-65.

SC-44F sci-funct, mem, exp, fluor, sealed batt, 3.5x6.5", Korea, similar to SC-44 but has interesting fluor display, value $65-75.

SC-60 sci-funct, mem, exp, red LED, sealed batt, 3.5x6.5", 1976 price $59, value $55-65.

SC-6010 sci-funct, mem, exp, red LED, sealed batt, 3.5x6.5", same as SC-60 except with more memories, 1976 price $69, value $55-65.

SCM-100 4-funct, mem, tube display,

4-AA rep batt, 3.25x6.0", Hong Kong, similar to the early 8000 series models, value $45-55.

Kosmos

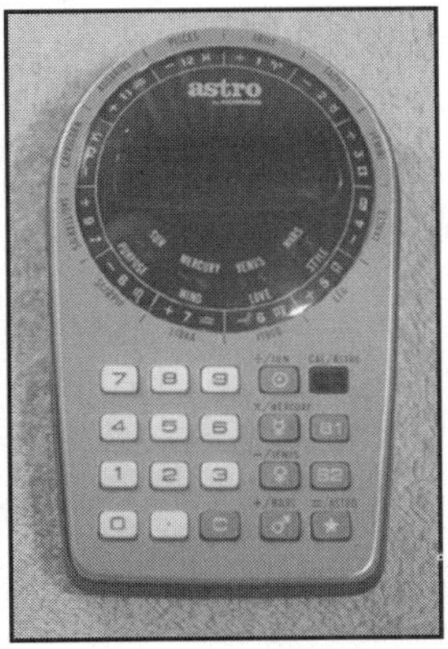

Astro 4-funct and biorhythm calculations, fluor, 2-AA rep batt, 3.0x4.5", unusual styling with a rounded top, same as Radio Shack 312, Taiwan, value $55-65.

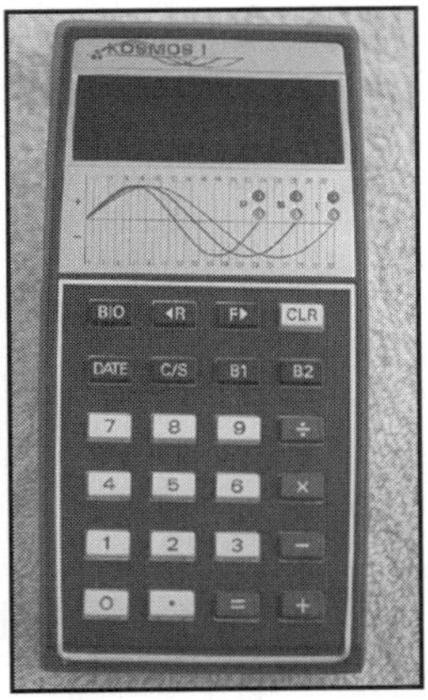

Kosmos 1 4-funct and biorhythm calculations, green fluor, 3-AA rep batt, 2.5x5.5", Japan, value $30-45.

Kosmos 2 4-funct and biorhythm calculations, fluor, 2-AA rep batt, 3.0x5.25", same case as Radio Shack EC-314, Taiwan, value $20-30.

Kovac

United Kingdom.

Mini 4-funct, tube display, 2-C rep batt, 5.25x8.25", batt strength indicator, c1973, Japan, value $55-65.

SM-858M 4-funct, mem, %, sq rt, green fluor, 4-AA rep batt, 3.75x6.25", c1974, Japan, value $55-70.

Lexicon

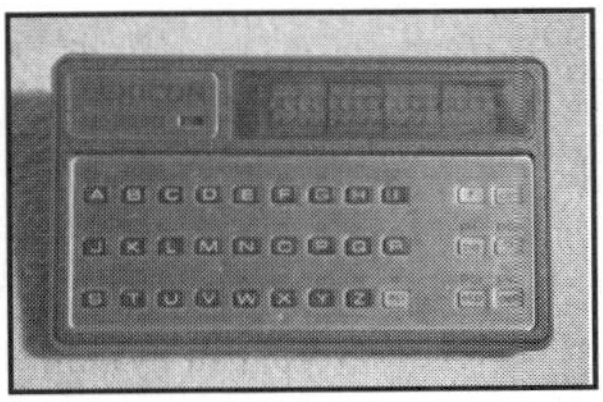

LK-3000 4-funct, mem, %, sgn chg, red LED, sealed batt, 6.25x4.0", horizontal, alpha-numeric keypad, could use various slip-in modules with capabilities to translate words from one language to another, made by Nixdorf and is the same as Nixdorf LK-3000, 1980 price $140, Malaysia, value $35-45.

Litronix

Litronix, Inc. was located in Cupertino, California (USA), the city made famous by Apple Computer. They originally were simply a manufacturer of LED displays and decided, like Bowmar before them, to branch into the more profitable calculator end-product. Some Litronix models have the word, "Checkmate" on the case.

Checkmate *see 1002 when there is no other model number with "Checkmate." Later Litronix models used "Checkmate" in conjunction with the number (for example, Checkmate 1700) Occasionally another model has only "Checkmate" on the front -- the 1102 -- however this is not always the case and is less common and a different case style than the 1002.*

1000 *aka Triton* 1000, 4-funct, red LED, 3-AA rep batt, 3.0x6.0", had decimal slide switch, similar to model 1100 but has unusual black colored case, significance of Triton name is unknown, value $35-45.

1002 *aka Checkmate*, 4-funct, LED, sealed batt, 3.0x5.5", probably the first Litronix model, almost 1.25" thick, boxy like an early Bowmar or Craig, very different from other Litronix models, Klixon keypad, slide switch for 2 or 4 decimal selection, second variation has a non-Klixon keypad and no mention of model # or Litronix company -- possibly a version for another marketing company?, both versions have "Checkmate" label on front, c1972, Malaysia, value $55-65.

1100 4-funct, red LED, 3-AA rep batt, 3.0x6.0", has decimal slide switch, similar to Triton 1000 but with brownish colored case, 1973 price $39.95, Malaysia, value $30-35.

1100A 4-funct, red LED, 3-AA rep batt, 3.0x6.0", decimal slide switch, c1973, Malaysia, value $20-30.

1101 4-funct, %, red LED, 4-AA rep batt, 3.0x6.0", similar case to 1100A, Malaysia, value $20-30.

1101P 4-funct, %, red LED, 3-AA rep batt, 3.0x6.0", similar case to 1100A, Malaysia, value $25-30.

1102 4-funct, %, red LED, 4-AA rep batt, 3.0x6.0", similar case to 1100A, constant slide switch, 1974 price $24.95, Malaysia, value $25-30.

1102A 4-funct, %, red LED, 3-AA rep batt, 3.0x6.0", constant slide switch, similar to 1102 but uses 3-AA rep batt instead of 4, "A" designation only marked on back label, Malaysia, value $25-35.

1502 *aka Avatar 1502*, 4-funct, mem, %, red LED, 9V rep batt, 3.0x5.75", dark colored case similar to 1602 and 1603, label says "Avatar by Lintronix," Malaysia, $40-50.

1602 *aka memory*, 4-funct, mem, %, red LED, 9V rep batt, 3.0x5.75", similar to 1603, Malaysia, value $45-55.

1603 *aka slide rule*, 4-funct, mem, %, sq funct, red LED, 9V rep batt, 3.0x5.75", similar to 1602, Malaysia, value $45-55.

1700 *aka Checkmate 1700*, 4-funct, red LED, 4-AA rep batt, 3.0x6.0", appears identical to 1100A except that it says Checkmate on the front instead of Litronix, Malaysia, value $25-35.

1720 *aka Checkmate 1720*, 4-funct, mem, %, sgn chg, red LED, 3-AA rep batt, 3.0x6.5", ivory case, c1975, Malaysia, value $40-50.

1720A *aka Checkmate 1720*, 4-funct, mem, %, sgn chg, red LED, 3-AA rep batt, 3.0x6.5", c1975, black case, difference between 1720 and 1720A may be only the color, Malaysia, value $40-50.

1740A *aka Checkmate* 1740, 4-funct, mem, %, sq funct, recip, sgn chg, red LED, 3-AA rep batt, 3.0x6.5", looks like 1720A, c1975, Malaysia, value $45-55.

2120 4-funct, mem, %, sgn chg, red LED, 3-AA rep batt, 3.0x6.5", looks like 1720A, Malaysia, value $45-55.

2140 4-funct, mem, red LED, 3-AA rep batt, 3.0x6.5", 1974 price $59.95, Malaysia, value $50-60.

2200 *aka memory plus*, 4-funct, mem, %, metric measurement conversions, red LED, 3-AA rep batt, first of the "new" case style, has 19 built-in conversion functions, one of the earliest calculators with conversion factors, Malaysia, value $35-45.

2200R 4-funct, mem, %, metric measurement conversions, red LED, sealed batt, same as 2200 except has sealed batt, Malaysia, value $40-50.

2220 *aka memory*, 4-funct, mem, %, sgn chg, red LED, 3-AA rep batt, 1974 price $49.95, Malaysia, value $35-40.

2220R *aka memory*, 4-funct, mem, %, sgn chg, red LED, sealed batt, 1974 price $59.95, same as 2220 except has sealed batt, Malaysia, value $35-40.

2230 *aka memory*, 4-funct, mem, %, sq rt, sgn chg, red LED, 3-AA rep batt, 1975 price $29.95, Malaysia, value $35-45.

2230R 4-funct, mem, %, sq rt, sgn chg, red LED, sealed batt, same as 2230 except has sealed batt, Malaysia, value $40-50.

2230/2235 4-funct, mem, red LED, 3-AA rep batt, appears to be same as 2235, Malaysia, value $35-45.

2235 4-funct, mem, red LED, 3-AA rep batt, similar to 2230 but has brown case instead of white, Malaysia, value $30-35.

2240RA *aka scientific*, 4-funct, mem, %, sq funct, recip, sgn chg, red LED sealed batt, 3.0x6.5", looks like 2200, Malaysia, value $35-45.

2250 *aka slide rule*, 4-funct, mem, sq funct, sgn chg, red LED, 3-AA rep batt, Malaysia, value $40-50.

2250R *aka slide rule*, 4-funct, mem, sq funct, sgn chg, red LED, sealed batt, 3.0x6.5", same as 2250 except has sealed batt, Malaysia, value $45-55.

2260 4-funct, sq funct, exponent, pi, paren, red LED, 3-AA rep batt, 3.0x6.5", Malaysia, value $45-55.

2260R *aka slide rule*, 4-funct, sq funct, exponent, pi, paren, red LED, sealed batt, 3.0x6.5", same as 2260 except has sealed batt, Malaysia, value $45-55.

2270 *aka statistical*, statistical functions, red LED, 3-AA rep batt, early statistical calculator, Malaysia, value $45-55.

2270R *aka statistical*, statistical functions, red LED, sealed batt, 3.0x6.5", same as 2270 except has sealed batt, Malaysia, value $45-55.

2280 *aka Memory II*, 4-funct, mem, %, red LED, 3-AA rep batt, 3.25x6.5", Malaysia, value $45-55.

2290R *aka programmable*, 4-funct, mem, %, programmable, red LED, sealed batt, 3.0x6.5", Malaysia, value $40-50.

Lloyd's

In the early to mid 1970's Lloyd's Electronics, Inc. of Compton, California (USA) introduced several dozen differ-

ent pocket calculator models, most using blue or green fluorescent displays. Lloyd's also sold stereo equipment and other consumer electronic products. Almost all Lloyd's calculator model numbers are preceded by the term "Accumatic." Some model numbers are preceded with an "E" such as E305, E310, and E321. With a few exceptions, most Lloyd's models fall into groups of similar models. Models 30 to 70 have a two-tone case. Models 303 to 310 have a slightly thinner case which is usually black and the display is slightly tilted towards the user. Models 311 to 334 also have the tilted display but a tan-colored case. Most 400-series have a futuristic stream-lined silver colored case. A few models like the 340 and 603 look nothing like the "typical" Lloyd's calculators. Most calculators were made in either Japan or Taiwan. Some models were manufactured in both. Origins listed are those found on models we have seen.

20 *aka EH-8822*, 4-funct, mem, %, fluor, 4-AA rep batt, 3.5x5.5", Taiwan, value $20-30.

30 *aka EH-9036*, 4-funct, %, fluor, 4-AA rep batt, 3.5x5.5", Taiwan or Japan, value $20-30.

30 *aka EH-9036-2*, this is a variation of the EH-9036 and includes sq rt, value $35-45.

30 *aka EH-9036-0018*, another variation of the EH-9036, has a minus-indicator light, Taiwan, value $55-65.

40 4-funct, mem, %, early LCD, 2-9V rep batt, 3.5x6.0", LCD display with see-through panel at top of calculator to help light LCD, same as Dataking LC-800 and Ibico 086, Mexico (of US parts), value $40-50.

50 *aka EH-9325*, 4-funct, mem, sq rt, fluor, 4-AA rep batt, 3.5x5.5", similar to models 20 to 40 but adds a metal face-plate, Japan, value $25-35.

55 *aka EH-8715*, similar to model 50 but adds square and recip, Taiwan, value $25-35.

100 4-funct, LCD, 4-C rep batt, 5.5x9.25", flip-up display cover, very early LCD made by Rockwell, possibly the first portable LCD calculator, value $60-90.

Liquid Crystal Displays (LCD) were used on calculators as early as 1972 (with Rockwell-made Lloyds and Sears calculators). Sharp developed their COS type of LCD in 1973. The LCD's benefit was the low power requirement allowing for smaller batteries. Today, virtually all calculators use LCDs.

200 *aka E681*, 4-funct, mem, %, blue fluor, 4-AA rep batt, 3.0x5.5", looks like an early Rockwell model (as does the Lloyd's 500), has tilted spring-loaded keys and a slide switch to select floating or fixed decimal place, 1973 price $99.95, label states "assembled in Mexico, primarily of United States parts", value $55-65.

303 4-funct, %, fluor, 4-AA rep batt, 3.5x5.5", Taiwan, value $20-25.

304 4-funct, %, sq rt, fluor, 4-AA rep batt, 3.5x5.5", Taiwan, value $20-25.

305 4-funct, %, sq rt, fluor, 4-AA rep batt, 3.5x5.5", similar to 304 but adds pi and constant, Japan, value $20-25.

306 4-funct, %, sq rt, fluor, similar to 305 but adds recip and square functions, value $20-25.

> *The first portable calculators sold to the public were made by Japanese companies (Canon, Sharp, Busicom, Sanyo, etc.) using American integrated circuit technology. The Japanese manufacturers were trying to break into the office calculator business machine market. These models cost up to $300-$400 in 1970 dollars and included the basic four mathematical functions.*

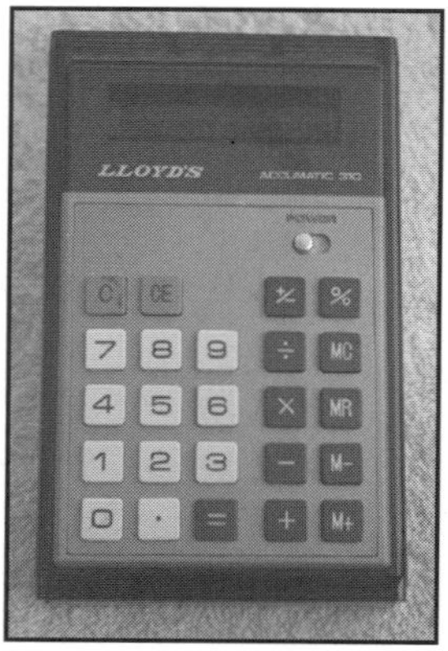

310 4-funct, %, mem, fluor, similar to 303 but adds memory, Japan or Taiwan, value $25-30.

311 4-funct, %, sq rt, mem, fluor, same case as in 320 series, 4-AA rep batt, 3.5x5.5", Japan, value $25-30.

320 4-funct, %, sq rt, recip, fluor, 4-AA rep batt, 3.5x5.5", Japan, value $25-30.

321 4-funct, %, sq rt, recip, paren, fluor, 4-AA rep batt, 3.5x5.5", Japan or Taiwan, value $25-35.

322 4-funct, %, sq rt, recip, paren, constant, fluor, 4-AA rep batt, 3.5x5.5", Japan, value $25-35.

333 sci-funct, fluor, 4-AA rep batt,

same case as 400-series models described below, Japan, value $35-40.

334 sci-funct, mem, exp, fluor, 4-AA rep batt, 3.5x5.5", first Lloyd's to use small keys to allow for sci-functions, Taiwan, value $35-45.

340 4-funct, %, sq rt, fluor, 3-AAA rep batt, 2.5x3.75", probably the smallest Lloyd's case style of the 1970's, odd method to get to battery cover -- you must slide down an outer trim piece to allow cover to open, Japan, value $45-55.

341 4-funct, mem, %, 3-AAA rep batt, 2.5x3.75", same case as 340, has memory "function" key which gives a dual "memory" role to other keys, Japan, value $50-60.

408 4-funct, %, sq rt, fluor, 4-AA rep batt, 3.5x5.5", 400-series (and model 333) have an interesting silver-colored case (which is exciting or ugly depending on your point of view), Taiwan, value $25-30.

419 4-funct, mem, fluor, 4-AA rep batt, similar to 408 but adds memory, Japan, value $25-35.

445 sci-funct, exp, fluor, 4-AA rep batt, 3.5x5.5", looks much like Lloyd's 333, Japan, value $35-45.

500 4-funct, %, mem, very interesting style, similar to Lloyd's 200, Mexico, value $65-75.

501 4-funct, mem, %, red LED, 9V rep batt, 3.0x5.25", different style from other Lloyds, Taiwan, value $45-55.

502 4-funct, red LED, 9V rep batt, 2.75x5.5", similar to Novus 826 type of cases, value $30-40.

603 4-funct, mem, %, sq rt, sgn chg, fluor, 3-AAA rep batt, 2.8x5.5", perhaps the thinnest Lloyd's calculator made in the 1970's (less than 0.5") and sporting an all-metal case, this model looks more like a Unisonic than a Lloyd's, Taiwan, value $35-45.

604 4-funct, red LED, 9V rep batt, 2.75x5.5", case similar to one by Novus or National Semiconductor, (a Lloyd's with LED displays is very unusual), USA, value $55-65.

610 4-funct, mem, %, sq rt, sgn chg, 3-AAA rep batt, 2.8x5.5", metal case similar to 603, Japan, Value S35-45.

616 4-funct, mem, %, sq funct, recip, sgn chg, paren, fluor, 3-AAA rep batt, 2.8x5.5", same thin metal case as 603, 1978 price $14.88, Taiwan, value $35-45.

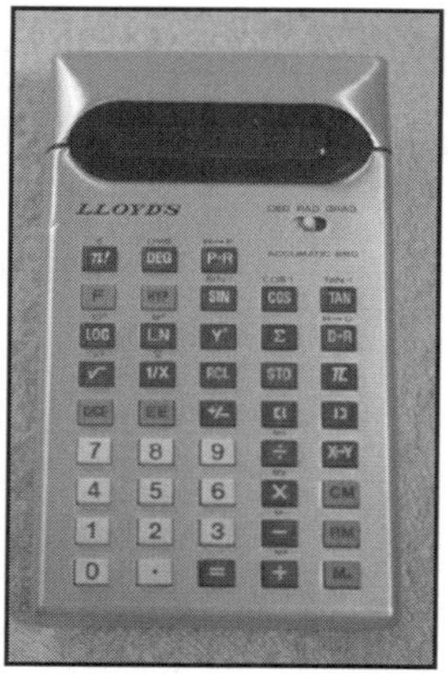

650 sci-funct, unusual 12-digit fluor display, 4-AA rep batt, 3.5x5.5", one of the most advanced Lloyd's calculators made in the 1970's, 43 input keys, Japan, value $65-75.

907 4-funct, mem, fluor, 4-AA rep batt, 3.5x5.5", almost identical to Lloyd's model 20 but for some reason has high model number, Japan, value $45-55.

999 sci-funct, blue fluor, 4-AA rep batt, 3.0x5.5", same case as 200 and 500, looks like a Rockwell design, 1974 price $199.95, value $55-65.

Logitech

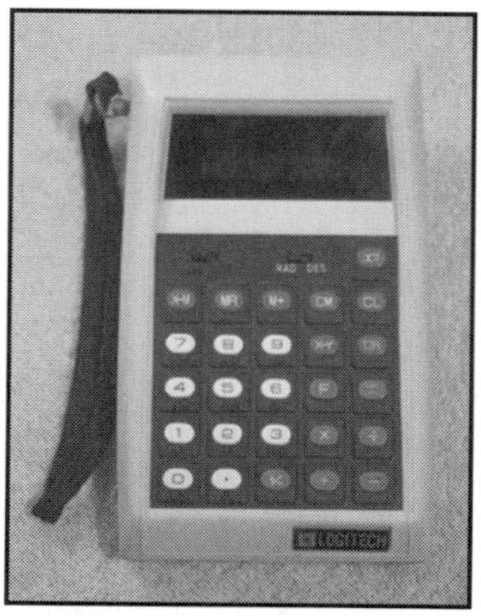

Logitech-1 sci-funct, mem, green fluor, 4-AA rep batt, 3.25x5.25", fabric wrist-strap, two-tone case, Taiwan, value $55-75.

Longines Symphonette

Longines Symphonette was apparently a 1970's musical record club which had various offers for its members. These models may have been offered in this manner.

LTP 5405 4-funct, red LED, 4-AA rep batt, 4.25x7.5x1.75", calculator and micro-cassette recorder, calculator circuit board from Bowmar, Japan, value $100-125.

Battery-AC Electronic Calculator 4-funct, red LED, sealed batt, 3.5x6.0", similar to Radio Shack EC-100, made by Texas Instruments, c1972-73, value $75-85.

Electronic Calculator 4-funct, red LED, 3.0x5.5", same as TI-2500

Datamath, made by Texas Instruments, green color, there were several versions with the basic same case but having different battery arrangement - one has no outside access to rechargeable batteries, another has a screwed-in hatch panel, a third has an easily removable battery cover (the first two styles are similar to the TI-1500, the third is like the TI-2500B), USA, value $45-55.

Mach

Mach I *aka Sliderulette,* 4-funct, green fluor, 4-AA rep batt, 3.25x5.25", appears identical to Unisonic 1212, in spite of name has no slide rule functions, Japan, c1972, value $50-60.

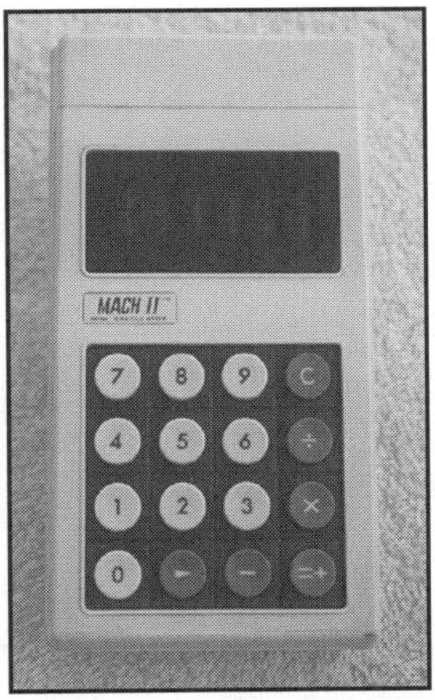

Mach II *aka Mini Calculator*, 4-funct, tube display, 4-AA rep batt, 3.0x6.0", unusual round spring-loaded keys like early Sanyo, Japan, value $40-50.

Mancal

European-market company.

732 4-funct, red LED, 4-AA rep batt, 2.75x5.25", unusual case design, Japan, value $50-60.

Manica

8 4-funct, tube display, 4-AA rep batt, 3.5x5.5", very thick (1.5"), interesting carrying strap, Taiwan, c1973, value $50-60.

Mannics

303 sci-funct, green fluor, 2-AA rep batt, 2.75x5.0", stylish case, Taiwan, value $45-55.

Master Calculator Company

Division of SG Corp, Grand Prairie, Texas (USA). They apparently made a few desk-top and handheld calculators in the early 1970's. Label state: "made with all USA components in the USA."

Mini Master 4-funct, red LED, sealed batt, 3.75x6.75", 4 slide switches, very thick and sturdy, 1971 price $345, USA, value $150-200.

Mathbook

806L 4-funct, %, green fluor, 2-AA rep batt, 3.25x5.0, same case as 817L, similar cases to various Teal models, Japan, value $40-50.

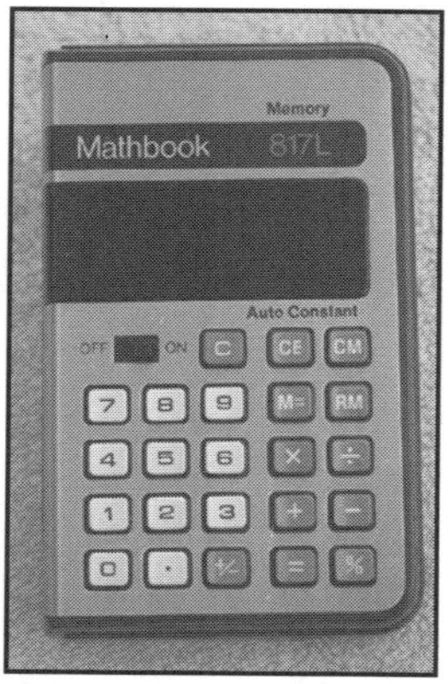

817L 4-funct, mem, %, sgn chg, green fluor, 2-AA rep batt, 3.25x5.0", same case as 806L, Japan, value $40-50.

Mathmatic

S-666 4-funct, red LED, 9V rep batt, 3.0x5.75", two-tone case, 4 strange "dummy" keys, Thailand, c1974, value $45-55.

S-888 4-funct, %, red LED, 9V rep batt, 3.0x5.75", two-tone case, 2 "dummy" keys, Thailand, value $45-55.

Mattel

USA toy and game maker.

JR Ewing game calculator related to a popular television show, red LED, 9V rep batt, Philippines, value $5-15.

Mayfair

Mayfair Sound Products; Chicago, Illinois (USA.)

2W01B 4-funct, blue fluor, 4-C rep batt,

4.5x7.25", same case as Soundesign 8300/Mach II, Japan, value $20-30.

MBO

West German calculator company.

570 *aka "Handy 570"* 4-funct, red LED, 9V rep batt, 2.5x4.75", text on back is German, West Germany, value $50-60.

838MD 4-funct, mem, %, sq funct, recip, fluor, 3-AA rep batt, 3.25x5.75", value $50-60.

Melcor

Melcor Electronics Corporation of Farmingdale, New York (USA) was one of the first US companies to enter the pocket calculator business. Like Bowmar, they were known for quality products but only made calculators for a few years. Most if not all Melcor models appear to have been manufactured in the United States. Some Melcor models were made specifically for IBM and have slogans such as "IBM Cost Effectiveness" on the front nameplate. With rare exceptions, all Melcor's have red LED displays.

40 *aka "Maximus 40"* 4-funct, sq rt, mem, red LED, 9V rep batt, 3.0x6.0", interesting red case, USA, value $65-75.

50 *aka "Maximus 50"* 4-funct, mem, red LED, 9V rep batt, 3.0x6.0", beige case, USA, value $65-75.

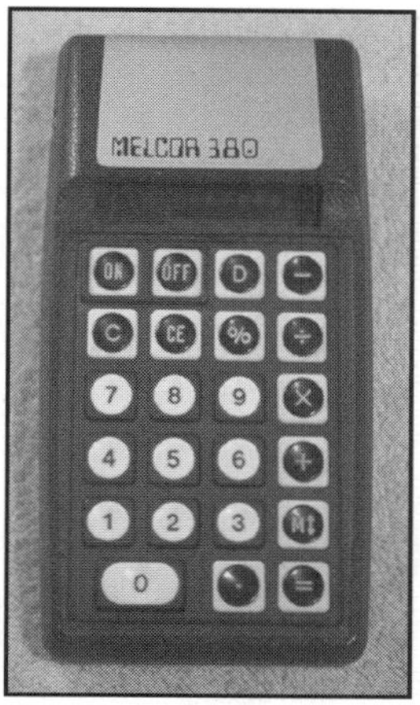

380 4-funct, mem, %, red LED, 9V rep batt, 3.0x6.0", USA, 1973 price $100, USA, value $45-55.

390 4-funct, mem, %, red LED, 9V rep batt, 3.2x6.0", c1973, 2 keypad variations, USA, value $45-55.

392 4-funct, mem, %, red LED, 9V rep batt, 3.2x6.0", same case as 390, USA, value $45-55.

400 4-funct, mem, %, sq rt, recip, red LED, 9V rep batt, 3.2x6.0", 1973 price $99.95, USA, value $45-55.

480 4-funct, mem, %, red LED, 9V rep batt, 3.0x6.0", similar to 380, USA, 1974, value $45-55.

500 4-funct, mem, %, red LED, 9V rep batt, 3.0x6.0", USA, value $45-55.
535 see SC-535.

550 4-funct, mem, %, sq rt, red LED, 9V rep batt, 3.0x6.0", same as 500 but has sq root, USA, value $45-55.

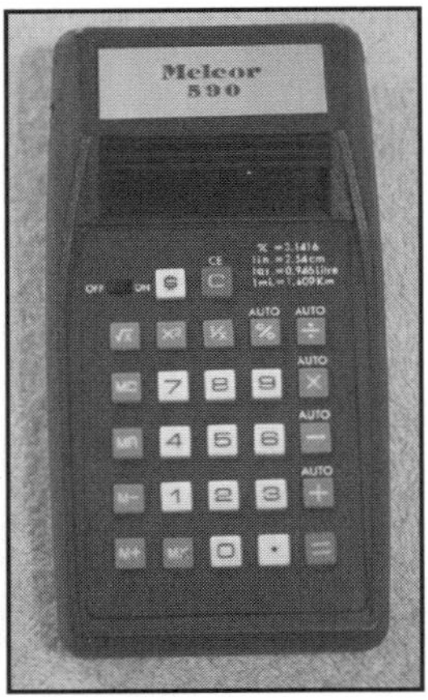

590 4-funct, conversions, sq rt, green fluor, 9V rep batt, 3.0x6.0", shape unlike any other known Melcor, rare fluor display on a Melcor, USA, value $75-85.

655 sci-funct, red LED, sealed batt, 3.5x6.5", twice as many functions as 635, only known Melcor with "F" function key, USA, 1975 price $129.95, value $75-85.

670 sci-funct, green fluor, 9V rep batt, 3.0x6.0", only a prototype (with unusual green display) is known, USA, c1974, value $150-180.

747 4-funct, mem, %, red LED, 9V rep batt, 3.0x4.5" black case, value $55-65.
1100 4-funct, %, red LED, 9V rep batt, 3.0x6.0", similar to 300 and 400 series, strange blue case, USA, value $65-75.

SC-535 sci-funct, red LED, sealed batt, 3.5x6.5", USA, 1974 price $89.95, value $50-60.

SC-635 sci-funct, red LED, sealed batt, 3.5x6.5", USA, c1974, value $50-60.

Compu-tech X 4-funct, sq rt, mem, red LED, 9V rep batt, 3.0x6.0", almost identical to Melcor Maximus 40, USA, value $85-95.

Metronic Laboratories

Metronic Laboratories, Wappingers Falls, New York (USA). Little known company.

Execucal M55 4-funct, orange fluor, 2-Eveready 523 4.5V batt, 4.25x7.0", unusual style, c1973, USA, value $90-110.

Micro Instrumentation & Telemetry Systems (MITS)

MITS of Albuquerque New Mexico (USA) is the same company that eventually made the Altair computer. This was the first computer to be sold to the general public in large numbers and is felt to have started the personal computer revolution. All their pocket calculators appear to have been manufactured in the USA.

150 4-funct, mem, %, sq rt, red LED, 6-AA rep batt, 3.25x5.75", 1973 price $149.95 assembled, or $119.95 as a kit, black case, USA, value $65-75.

605M 4-funct, mem, %, 6 digit red LED, 3.25x5.75", 1973 price $59.95 or $49.95 as a kit, USA, value $65-75.

905M 4-funct, mem, %, 8 digit red LED, 3.25x5.75", similar to 605M, 1973 price $69.95 or $59.95 as a kit, USA, value $65-75.

908M 4-funct, mem, %, sq funct, recip, red LED, 3.25x5.75", 1973 price $129.95 assembled or $99.95 as a kit, USA, value $70-80.

941M 4-funct, mem, %, metric conversions, red LED, 3.25x5.75", 1973 price $149.95 assembled or $129.95 as a kit, USA, value $70-80.

"I can clearly remember the first time I saw a pocket calculator. In 1972 I stood in a crowd of people in a department store trying to get a glimpse of a little machine that could actually divide numbers. Everyone in line actually got a chance to try it. It was amazing!"
--Bruce Flamm

1206 4-funct, 6 digit red LED, 5-AA rep batt, 3.0x5.5", very thick (1.5"), actually sold in a velvet-lined "jewelry" box, 1973 price $59.95 assembled or $49.95 as a kit, USA, value $70-90.

1209 4-funct, 9 digit red LED, 5-AA rep batt, 3.0x5.5", very thick (1.5"), similar to 1206, 1973 price $79.95 assembled or $69.95 as a kit, USA, value $70-90.

1212 4-funct, 12 digit red LED, 5-AA rep batt, 3.0x5.75", boxy shape, very thick (1.5"), similar to 1206, 1973 price $99.95 or $89.95 as a kit, USA, value $70-90.

Microlith

205 *aka Scientific*, sci-funct, green fluor, 9V rep batt, 3.0x5.25", very early example of an "F" function key, Hong Kong, c1974, value $65-75.

Miida

8 4-funct, fluor, sealed batt, 4.0x6.0", 1973 price $109.95 Japan, value $30-40.

One of the first Busicom electronic calculators (their 141-PF desktop printing model) used the Intel 4004, the grandfather of the 8088 - the IC chip used in the first IBM personal computer years later. The 4004 is the great-great (+2) grandad of the modern Pentium chip.

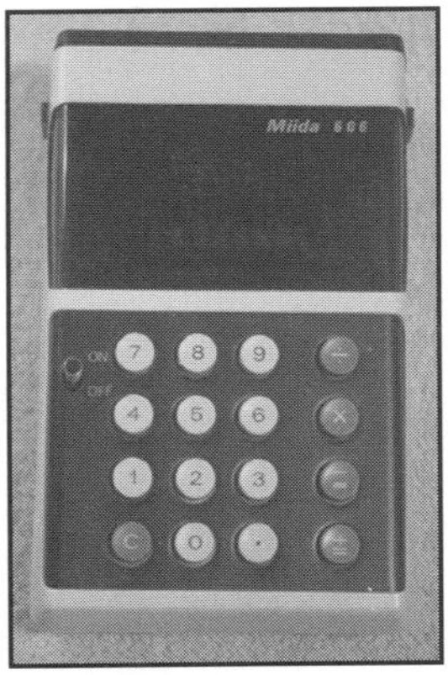

606 4-funct, fluor, 4-AA rep batt, 4.0x6.25", battery holder slides in top, Mexico, value $40-50.

808 4-funct, fluor, sealed batt, 4.0x6.0", c1973, Japan, value $25-35.

809 4-funct, sq rt, green fluor, 2-AA rep, 3.0x5.25", one of few known Miida's with square data entry keys, Japan, c1974, value $55-65.

828 4-funct, mem, fluor, sealed batt, 4.0x6.0", c1974, Japan, value $30-40.

838 4-funct, sq rt, sgn chg, fluor, sealed batt, 4.0x6.0", very similar to 868M, c1975, Japan, value $45-55.

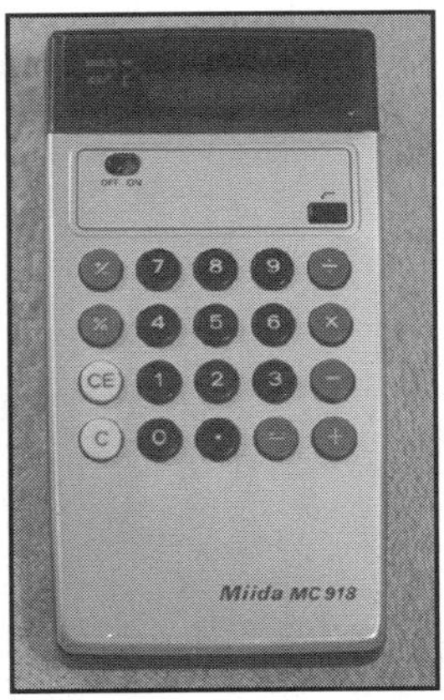

918 4-funct, %, green fluor, 2-AA rep

batt, 3.0x5.75", strange sq rt key located well above the keypad, interesting metal faceplate, c1976, Japan, value $55-65.

988 4-funct, %, mem, green fluor, 2-AA rep batt, 3.0x5.75", similar to 918 but has decimal slide switch and memory, c1976, Japan, value $55-65.

MC855M 4-funct, mem, sgn chg, sq rt, blue fluor, 2-AA rep batt, 4.0x6.0", c1975, Japan, value $35-45.

MC868M 4-funct, mem, sq rt, sgn chg, fluor, sealed batt, 4.0x6.0", similar case to MC855M, c1975, Japan, value $35-45.

Minerva

Minerva International; Franklin, Tennessee, USA.

825 4-funct, red LED, 4-AA batt, 2.75x5.0", small and interesting molded case, tan, USA, value $65-75.

Mintron

Mintron calculators were made by Minsung Electronics, LTD of Seoul Korea. Some models were made specifically for Korean Airlines and may have been given to passengers as a promotion for taking expensive overseas flights. Some models such as the 812D and 822DR have been found with "Korean Airlines" printed on the front.

812D 4-funct, sq rt, green fluor, 2-AA rep batt, 3.0x5.25", "Korean Airlines" might appear on front, Korea, value $35-45.

822DR 4-funct, sq rt, green fluor, sealed batt, 3.0x5.0", very thin all-metal case, Korea, value $35-45.

845D 4-funct, mem, %, tube display, 3.0x5.25", Korea, value $25-35.

M1205D 4-funct, mem, %, sq rt, sgn chg, tube display, 4-AA rep batt, 5.5x7.5", Korea, value $30-40.

S812D sci-funct, green fluor, 2-AA rep batt, 3.0x5.25", 2-tone case, early example of an "F" function key to double the number of available keys, Korea, value $55-65.

MITS

See Micro Instrumentation & Telemetry Systems.

Monroe-Litton

A division of Litton Industries, Morris Plains, New York. Some calculators may be labeled "Litton-Monroe, The Calculator Company, a division of Litton Industries." Monroe, one of the great American calculator companies during the first half of the twentieth century, was famous for desk-top mechanical and electro-mechanical calculators. They apparently merged with Litton Industries in the late 1960's and went on to produce mainly electronic desktop calculators but also a few "pocket" models. There is also a link with Compucorp as their models 324, 326, and 360 were the same as Compucorp's models.

10 4-funct, paper tape display, sealed batt, 4.0x8.5", very stylized case based on the Canon Pocketronic 1, was made by Canon for Monroe, 1972 price $379, Japan, value $80-100.

20 4-funct, red LED, sealed batt, 3.5x6.0", very stylish case, 1973 price $199, USA, value $60-70.

30 4-funct, %, red LED, sealed batt, 3.5x6.0", c1973, USA, value $40-50.

Of the scores of U.S. companies making pocket calculators in the early 1970's, only two, Texas Instruments and Hewlett-Packard, survived the "great calculator war." But neither TI nor HP actually manufacture calculators in the U.S. anymore.

98 4-funct, mem, %, recip, sq funct, green fluor, 4-AA rep batt, 3.25x6.0", Japan, c1973, value $55-65.

99 sci-funct, green fluor, 4-AA rep batt, 3.25x6.5", an early scientific model, Japan, c1973, value $65-75.

324 *Same as Compucorp 324-G.*

326 *Same as Compucorp 326.*

360 *Same as Compucorp 360.*

Monte Carlo

Monte Carlo 4-funct, %, red LED, 2.0x3.5", sealed batt, black case, script lettering on keys, Japan, value $40-50.

Monteverdi

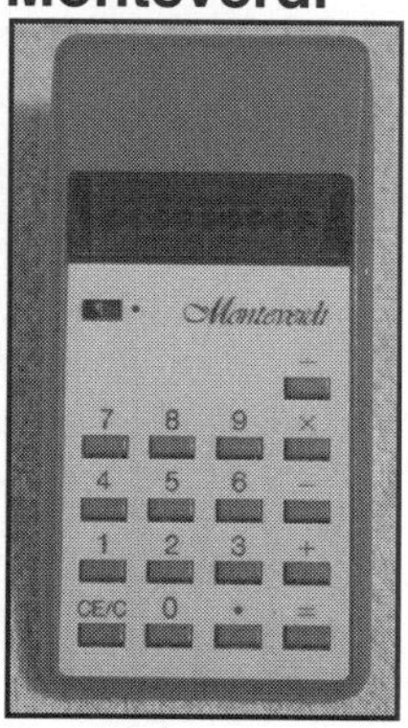

Monteverdi 4-funct, red LED, 9V rep batt, 2.75x5.5", similar to National Semiconductor models, c1974, USA, value $10-20.

Montgomery Ward

American department store which also sold calculators through a general merchandise catalog. Montgomery Ward labels were usually placed on calculators already made by other companies.

Electronic I 4-funct, red LED, 9V rep batt, 3.25x5.5", same as Rapid Data Rapidman 800, c1973, Canada, value $35-45.

P8F *aka model TXI-8644A*, 4-funct, red LED, 4-AA rep batt. 3.0x5.75", made by TI but with an unusual body style, c1974, USA, value $50-60.

P8P 4-funct, %, red LED, 4-AA rep batt, 3.0x5.75", apparently made by TI but with an unusual body style, like P8F but adds % and decimal slide switch, c1974, USA, value $50-60.

P10 *aka Mathbox, model DNS-8678A*, 4-funct, red LED, 9V rep batt, 2.75x5", same as Novus 650, at least 2 case color variations - ivory and black, c1974, USA, value $15-25.

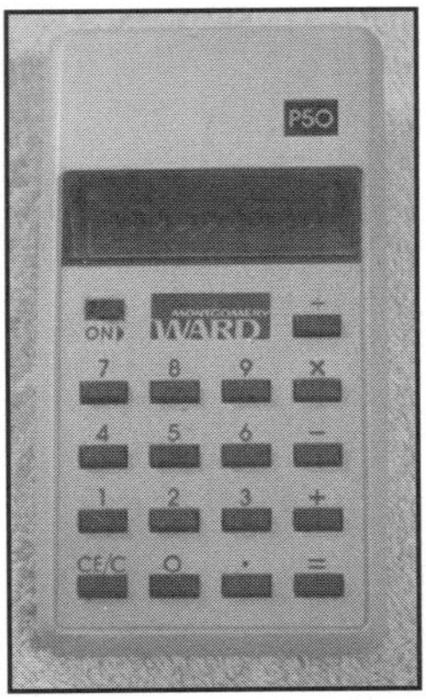

P50 *aka model DNS-8660A*, 4-funct, red LED, 9V rep batt, 2.75x5", same as Novus 850, c1974, USA, value $15-25.

P60 *aka GLE-8692A*, 4-funct, %, fluor, 4-AA rep batt, 3.5x5.5", same as Lloyd's 30, Japan, value $20-30.

P90 *aka DAN-8670A*, 4-funct, %, red LED, 9V rep batt, 2.75x4.5", same as APF Mark 40, c1974, Japan, value $20-30.

P100 *aka TXI-8661A*, 4-funct, %, red LED, 3-AA rep batt, 2.75x5.0", looks like TI Exactra models, USA, value $25-35.

P130 *aka DAN-8668A*, 4-funct, mem, %, red LED, 9V rep batt, 3.0x5.0", Japan, value $25-35.

P200 *aka TXI-8662A*, 4-funct, mem, %, red LED, 3-AA rep or sealed batt, 3.25x6.5", looks like TI models, c1973, USA, value $50-60.

P201 *aka DAN-8659A*, 4-funct, mem, %, red LED, 9V rep batt, 3.0x6.0", looks like APF models, USA, value $20-30.

P202 *aka DAN-8656A* or DAN-8656B, 4-funct, mem, %, sq rt, recip, fluor, 9V rep batt, 3.0x5.75", looks like APF models, Japan or USA, value $20-30.

P300 *aka TXI-8663A*, 4-funct, sq rt, recip, sgn chg, exp, red LED, sealed batt, 3.0x6.0", similar to TI SR-10, c1974, USA, value $45-55.

P330 *aka DAN-8665A*, sci-funct, red LED, 9V rep batt, 3.0x6.0", same case as APF Mark 50, 1976 price $27, USA, value $30-40.

Most hand-held calculators use the algebraic entry system in order to perform calculations. Hewlett-Packard is one of the very few manufacturers that use Reverse Polish Notation (RPN). The difference lies in how the numbers and operations are entered. With algebraic the user would type "3" "+" "4" "=". With RPN, the user would use the "enter" key and type "3" "enter" "4" "=".

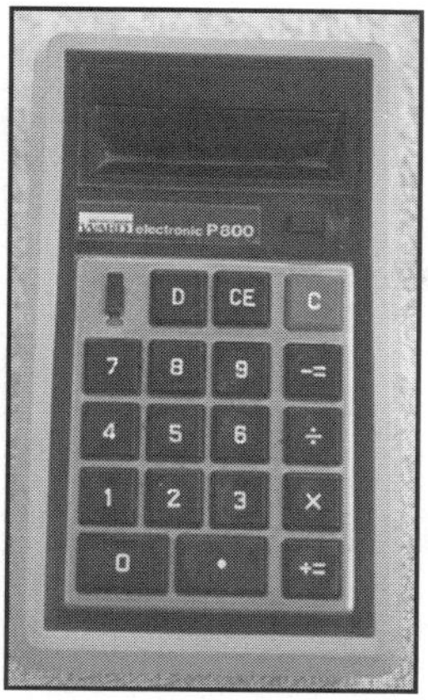

P800 *aka TXI8642A*, 4-funct, red LED, sealed batt, Klixon keypad, 3.5x6.0", c1972, USA, value $40-50.

Morse Electrophonic

Cal-801 4-funct, fluor, 4-C rep batt, 4.5x7.5", same case as Soundesign 8300/Mach II and Mayfair 2W01B, c1972, Hong Kong, value $30-40.

Morse International

Probably a different company than Morse Electrophonic.

Morse 8 4-funct, red LED, sealed batt, 1973 price $109.50, value $50-65.

MPI

360 4-funct, mem, %, red LED, 9V rep batt, 2.5x4.5", silver-colored metal faceplate, black case, similar to Nobility K14/350, Hong Kong, value $20-30.

National

See Panasonic.

National Cash Register (NCR)

American company.

1844 4-funct, red LED, sealed batt, 2.5x4.75", incredibly small, made by Nippon similar to the Busicom Handy LE-120 series, c1971-72, Japan, value $200-300.

National Semiconductor

American integrated circuit maker. Also used NSC Electronics on nameplate. The calculator division eventually was renamed Novus with their models listed in that section of this book. Some identical calculators were sold under both National Semiconductor and Novus labels. Thus the same calculator could be sold at two different prices. This may have allowed them to sell their calculators at both department stores and discount stores with less conflict. Country of origin may have changed with later production runs of same calculator. See Novus for separate listing of calculators with that nameplate.

200 4-funct, mem, %, sq, funct chg, fluor, 3-AAA rep bat, 2.75x5.5", flat model, Hong Kong, value $20-25.

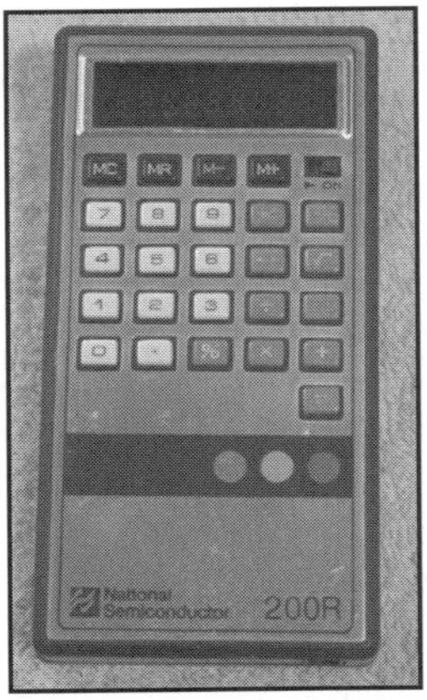

200R 4-funct, mem, %, sq, funct chg, fluor, sealed batt, 2.75x5.5", flat model with power adapter stand, Taiwan, value $25-30.

201 sci-funct, mem, %, sq, sgn chg, fluor, 3-AAA rep bat, 2.75x5.5", flat model, Hong Kong, value $45-55.

202 financial-funct, mem, %, sq, funct chg, fluor, 3-AAA rep bat, 2.75x5.5", flat model, Hong Kong, value $45-55.

203R 4-funct, mem, %, sq rt, recip, paren, fluor, 3-AAA rep batt, 2.75x5.5", similar case to 200, Taiwan, value $20-25.

500 4-funct, mem, green fluor and paper printer, sealed batt, 3.0x5.5", very small printer-calculator, Japan, value $40-50.

> *The world's first calculator which could deal with fractions was the Casio AL-10. Using a special key, it allowed you to enter a fraction like $^1/_2$ directly.*

600 4-funct, 6-digit red LED, 9V rep batt, 2.75x5.0", same case as 900, late 1973 price $29.95, USA, value $15-20.

750 4-funct, red LED, 9V rep batt, produced in large quantities, 2.75x5.0", c1978, Hong Kong, value $10-15.

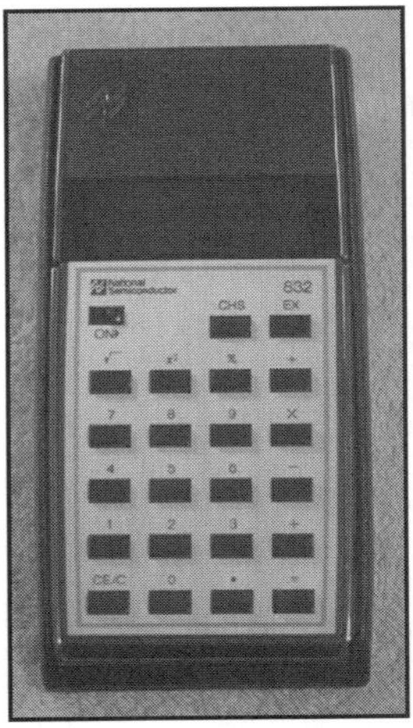

832 4-funct, red LED, 9V rep batt, 3.0x6.0", Malaysia, value $20-30.

835 4-funct, mem, sq rt, %, red LED, 9V rep batt, 2.75x5.5", similar case to 750, Hong Kong, value $15-20.

835A 4-funct, mem, %, red LED, 9V rep batt, 2.75x5.5", similar case to 750,

Hong Kong, value $10-20.

842 4-funct, mem, %, sq rt, red LED, 9V rep batt, 3.0x6.0", similar case to 832, USA, value $20-30.

850 4-funct, red LED, 9V rep batt, 2.75x5.5", similar case to 750, Hong Kong, value $35-40.

850A 4-funct, %, red LED, 9V rep batt, 2.75x5.5", like 850 but has % and is more common, 1978 price $5.89, Hong Kong, value $15-20.

852 sci-funct, mem, exp, red LED, 9V rep batt, 3.0x6.0", similar case to 832, Hong Kong, value $20-30.

900 4-funct, red LED, 9V rep batt, 2.75x5.0", white case, same case as 600, 1974 price $39.95, USA, value $25-30.

4615 sci-funct, mem, exp, programmable, red LED, sealed batt, 3.0x6.0", Malaysia, value $45-55.

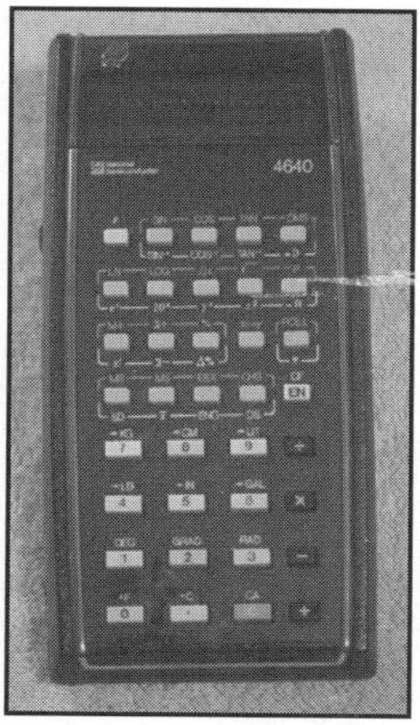

4640 sci-funct, red LED, sealed batt, 3.0x6.0", 4615-type case, USA, value $45-55.

4650 sci-funct, mem, exp, parenthesis, red LED, sealed batt, 3.0x6.0", 4615-type case, USA, value $45-55.

4660 sci-funct, mem, exp, red LED, sealed batt, 3.0x6.0", 4615-type case, USA, value $45-55.

Calculator Watch 4-funct, red LED, button rep batt, unusual flip cover over keypad, c1976, value $200-600.

CM IV 4-funct, mem, sq rt, %, red LED, 9V rep batt, 2.75x5.5", appears identical to 835 but may not have been made by National Semiconductor, value $40-50.

Mathematician sci-funct, mem, exp, red LED, 9V rep batt, 3.0x6.0", value $25-35.

Scientist sci-funct, mem, exp, red LED, sealed batt, 3.0x6.0", Hong Kong, value $35-45.

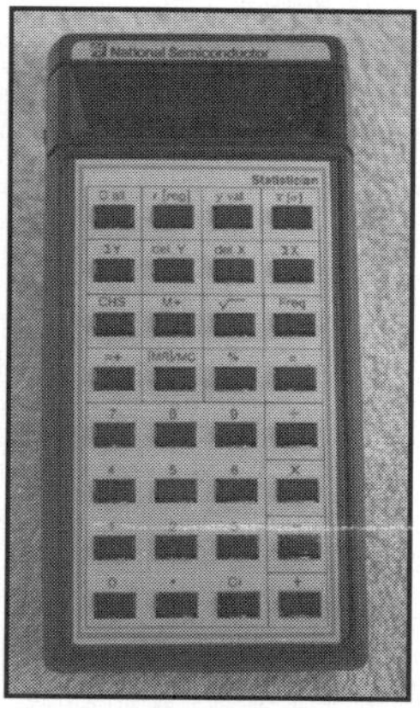

Statistician financial funct, mem, red LED, 9V rep batt, 3.0x6.0", similar case to Mathematician, Singapore, value $25-35.

Quiz Kid children's educational calculator, had several variations of body styles and functions under the Quiz Kid model name, c1976, value $10-20.

Whiz Kid 4-funct, red LED, 9V rep batt, 2.75x5.0", similar case to 600, value $10-20.

NCR

See National Cash Register.

Netronics

Metronics Research and Development, Ltd, of Spring Valley, NY (USA).

1000 sci-funct, red LED, sealed batt, 3.5x6.5", similar case to Melcor SC-635, seen as unassembled kit for $89.95, c1975, USA, value $65-75.

N2000/MX sci-funct, red LED, sealed batt, 3.5x6.5", similar case to Melcor SC-635, USA, value $65-75.

Nixdorf

LK-3000 4-funct, mem, %, sgn chg, red LED, sealed batt, 6.25x4.0", horizontal, alpha-numeric keypad, could use various slip-in modules with capabilities to translate words from one language to another, similar to Lexicon LK-3000, Malaysia, value $35-45.

The Hewlett-Packard HP-35 was so expensive and in such demand that HP designed and sold a $24.95 locking cradle which allowed you to securely attach your $395 scientific calculator to your desk. For even greater mobility, you could lock the cradle to the leg of your laboratory table using the accompanying 6-foot steel cable.

Nobility

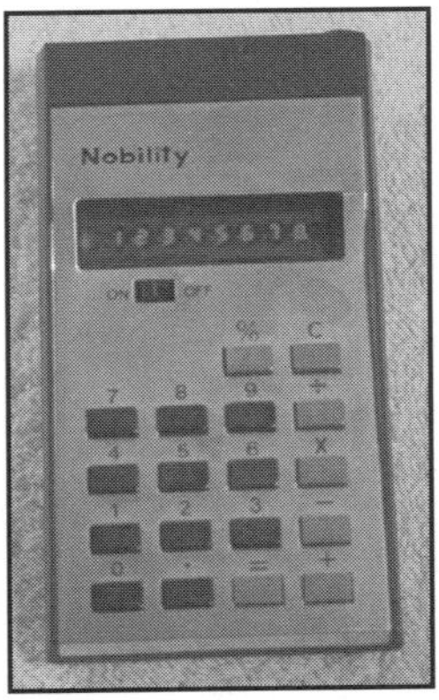

K14/350 4-funct, %, red LED, 9V rep batt, 2.5x4.75", cheap little model, Hong Kong, value $10-15.

3000 4-funct, mem, %, red LED, 9V rep batt, 2.75x5.25", cheap little model, this popular calculator was apparently sold under different labels including Bohsei 3000, Tronica 3000, Unitrex 1000, or Janon 3000, Hong Kong, value $5-10.

Novus

Novus became the consumer product division of National Semiconductor (USA). Country of origin may have changed with later production runs of same calculator. Also see National Semiconductor.

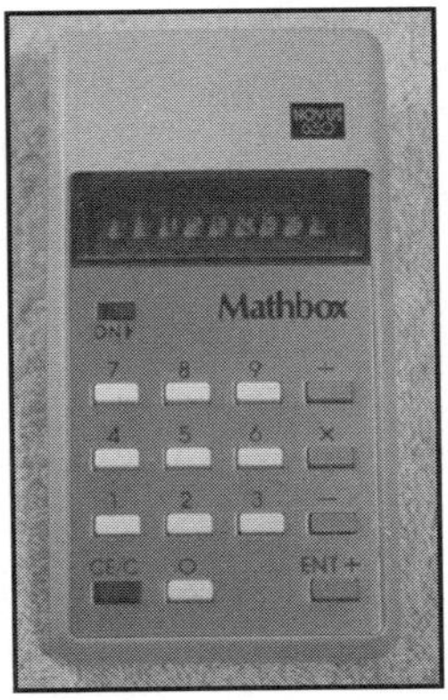

650 *aka Mathbox*, 4-funct, 6-digit red LED, 9V rep batt, 2.75x5.0", 1975

price $17, USA, value $10-15.

750 4-funct, red LED, 9V rep batt, 2.75x5.0", similar case to 850, USA, value $20-25.

820 4-funct, red LED, 9V rep batt, 2.75x5.0", similar case to 650, USA, value $15-20.

821 4-funct, %, red LED, 9V rep batt, same case as 820 except includes %, USA, value $25-35.

822 *aka The Professional*, 4-funct, %, red LED, 9V rep batt, 2.75x5.5", c1975, USA, value $30-40.

823 4-funct, mem, %, red LED, rep batt, 3.0x5.0", stylish case, 1974 price $49.95, USA, value $20-30.

826 4-funct, mem, %, red LED, 9V rep batt, 2.75x5.5", similar case to 822, c1975, USA, value $15-20.

830 *aka Datachecker*, 4-funct, other data functions, red LED, 9V rep batt, 2.75x5.5", similar case to 835, Malaysia, value $25-35.

831 4-funct, %, sq rt, red LED, 9V rep batt, 2.75x5.5", similar case to 822, value $20-30.

835 4-funct, mem, sq rt, %, red LED, 9V rep batt, 2.75x5.5", similar case to 822, Hong Kong, value $15-20.

850 4-funct, red LED, 9V rep batt, 2.75x5.0", similar to 650, has 2 minor style variations mainly with the front and back face plates, c1974-76, 1976 price $7.88, USA, value $10-20.

950 4-funct, red LED, 9V rep batt, 2.75x5.0", similar to 650 but fewer were made, USA, value $30-45.

3500 *aka Sliderule*, sci-funct, mem, exp, red LED, 9V rep batt, 3.0x6.0", USA, value $45-55.

4510 *aka Mathematician*, sci-funct, mem, exp, red LED, 9V rep batt, 3.0x6.0", similar case to 3500, has 2 minor style variations with the color and key markings, c1975, Malaysia, value $25-35.

Bowmar and Litronix were two US-based companies which led the calculator field with their innovative designs which they were constantly improving on. Their heritage was actually very similar to one another. Both were originally manufacturers of Light Emitting Diode (LED) displays before moving into the more lucrative calculator market.

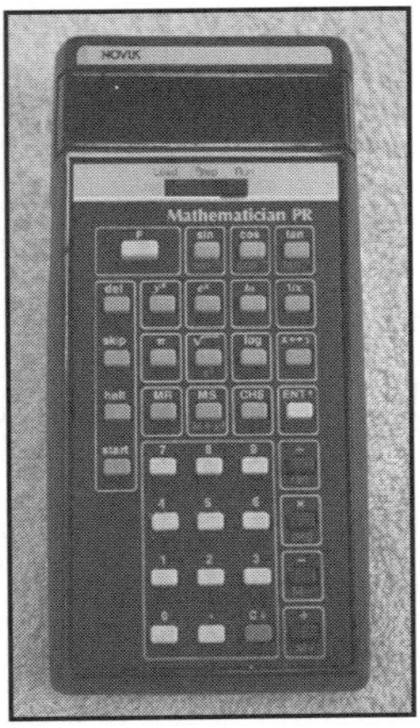

4515 *aka Mathematician PR*, sci-funct, mem, exp, programmable, red LED, sealed batt, 3.0x6.0", c1975, USA, value $25-35.

4520 *aka Scientist*, sci-funct, mem, exp, programmable, red LED, sealed batt, 3.0x6.0", similar case to 4515, 1975 price $60, USA, value $25-35.

4525 *aka Scientist PR*, sci-funct, mem, exp, programmable, red LED, sealed batt, 3.0x6.0", similar case to 4515, c1975, USA, value $25-35.

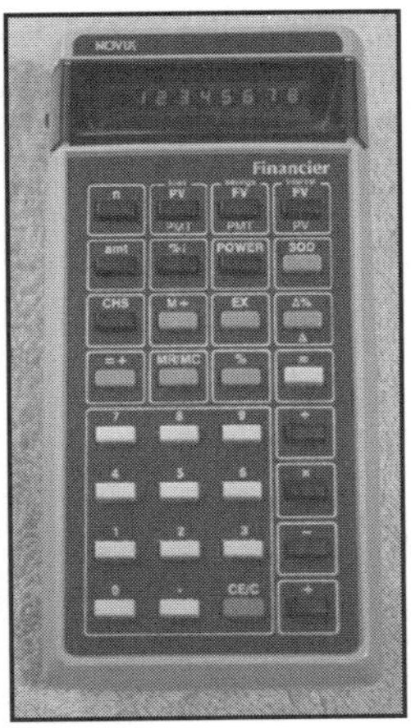

6020 *aka Financier*, financial funct, mem, red LED, 9V rep batt, 3.0x6.0", similar case to 3500, 1975 price $79.95, USA, value $25-35.

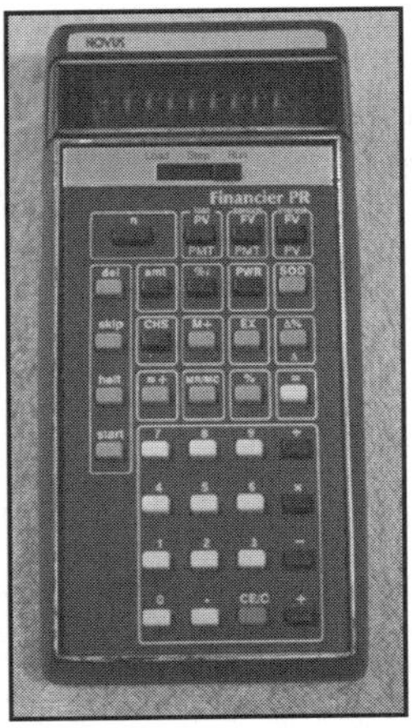

6025 *aka Financier* Programmable, financial funct, mem, exp, programmable, red LED, sealed batt, 3.0x6.0", similar case to 4515, c1975, USA, value $35-45.

6030 *aka Statistician*, statistical funct, mem, red LED, 9V rep batt, 3.0x6.0", similar case to 3500, USA, value $35-45.

Attache 4-funct, red LED, special long 9V rep batt, 3.5"x5.75", thin calculator in wallet case, c1975, USA, value $20-30.

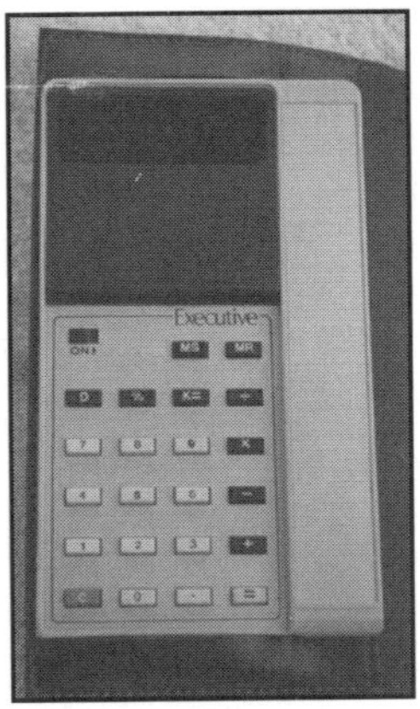

Executive 4-funct, mem, %, red LED, special long 9V rep batt, 3.5"x5.75", thin calculator in wallet case, c1975,

USA, value $20-30.

Mathematician *see 4510.*

Olivetti

This large Italian calculator company made a few handheld models in the early 1970's.

BC-D18 *aka Divisumma-18*, 4-funct, printer only, rep batt pack, 4.75x12", wt. 3 pounds, bold yellow color, a work of art, Italy, c1972, value $75-95.

Olympia

Olympia-Werke AG., West Germany.

108MS 4-funct, mem, green fluor, 1-AA rep batt, 3.0x5.0", value $30-40.

816MS 4-funct, mem, %, sq funct, recip, sgn chg, pi, fluor, 1-AA rep batt, 3.0x4.75", similar to Caltek 830D, uncreative design uncommon to other stylish Olympia calculators, Korea, value $25-35.

CD-44S 4-funct, mem, %, sq rt, sgn chg, fluor, 2-AA rep batt, 3.0x5.0", Japan, value $35-45.

CD-45 4-funct, %, sq rt, green fluor, 2-AA rep batt, 2.75x4.75", Japan, value $35-45.

CD-46 4-funct, mem, %, sq rt, sgn chg, fluor, 2.75x4.75", same as Panasonic 8203, Japan, value $30-40.

CD-51 4-funct, sgn chg, red LED, 4-AA rep batt, 3.2x5.5", Hong Kong, value $30-40.

CD-71 4-funct, mem, green fluor, sealed batt, 3.25x6.0", very heavy but has wrist strap, West Germany, c1973, value $55-75.

CD-75 4-funct, mem, %, sgn chg, fluor, sealed batt, 3.0x6.0", black, very slim, attractive style, Japan, value $60-75.

CD-80 4-funct, tube, 4-AA sealed batt, 4.0x6.25", similar to panasonic 850, Japan, value $60-80.

CD-100 4-funct, tube, 4-C rep batt, 7.0x8.0", similar style case and key design as Panasonic 805, 1973 price $149.50, Japan, value $35-45.

Omron

Omron Tateisi Electronics (Japan). Omron is in a class by itself. The cases are more colorful than any other brands. Unlike most early pocket calculators, Omrons are often bright orange, yellow, or even two-tone. Many models have wrist straps. The 88 and 89 series actually have a strange wedge shape with the top being much wider than the bottom, presumably to make them a better fit for the hand. Colorful circular buttons are found on most Omron keypads and the battery cover is actually on the front of some models. Most have 6 or 8 digit fluor displays although the one model has 14 digits. If you collect calculators, you'll love Omrons!

8 *aka 88R*, 4-funct, %, sq rt, blue fluor, 2-AA rep batt, 3.0x5.75", unique tapered shape for easy hand holding, similar to 88, Japan, value $35-45.

8M *aka 8300*, 4-funct, mem, %, sq rt, sgn chg, blue fluor, 2-AA rep batt, 2.5x4.25", unusual for Omron in its common shape, Japan, value $30-40.

8SR sci-funct, green fluor, 2-AA rep batt, 3.0x4.5", 2-tone case, early example of "F" function key, Japan, value $45-55.

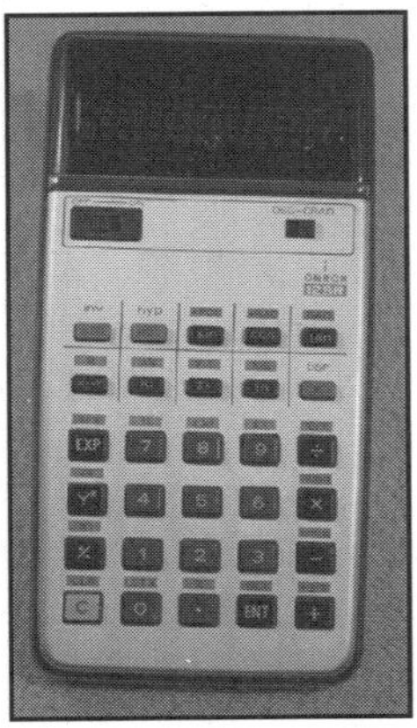

12SR *aka slide rule*, sci-funct, green fluor, 3-AA rep batt, 3.25x6.25", huge 14 digit display, this is the most complex Omron model known, Japan, value $65-75.

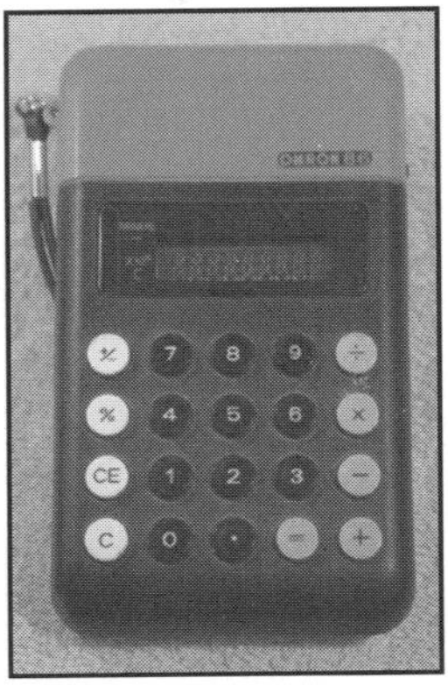

86 4-funct, %, sgn chg, fluor, 2-AA rep batt, 3.0x5.25", Japan, value $35-45.

86M 4-funct, mem, %, sgn chg, fluor, 2-AA rep batt, 3.0x6.0", orange and yellow case color variations, Japan, value $35-45.

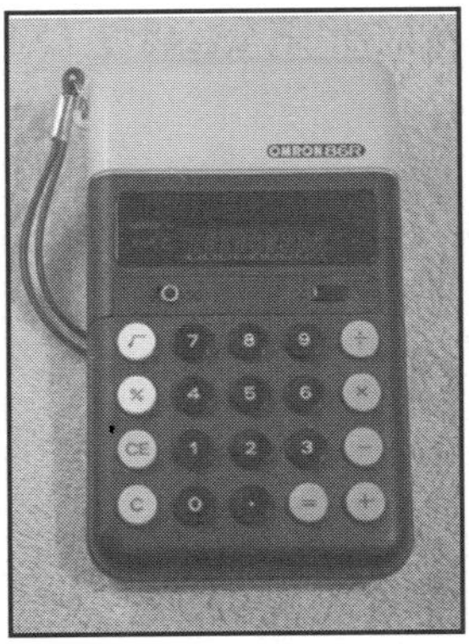

86R 4-funct, %, sq rt, sgn chg, fluor, 2-AA rep batt, 3.0x5.2", similar case to86, Singapore, value $35-45.

86SR sci-funct, mem, fluor, 2-AA rep batt, 3.0x5.25", similar case to 86R except has a function key allowing sci-funct, Japan, value $45-55.

88 4-funct, %, sgn chg, fluor, 2-AA rep batt, 3.0x5.75", unique tapered shape for easy hand holding, yellow color, Japan, value $40-50.

88M 4-funct, sq rt, mem, green fluor, 2-AA rep batt, 3.0x6.25", wedge-shaped like 88 but larger size, black which is unusual for Omron, Japan, value $45-55.

88R *see 8.*

88SR sci-funct, fluor, 4-AA rep batt, 3.8x6.25", Japan, value $55-65.

89M 4-funct, sq rt, mem, green fluor, 2-AA rep batt, 3.0x6.25", very similar to 88M, Japan, value $45-55.

606 4-funct, 6 digit fluor display, 2-AA rep batt, 3.0x5.2", similar case to 86, 1976 price $7.95, Singapore, value $35-45.

860 4-funct, sq rt, green fluor, 2-AA rep batt, 3.0x4.5", 2-tone case, looks like 8SR but has no sci-funct except sq rt, Japan, value $45-55.

865R sci-funct, fluor, 2-AA rep batt, 3.25x5.25", 1976 price $25, value $45-55.

8300 *see 8M.*

Ordibel Collators

Executive 4-funct, red LED, sealed batt, 3.5x6.0", 1973 price S145, value $60-75.

Panasonic

Also made/sold models with National nameplate -- primarily in Japan. Some of the early Panasonic models are quite unusual.

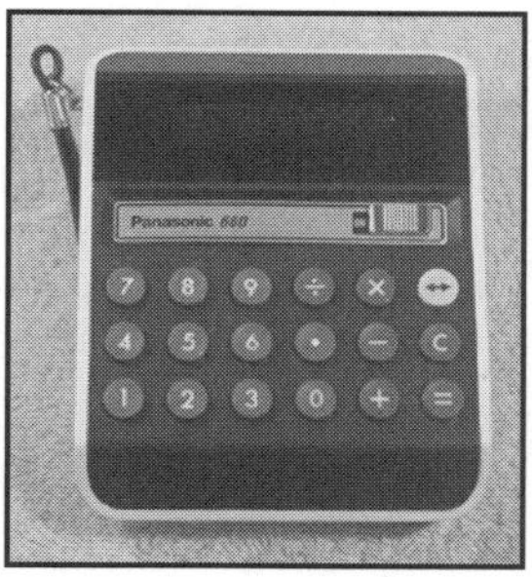

660 *aka JE-660U*, 4-funct, 6 digit fluor with 12 digit capability, 4-AA rep batt, 3.7x4.5" stylish case, 1974 price $59.95, Japan, value $45-55

801 *aka JE-801A*, 4-funct, tube display, 4-C rep batt, 6.75x7.5", decimal slide switch, 1972 price $229, Japan, value $45-55.

805 4-funct, tube, 4-C rep batt, 7.0x7.5", similar style case and key design as Olympic CD-100, 1973 price

$169, Japan, value $35-45.

830 *aka JE-830U*, 4-funct, green fluor, 2-D cell rep batt, 5.75x6.0", gloss white case, 1974 price $69.95, Japan, value $60-70.

840 *aka JE-840U*, 4-funct, green fluor, 4-AA rep batt, 3.25x5.5", slot for thumb, carrying strap, 1974 price $49.95, Japan, value $65-75.

850 *aka JE-850U*, 4-funct, tube display, sealed batt, 4.0x6.0", very stylized almost sculpted case, same case as 855, Japan, 1972 price $139.95, value $60-70.

855 *aka JE-855U*, 4-funct, mem, tube, sealed batt, 4.0x6.0", very stylized almost sculpted case, same case as 850, 1973 price $149.95, Japan, value $60-70.

860 *aka JE-860U*, 4-funct, tube display, sealed batt, 4.0x6.0", same case as 850, 1973 price $149.95, Japan, value $60-70.

880 *aka JE-880U, 4-funct, fluor, 4-AA rep batt, 3.25x5.25", Japan, value $35-45.*

883 *aka JE-883U*, 4-funct, fluor, 4-AA rep batt, 3.25x5.25", 1973 price $99.95, Japan, value $40-50.

885 *aka JE-885U*, 4-funct, mem, green fluor, 4-AA rep batt, 3.25x5.5", thumb-slot similar to 840, carrying strap, Japan, c1973, value $65-75.

1001 *aka JE-1001*, 4-funct, tube display, 4-C rep batt, 6.75x7.5", same as 801 but has 11 tubes instead of 9, decimal slide switch, 1973 price $159.95, Japan, value $45-55.

1403 *aka JE-1403U*, sci-funct, fluor, 3-AA rep batt, 3.5x6.0", Japan, value $45-55.

2001 *aka JE-2001*, 4-funct, %, mem, red LED, 3.0x6.0", sealed batt, unusual style similar to model 850 but smaller, 1974 price $99.95, Japan, value $45-55.

2003 aka JE-2003, 4-funct, %, sq, mem, red LED, 3.0x6.0", sealed batt, same as 2001 but has sq rt, Japan, value $45-55.

8203 *aka JE-8203U*, 4-funct, mem, %, sq rt, sgn chg, fluor, 2-AA rep batt, 2.8x4.7", Japan, value $25-35.

JE-1803 4-funct, mem, %, green fluor and paper printer, sealed batt, 3.5x9.0", similar to small Canon printers, value $25-35.

JE-2002U 4-funct, mem, sq rt, pi, red LED, sealed batt, 3.0x6.0", very thin, unusual looking, Japan, value $70-80.

JE-8220U 4-funct, mem, %, sq rt, sgn chg, fluor, 2-AA rep batt, 2.8x4.7", Japan, value $25-35.

JE-8221U 4-funct, %, sq rt, sgn chg, pi, fluor, 2-AA rep batt, 2.8x4.7", Japan, value $30-40.

Electric Ruler 4-funct, mem, %, green fluor, 2-AA rep batt, 8.75x2.25", horizontal, has wheel on nose of unit that will measure distance traveled -- for maps, blueprints, patterns, etc. -- 1979 price $89.95, Japan, value $65-85.

Panac S-1 *aka JE-5001 (National on nameplate)*, sci-funct, fluor, 4-AA rep batt, 3.5x5.75", value $45-55.

Panac M-3 *aka JE-8203*, 4-funct, mem, %, sq rt, sgn chg, fluor, 2-AA rep batt, 2.8x4.7", National on nameplate, similar body to 8203, Japan, value $35-45.

Panac SD-1 *aka JE-1401*, sci-funct, fluor, 3-AA rep batt, 3.5x5.75", National on nameplate, Japan, value $40-50.

Peripheral Magnetics

Peripheral Magnetics; Los Angeles, California (USA). Connection of this "Abatron" name with Business Electronics' use (see other listing) is unknown.

Abatron 800 4-funct, red LED, 6-AA rep batt, 3.5x6.0", 1973 price $100, value $50-60.

Pico

PA-80D 4-funct, %, fluor, 2-AA rep batt, 2.25x3.25", very small, looks like Vista models, c1975, Japan, value $40-50.

PA-80N 4-funct, %, purple LED, 2-AA rep batt, 2.25x3.25", very small, looks like Vista models, same case as PA-80D, c1975, Japan, value $40-50.

Pioneer

See Rapid Data.

Plustron

An English company.

308 4-funct, red LED, 9V rep batt, 3.0x4.0", gray body with round blue and white keys, value $40-50.

Plustronic

Plustronics was a distributor of calculators in England. This model evidently was labeled directly for them.

SM838M 4-funct, mem, green fluor, sealed batt, 3.75x6.25", almost 0.5 pound, strange slide switch for "auto m," Japan, c1974, value $75-95.

Price Research Associates (PRA)

PRA was started by Ed Price after his Summit calculator company closed down in 1974. They introduced the Wisp in very small quantities before they also went out of business.

> ***In mid-1973, the head of Bowmar's Consumer Products division predicted the US would soon be a nation of two-calculator families. At the time, Bowmar claimed half of all the consumer calculator sales in the United States.***

Wisp 4-funct, %, red LED, 9V rep batt, 2.25x3.5, very small and lightweight, made in several bright colors including yellow, c1974-75, USA, value $110-130.

PrintaBowmar

PrintaBowmar SA de CV, Division Calculadoras Electronicas, Mexico. Unknown relation to the Bowmar company of USA who made the famous Bowmar Brain calculators.

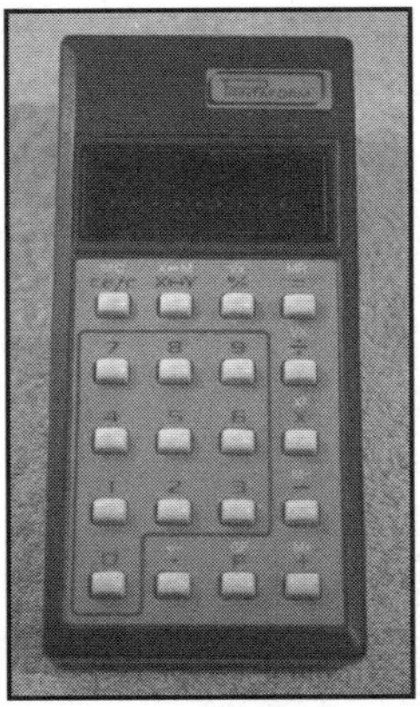

1530 *aka Printaform 1530* 4-funct, mem, sq rt, red LED, 9V rep batt, 2.75x6.0", Rockwell-like keypad, in spite of the name this is not a printing calculator, label is in Spanish, Mexico, value $85-95.

Prinztronic

An English company and possibly just the brand name for the Dixon chain of electronic and photographic stores in

England. Some calculators are labeled Dixon-Prinztronic.

88P 4-funct, %, green fluor, 4-AA rep batt, 3.5x5.5", similar case to Unimark 805T and Karstadt MR40, Japan, value $45-55.

C20 4-funct, red LED, 4-AA rep batt, 3.75x6.0", c1973, Taiwan, value $45-55.

SR-99P 4-funct, %, sq rt, green fluor, 2-AA rep batt, 3.0x4.75", similar case to Teal 806 or 817, Japan, value $45-55.

X15 4-funct, red LED, 9V rep batt, 2.75x5.25", has "vat" (value added tax) key, similar to Radofin design, Hong Kong, value $45-55.

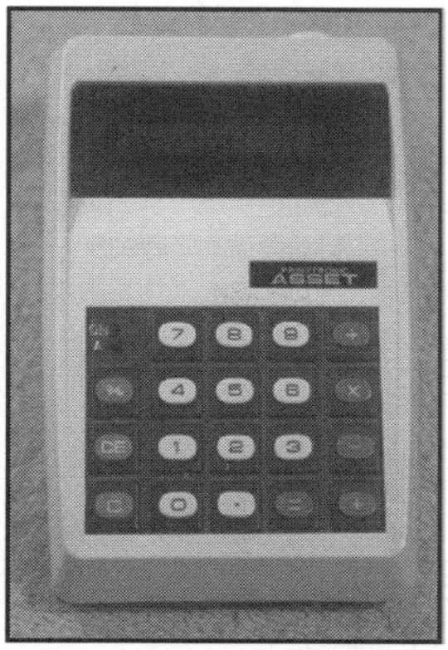

Asset 4-funct, fluor, 4-AA rep batt, 3.0x4.0, similar to Commodore MM series, value $45-55.

Financial 4-funct, %, sq rt, sgn chg, green fluor, 4-AA rep batt, 3.0x5.5", looks like Qualitron models, c1976, Taiwan, value $45-55.

M 4-funct, mem, %, red LED, 4-AAA rep batt, 2.0x4.75", brown color, similar to Sinclair Cambridge but slightly smaller, Hong Kong, value $60-70.

MC95 4-funct, mem, sgn chg, 8 digit mini tube display with 16 digit calculating readout capability, sealed batt, 4.5x6.75", similar to Sharp case designs, Japan, value $75-95.

Micro 4-funct, purple LED, 4-AA rep batt, 3.0x4.0", same case as Sharp EL-801, c1972-73, Japan, value $65-75.

Scientific *aka SC500M*, sci-funct, green fluor, 4-AA rep batt, 2.5x5.5", Taiwan, value $45-55.

Prismatic

500 *aka P500*, 4-funct, mem, %, early LCD, 2-9V rep batt, 3.5x6.0", early LCD display with see-through panel at top of calculator to help light LCD, same as Dataking LC-800 and Lloyd's 40, Mexico (of US parts), value $40-50.

Privileg

Privileg was the brand name for Quelle International, a European based marketing company which sold calculators made by others under their Privileg name.

85 4-funct, %, red LED, 9V rep batt, 3.0x6.0", odd flat keys, looks like Hanimex 305, value $50-60.

583 DE sci-funct, green fluor, 2-AA rep batt, 3.0x5.25", value $40-50.

585 DE sci-funct, green fluor, 2-AA rep batt, 3.0x6.0", value $45-55.

848 MD 4-funct, mem, %, paren, pi, sq funct, recip, green fluor, 2-AA 3.0x5.5", value $35-45.

1081ESR-E sci-funct, red LED, 2-AA rep batt, 2.75x5.75", label on back in German, value $40-50.

SR 30 sci-funct, red LED, 9V rep batt, 3.0x6.0", value $40-50.

SR60D-NC sci-funct, green fluor, 3-AA rep batt, 3.25x6.5", value $45-55.

Sensor *aka 867MD*, 4-funct, mem, %, sq funct, recip, green fluor, 9V rep batt, 3.25x5.0", unique touch-sensitive on/off button, value $55-70.

Super 2002 4-funct, red LED, 5-AA rep batt, 3.0x5.25", fits in 7.0x9.0" desk-top docking unit that has a paper and pencil holder, West Germany, value $70-90.

Mini Computer 4-funct, red LED, 2.5x4.75", same case as Busicom 120A, Japan, value $80-120.

Pulsar

Calculator Watch 4-funct, mem, %, red LED, button rep batt, 1.6x1.6", several case metals were available - in 1975 an 18 kt. solid gold case model sold for $3950, in 1977 a 14 kt. gold filled case model sold for $495, and a stainless steel version sold for $550 in 1976 and $395 in 1977, value $250-$600 for the steel and 14 kt. gold versions.

Pye

English company.

630 4-funct, fluor, sealed batt, 3.0x5.75", c1974, value $40-50.

640 4-funct, mem, %, fluor, sealed batt, 3.0x5.75", c1974, value $45-55.

650 4-funct, mem, %, sq funct, recip, fluor, sealed batt, 3.0x5.75", c1974, value $45-55.

Quali

Taiwan Company

112 4-funct, mem, red LED, 4-AA rep batt, 3.0x5.5", early Klixon-like keypad, strange "n-m" slide switch, Taiwan, value $85-95.

Qualitron

Distributed in the US by California Qualitron Corp.

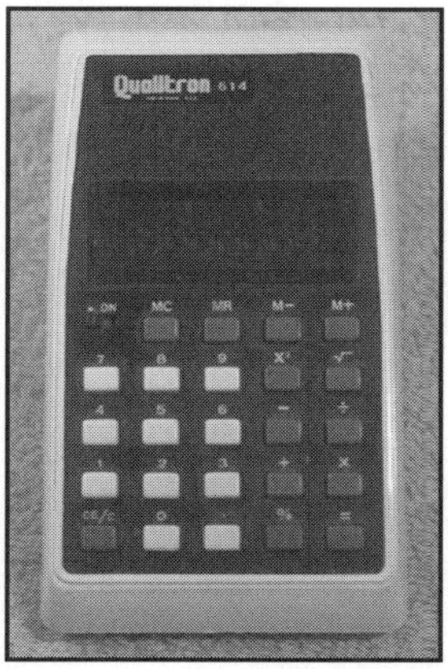

614 4-funct, mem, sq rt, red LED, 9V rep batt, 2.5x4.5", Taiwan, value $45-55.

907 4-funct, %, red LED, 9V rep batt, 3.0x5.5", Taiwan, value $30-40.

910 *aka Slimline 910*, 4-funct, mem, red LED, 9V rep batt, 3.0x5.5", Taiwan, value $45-55.

1437 4-funct, %, green fluor, 4-AA rep batt, 3.0x5.75", Taiwan, value $40-50.

1439 *aka Financial,* financial functions, green fluor, 4-AA rep batt, 3.0x5.75", Taiwan, value $40-50.

1442 4-funct, mem, %, green fluor, 4-AA rep batt, 3.0x5.75", looks like 1437, Taiwan, value $40-50.

The International Association of Calculator Collectors was founded in 1992 by Bruce Flamm and Guy Ball and is the only organization in the world dedicated to the collectors of calculators. Along with their newsletter, they host two calculator-themed web sites.

1443 4-funct, mem, sq rt, green fluor, 4-AA rep batt, 3.0x5.5", looks like 1437 but has mem and sq rt, Taiwan, value $35-45.

1445 sci-funct, green fluor, 4-AA rep batt, 3.0x5.75", looks like 1437, Taiwan, value $40-50.

2443R 4-funct, mem, %, sq rt, green fluor, sealed batt, 3.0x5.75", Taiwan, value $40-50.

2446R *aka Slide Rule*, 4-funct, sq rt, recip, mem, green fluor, sealed batt, 3.0x5.5", in spite of name has no trig or log functions, Taiwan, value $45-55.

2543 4-funct, mem, %, sq rt, sgn chg, fluor, 3-AAA rep batt, 2.75x5.25", thin, same case as National Semiconductor 200, Taiwan, value $35-45.

QI-1014 4-funct, mem, %, sq funct, recip, sgn chg, red LED, 4-AA rep batt, 3.0x5.75", looks like 1437, Taiwan, value $40-50.

QI-1064 4-funct, mem, %, sq funct, recip, sgn chg, red LED, 4-AA rep batt, 3.0x5.75", looks like 1437, Taiwan, value $40-50.

Elegance 4-funct, mem, sq rt, green fluor, sealed batt, very thin all-metal case, Taiwan, value $45-55.

Executive 4-funct, mem, %, sq rt, sgn chg, blue fluor, sealed batt, 2.8x5.5", very thin, metal case, same case as Rockwell 24K, Taiwan, value $40-50.

Quelle

See Privileg.

R and S

European-market company.

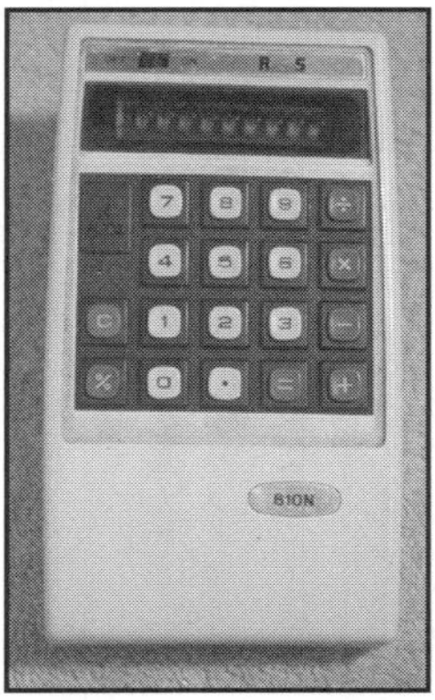

810N 4-funct, %, red LED, 3-AA rep batt, 3.0x5.25", Korea, value $35-45.

Radio Shack

American electronics store chain and catalog mass marketer. Radio Shack labels were usually placed on calculators already made by other companies so they often resemble models made by others.

EC-21 *aka Blackjack*, 4-funct, sq rt, paren, blackjack-21 game functions, fluor, 3-AAA rep batt, thin, metal case, 3.25x5.5", Taiwan, value $25-35.

EC-100 4-funct, red LED, 4-AA rep batt, 3.5x6.0", unusual case, same as Longines Symphonette Battery-AC, Klixon keypad, made by TI, 1973 price $129.95, USA, value $85-95.

EC-200 4-funct, red LED, 4-AA rep batt, 3.5x5.75", unusual case similar to EC-100, Klixon keypad, 1974 price $89.50, USA, value $85-95.

EC-201 *aka Electronic Memory Calculator*, 4-funct, mem, %, sgn chg, red LED, 9V rep batt, 2.75x5.25", Hong Kong, value $25-35.

EC-219 4-funct, mem, %, blue fluor, 2-AA rep batt, 3.0x5.75", Hong Kong, value $20-30.

EC-220 4-funct, %, red LED, 9V rep batt, 3.0x6.0", similar case to EC-415, 1976 price $16.95, Mexico, value $40-50.

EC-221 4-funct, %, red LED, 9V rep batt, 2.75x5.25", similar case style to Radofin Valuman and Unitrex 95SL, 1977 price $10.95, Hong Kong, value $35-45.

EC-223 4-funct, clock and watch function, same as Casio CQ-1, fluor, 1-AA rep batt, 2 button rep batt, 2.5x5.75", Japan, value $60-70.

EC-225 4-funct, red LED, 4-AA rep batt, 3.0x6.5, same as General EZ-2000, Canada, value $40-50.

EC-226 4-funct, mem, %, red LED, 9V rep batt, 3.0x5.75", looks like EC-219, Hong Kong, value $20-30.

EC-230 4-funct, %, red LED, 9V rep batt, 3.0x5.0", very unique case style, same case as Corvus 400, 1976 price $19.95, USA, value $35-45.

EC-231 4-funct, %, sq rt, fluor, 2-AA rep batt, 3.0x5.25", 1977 price $14.95, value $30-40.

EC-240 *aka Statesman Thin*, 4-funct, %, sq rt, green fluor, sealed batt, 3.0x5.25", thin, metal case, similar to EC-245, 1977 price $29.95, Taiwan, value $35-45.

EC-241 4-funct, mem, %, fluor, 9V rep batt, 3.0x5.5", 1977 price $12.95, value $30-40.

EC-242 4-funct, mem, %, red LED, 9V rep batt, 3.0x5.75", looks like EC-219, 1978 price $8.88, Hong Kong, value $20-30.

EC-243 4-funct, mem, %, sq rt, green fluor, 2-AA rep batt, 3.0x5.75", looks like EC-219, 1978 price $14.95, Hong Kong, value $20-30.

EC-245 *aka Statesman Thin*, 4-funct, mem, %, sq funct, recip, sgn chg, green fluor, sealed batt, 3.0x5.5", thin, metal case, similar to EC-240, 1977 price $34.95, Taiwan, value $35-45.

EC-250 4-funct, %, red LED, 3-AA rep batt, 3.0x6.0", same case style as Bowmar MX-55, USA, value $30-40.

EC-275 4-funct, %, red LED, 3-AA rep batt, 2.75x6.0", hard plastic slip cover protects the keys, 1975 price $49.95, Mexico, value $40-50.

EC-281 sci-funct, blue fluor, 4-AA rep batt, 3.25x6.0", 1978 price $29.95, Taiwan, value $40-50.

EC-300 4-funct, mem, %, red LED, 4-AA rep batt, 3.5x5.75", unusual boxy shape, 1974 price $114.95, USA, value $45-55.

EC-312 *aka Astro*, 4-funct and biorhythm calculations, fluor, 2-AA rep batt, 3.0x4.5", unusual styling, same as Kosmos Astro, Taiwan, value $55-65.

EC-314 *aka Biorhythm Computer/ Calculator*, 4-funct and biorhythm calculations, fluor, 2-AA rep batt, 3.0x5.25", same case as Kosmos 2, Taiwan, value $20-30.

Collectors use the term "LED/tube-type" in describing the type of calculators they collect. The term dates and indicates calculators from the early 1970's, prior to modern Liquid Crystal Display (LCD).

EC-350 4-funct, mem, %, red LED, 4-AA rep batt, 3.0x6.0", 1975 price $69.95, USA, value $50-60.

EC-375 4-funct, mem, %, sq rt, fluor, 4-AA rep batt, 3.75x6.5", 1976 price $39.95, Japan, value $40-50.

EC-380 4-funct, mem, %, sq rt, sgn chg, fluor, 2-AA rep batt, 3.0x5.5", similar to EC-231, 1977 price $24.95, Japan, value $20-30.

EC-400 4-funct, mem, %, sq rt, recip, sgn chg, red LED, sealed batt, 3.25x5.25", similar to Bowmar MX-90, 1975 price $99.95, USA, value $40-50.

EC-415 4-funct, mem, %, sq funct,

sgn chg, recip, red LED, 9V rep batt, 3.0x6.0", similar case to EC-220, 1976 price $29.95, Mexico, value $40-50.

EC-420 4-funct, mem, %, sq funct, sgn chg, pi, recip, blue fluor, 2-AA rep batt, 2.75x3.25", 1977 price $19.95, Taiwan, value $25-35.

EC-421 4-funct, mem, %, sq funct, sgn chg, pi, paren, green fluor, 2-AA rep batt, 3.0x5.25", looks like EC-420, 1978 price $19.95, Taiwan, value $35-45.

EC-425 4-funct, sq funct, recip, exp, sgn chg, red LED, sealed batt, 3.0x6.0", same as TI SR-10, 1975 price $79.95, USA, value $45-55.

EC-450 sci-funct, red LED, sealed batt, 3.25x5.25", similar to Bowmar MX-100, 1975 price $129.95, USA, value $45-55.

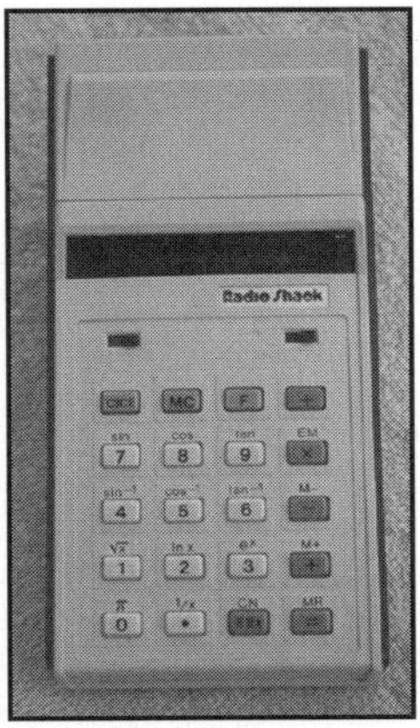

EC-475 sci-funct, red LED, 9V rep batt, 3.0x6.2", similar case style to model by General Instruments -- probably made by them also, 1976 price $59.95, Canada, value $45-55.

EC-480 sci-funct, fluor, 2-AA rep batt, 2.75x5.25", 1977 price $29.95, value $35-45.

EC-485 sci-funct, green fluor, 4-AA rep batt, 3.25x6.0", same features as EC-495 except with slightly different case, Taiwan, value $40-50.

EC-490 sci-funct, fluor, sealed batt, 3.25x6.25", same case with different type of keys as Rockwell 63R, 1976 price $99.95, Mexico, value $40-50.

EC-495 sci-funct, green fluor, 4-AA rep batt, 3.25x6.0", same features as EC-485 except with slightly different case, 1978 price $39.95, Japan, value $40-50.

EC-2001 4-funct, mem, %, 10 digit blue fluor, 2-D rep batt, 6x6.5", same case as Royal D-120, Compex EC-1000W, and Unisonic 1000M, 1978 price $29.95, Taiwan, value $15-25.

EC-2010 4-funct, mem, %, 10 digit blue fluor, 2-D rep batt, 6.0x6.5", similar styling to EC2001, Taiwan, value $15-25.

EC-3000 4-funct, %, paper printer only, 4-AA rep batt, 4.25x6.75, similar to Facit 1140 and Addo 9218, 1977 price $119.95, value $50-60.

EC-3005 4-funct, mem, %, sq rt, paren, green fluor, 4-AA rep batt, 3.25x8.0", Hong Kong, value $25-35.

EC-4000 sci-funct, programmable functions, red LED, sealed batt pack, 3.0x5.75", same as TI Programmable 57, 1978 price $79.95, USA, value $35-45.

Hewlett-Packard's HP-65 provided back-up for the on-board computer used by American astronauts during the Apollo missions. On one of the missions in outer space, astronauts calculated critical course correction maneuvers on their HP-65 programmable hand-held during the rendezvous of the US Apollo and Russian Soyuz spacecraft.

EC-4001 sci-funct, programmable, purple LED, 9V rep batt, 2.0x4.5", white, looks like Sinclair Cambridge Programmable, c1978, England, value $55-70.

BlackJack 21 *see EC-21.*

Teaching Calculator 4-funct, various teaching functions, fluor, 2-AA rep batt, value $15-25.

4-in-1 Electronic game calculator, red LED, 5-AA rep batt, 3.5x6.5", Hong Kong, value $15-25.

Radofin

8P 4-funct, %, red LED, 9V rep batt, 2.5x5.0", same case as 1610, Hong Kong, value $35-45.

1515 4-funct, %, green fluor, 2-AA rep batt, 2.6x5.2", Hong Kong, value $40-50.

1525 4-funct, mem, %, green fluor, 9V rep batt, 2.5x5.0", similar case to 8P, Hong Kong, value $35-45.

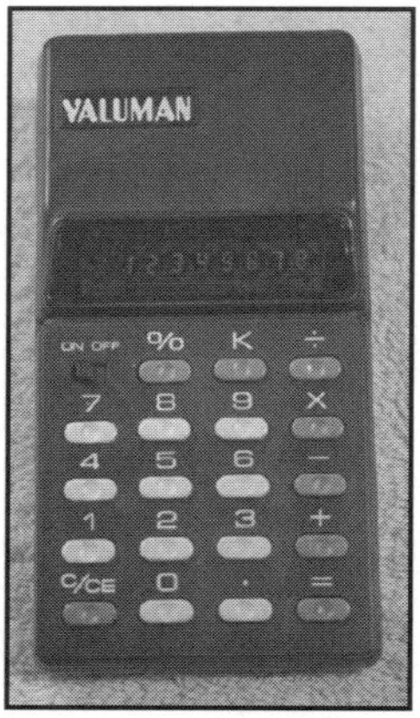

1610 *aka Valuman*, 4-funct, %, red LED, 9V rep batt, 2.5x5.0", same case as 8P, Hong Kong, value $40-50.

1630 *See SR1630.*

1720 4-funct, mem, red LED, 3.25x6.0", 6-AAA rep batt, Hong Kong, value $40-50.

1750 4-funct, mem, %, sq funct, recip, sgn chg, red LED, 6-AAA rep batt, 3.25x6.0", thin case in wallet pouch, similar to Novus wallet styles, Hong Kong, value $35-45.

Some manufacturers made calculators with 6-digit displays instead of the common 8. This saved on display and internal IC components as well as lowered power consumption to the batteries. In addition, 6-digit calculators were not covered by Japanese quota-induced export restrictions during 1972.

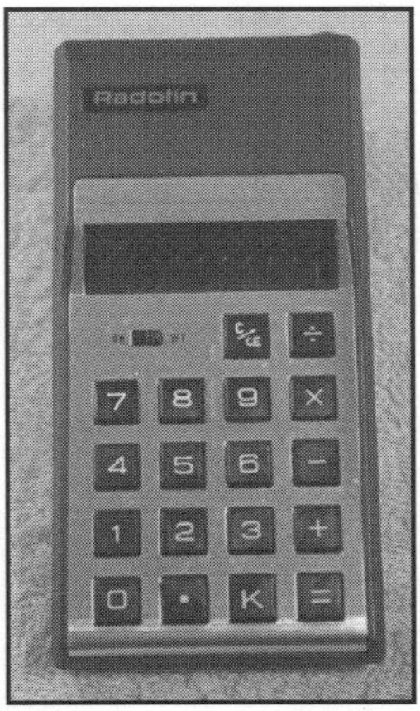

2200 4-funct, red LED, 9V rep batt, 2.75x5.25", Hong Kong, value $35-45.

SR1630 4-funct, mem, %, sq funct, recip, red LED, 9V rep batt, 2.75x5.25", Hong Kong, value $40-50.

Ragen Precision Industries

In late 1971, Ragen Precision (USA) announced plans to market a very small calculator in January 1972. The price would be $100 and use the as-yet unproven LCD display technology. While there was a lot of publicity surrounding this model (Micro-Mini), it is unknown if the company ever delivered on its claims.

Micro-Mini 4-funct, LCD, rep batt, 3.0x4.0", c1971-73, USA, value $120-150.

Rapid Data

One of the few Canadian companies that made early pocket calculators.

> ***"In 1973, my first electronic calculator was large and boxy and cost $50. for just the four basic functions. I was thrilled to find one so cheap. I had been waiting so long for a reasonable price."***
> ***--Guy Ball***

800 *aka Rapidman 800*, 4-funct, red LED, 9V rep batt, 3.25x5.5", introduced in Spring 1972, probably first model to sell for under $100, Canada, value $35-45.

804 *aka Rapidman 804*, 4-funct, red LED, 9V rep batt, 3.5x5.75", Canada, value $30-40.

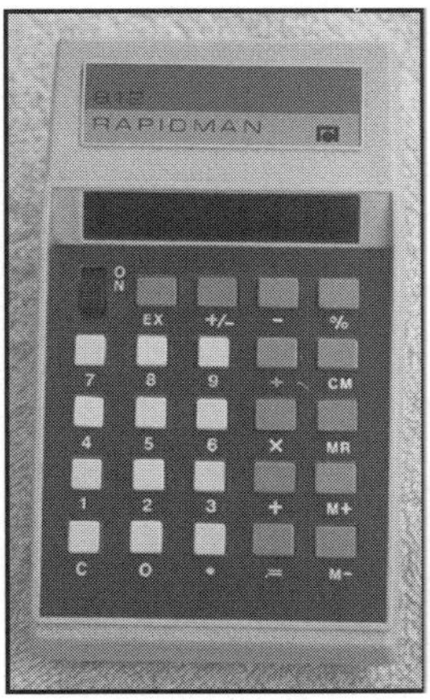

812 *aka Rapidman 812*, 4-funct, mem, %, exp, sgn chg, red LED, 9V rep batt, 3.5x5.75", similar case to 804, Canada, value $35-45.

Pioneer 1 4-funct, red LED, 9V rep batt, 3.25x5.5", same case as Rapidman 800 but in white color, 1973 price $60, Canada, value $45-55.

Rapidex

European-market company.

710 *aka RA-710*, 4-funct, mem, %, sq rt, sgn chg, fluor, 2-AA rep batt, 3.0x5.5", Singapore, value $45-55.

RBM

Scientific 4-funct, mem, %, sq, recip, red LED, sealed batt, similar case to Columbia Scientific models, USA, value $55-65.

Realtone

Realtone may be a division of, or otherwise connected with, the Soundesign company.

8412 *aka Micro Memory*, 4-funct, mem, %, tube, 4-AA rep batt, 3.5x6.0", Japan, value $45-55.

KP-470 4-funct, mem, %, sq funct, recip, sgn chg, 10 digit fluor, 3-AA rep batt, 3.25x6.75", looks like Kings Point KP-200, Hong Kong, value $45-55.

Regan

Regan Industries of Glendale, California (USA). No other information. Unknown relationship to RES.

RA900P 4-funct, tube display, sealed batt, 3.5x5.5", thick model with large keys, same as RES Mark IX except some keys in different color, two variations of RA900P also show keys in different colors, c1971-72, USA, value $70-80.

RES

Radiant Energy Systems of Newbury Park, California, (USA). Unknown relationship to Regan which had a "duplicate" calculator.

Mark IX 4-funct, tube display, sealed batt, 3.5x5.5", thick model with large keys, same as Regan RA900P except some keys in different color, two variations of Mark IX also show keys in different colors, c1971-72, USA, value $70-80.

RFT

East German company.

Konkret 100 4-funct, red LED, 4-AA rep batt, very unusual orange color, interesting case style, East Germany, value $80-100.

Minerex 75 4-funct, red LED, sealed batt, 3.25x5.0", used "docking bay" for recharging and desk-top use, East Germany, value $50-60.

MR-201 4-funct, sealed batt, 3.0x6.0", East Germany, value $45-55.

Ricoh

Japanese company.

RC-8F 4-funct, mem, %, sgn chg, green fluor, 2-AA rep batt. 1975 price $16.95, Japan, value $25-35.

RMS International

Only one unique-looking model is known made by Westlake Village California (USA) company. This may have been a "garage" operation quickly forced out of business by rapidly falling calculator prices in mid-1970's.

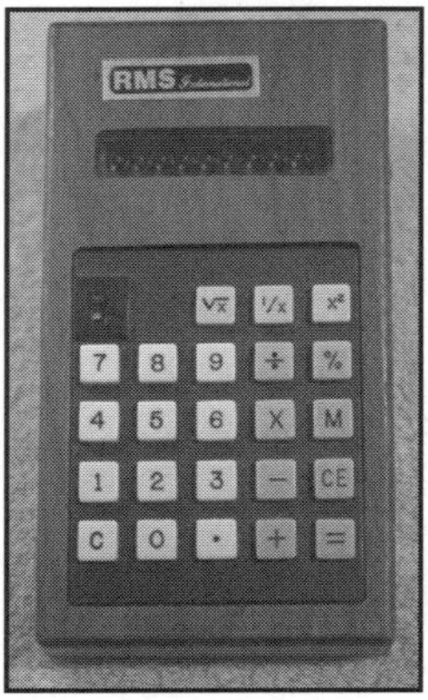

Zeta 7 4-funct, memo, sq rt, red LED, sealed batt, 3.0x6.0", this pocket calculator's case is actually made of real wood and is very well constructed! Appears to be balsa or other light wood with joints perfectly sanded, label says, "hand-crafted in the USA", c1972, value $300.

Rockwell

Integrated circuit maker that helped with ICs for the first Sharp calculators in the late 1960's. After purchasing the calculator maker Unicom, they eventually began making and selling their own models. Many Rockwell models share a characteristic keypad which is quite different from other brands.

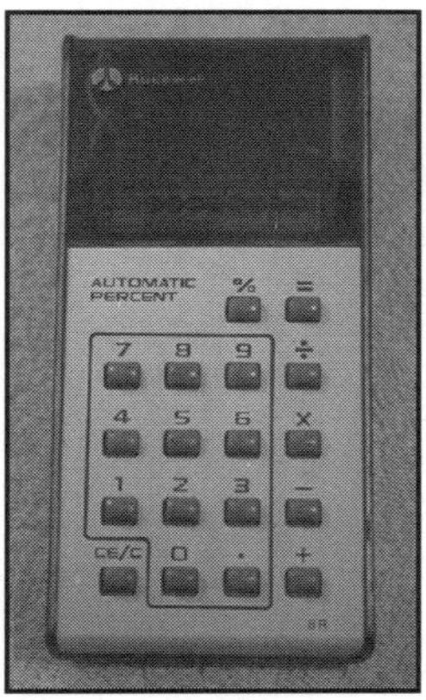

8R 4-funct, %, red LED, 9V rep batt, 3.0x6.0", 1975 price $16.88, Mexico or Hong Kong, value $10-15.

9TR 4-funct, %, red LED, 9V rep batt, 3.0x6.0", green case and keys, note on box states it is a "custom model manufactured for True Value Hardware Stores," very uncommon Rockwell model, Mexico, value $40-50.

10R 4-funct, red LED, 9V rep batt, 3.0x6.0", looks like 8R, 1974 price $29.95, Mexico, value $15-25.

12R 4-funct, sq rt, red LED, 9V rep batt, 3.0x5.5", looks like 8R, 1975 price $29.95, Mexico, value $15-25.

14RD 4-funct, %, fluor, 4-AA rep batt, 3.0x6.0", looks like 8R, keypad is different, less common than 14RD-II, Japan, value $35-45.

14RD-II 4-funct, %, fluor, 4-AA rep batt, 3.0x6.0", like 14RD but has 9 digit instead of 8 digit display, Japan, value $25-35.

18R 4-funct, mem, %, red LED, 9V rep batt, 3.0x6.0", looks like 8R, 1975 price $19.88, Mexico or Hong Kong, value $15-25.

20R 4-funct, mem, %, red LED, 9V rep batt, 3.0x6.0", looks like 8R, 1974 price $49.95, Mexico, value $15-25.

21R 4-funct, mem, %, red LED, 9V rep batt, 3.0x6.0", looks like 8R, 1975 price $49.95, Mexico, value $15-25.

22K 4-funct, mem, %, sq rt, sgn chg, blue fluor, 3-AAA rep batt, 3.0x5.5", very thin, metal case, came in wallet, same case as 22MS, 1978 price $11.99, Japan, value $35-45.

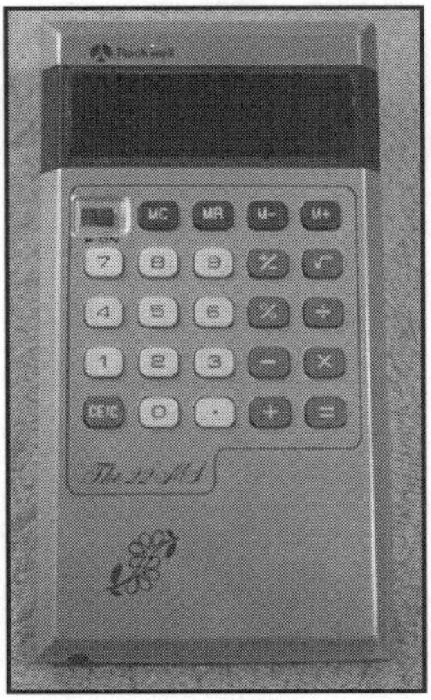

22MS 4-funct, mem, %, sq rt, sgn chg, blue fluor, 3-AAA rep batt, 3.0x5.5", very thin, metal case, came in wallet, Japan, value $35-45.

24K 4-funct, mem, %, sq rt, sgn chg, blue fluor, sealed batt, 2.8x5.5", very thin, metal case, came in wallet, 1975 price $40, Taiwan, value $35-45.

24K II 4-funct, mem, %, sq rt, sgn chg, blue fluor, sealed batt, 3.0x5.5", very thin, metal case, came in wallet, similar case style to 22K as opposed to 24K, Japan, value $35-45.

24MS 4-funct, mem, %, sq rt, sgn chg, blue fluor, sealed batt, 3.0x5.5", very thin, metal case, came in wallet, same case as 24K, Japan, value $35-45.

24MS II 4-funct, mem, %, sq rt, sgn chg, blue fluor, sealed batt, 3.0x5.5", very thin, metal case, came in wallet, similar case style to 22K as opposed to 24MS, Japan, value $35-45.

24RD 4-funct, mem, %, sq rt, sgn chg, fluor, 4-AA rep batt, 3.0x6.0", 1975 price $24.88, Japan, value $20-30.

24RD-II 4-funct, mem, %, sq rt, sgn chg, blue fluor, 4-AA rep batt, 3.0x6.0", similar case as 24RD with a minor display difference, Japan, value $20-30.

30R 4-funct, mem, %, sq funct, recip, sgn chg, red LED, 9V rep batt, 3.0x6.0", looks like 8R, 1974 price $59.95, Mexico, value $15-25.

31R 4-funct, mem, %, sq funct, recip, sgn chg, red LED, sealed batt, 3.0x6.0", looks like 8R, Mexico, value $15-25.

44RD sci-funct, green fluor, 4-AA rep batt, 3.0x6.0", the only known small-cased Rockwell with sci-funct, Japan, c1975, value $40-50.

"i remember staying up almost all night using pencil and paper to do "long division" when I took physics in college in 1971. This seemed like an incredible waste of time, but if you wanted a good grade, it was the price you had to pay. Of course, we could use our slide rules for division, but you can't get many decimal places out of a slide rule. I drank a lot of coffee to stay awake. About a year later, I got my first pocket calculator. It's probably hard for kids today to understand what that calculator meant to me."
--Bruce Flamm

51R *aka Converter*, 4-funct, mem, conversion functions, blue fluor, sealed batt, 3.25x6.25", 1974 price $99.95, Mexico, value $35-45.

61R *aka Advanced Slide Rule*, sci-funct, fluor, sealed batt, 3.25x6.25", 1974 price $99.95, Mexico, value $35-45.

63R *aka Scientific Slide Rule*, sci-funct, fluor, sealed batt, 3.25x6.25", similar case style to 61R, 2 variations of keys were used, 1975 price $89.95, Mexico, value $40-50.

64RD sci-funct, green fluor, 4-AA rep batt, 3.5x6.0", similar to 44RD but larger, Japan, c1975, value $40-50.

74K sci-funct, blue fluor, sealed batt, 3.0x5.5", very thin, metal case, came in wallet, similar case to 22MS, 1976 price $60, Japan, value $35-45.

While most people in the US are familiar with the brandname of Texas Instruments, Sharp, Casio and Hewlett-Packard, few are familiar with brands originating in Europe. Some of these names include Aristo from Germany, Anita from Britain, Vanguard from Spain, Elka from Bulgaria, Vito from Switzerland, and Facit from Sweden.

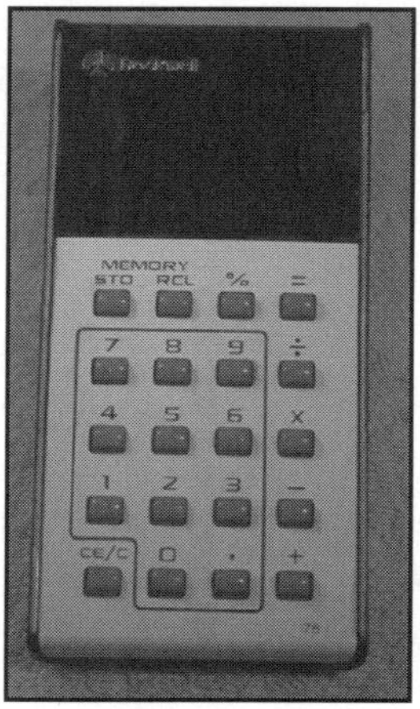

'76 4-funct, mem, %, red LED, 9V rep batt, 3.0x6.0", blue and white case with red keys, c1975-76 designed to commemorate USA Bicentennial, Mexico, value $35-45.

202 *aka Slide Rule*, sci-funct, fluor, 4-AA rep batt, 3.25x6.0", built-in calculator stand, Unicom Systems logo on back, Mexico, value $40-50.

203 *aka Metric Converter*, 4-funct, mem, conversion functions, fluor, 4-AA rep batt, 3.25x6.0", built-in calculator stand, looks like 202, Unicom Systems logo on back, Mexico, value $40-50.

204 *aka Financier*, financial functions, fluor, 4-AA rep batt, 3.25x6.0", built-in calculator stand, looks like 202, Unicom Systems logo on back, Mexico, value $50-60.

Roger

See Tohotronic.

Royal

Royal Typewriter Company, Hartford, Connecticut (USA). In the late 1960's the electronics revolution caused turmoil in the business machines industry. Mechanical calculators were quickly becoming obsolete. Some companies folded and others merged. Royal became part of Litton Industries. European companies Adler, Triumph, and Imperial seem to be linked to Royal either as the same company or sister divisions of Litton.

Award GT8 4-funct, mem, %, green fluor, 4-AA rep batt, 3.5x6.0", two-tone case, Japan, value $55-65.

Award MGT 4-funct, mem, %, green fluor, 4-AA rep batt, 3.5x6.0", uncommon design, has unusual spring-loaded pull-out battery holder, Japan, value $55-65.

Countess Royal *aka UA-117*, 4-funct, %, green fluor, 3-AAA rep batt, 2.5x3.75", powder blue plastic case, "ladies model," Japan, value $25-35.

D120 4-funct, mem, %, 10 digit blue fluor, 2-D rep batt, 6.0x6.5", same case as D330, Taiwan, value $20-30.

D330 4-funct, mem, %, 10 digit blue fluor, 2-D rep batt, 6.0x6.5", same case as D120, Taiwan, value $20-30.

D330 II *aka business calculator*, 4-funct, mem, %, 10 digit blue fluor, 2-D rep batt, 6.0x6.5", same case as D120, Taiwan, value $20-30.

Digital III 4-funct, 4 digit tube display with 8 digit calculating and readout ability, very unusual "keypad" concept using a wired stylus to electrically contact numbered gold plates on the calculator (no buttons), sealed batt, 3.25x6.75, early 1972 price $99, USA, value $90-110.

Digital IV 4-funct, red LED, sealed batt, same case and "keypad" concept as Digital III except used 8 digit red LED display, 3.25x6.75, c1972, USA, value $100-140.

Digital 5 4-funct, green fluor, sealed batt, 3.5x6.0", appears same as Digital 5-T except for batt, Japan, value $40-50.

Digital 5-T 4-funct, green fluor, 4-AA rep batt, 3.5x6.0", black case with uncommon styling, Malaysia, value $40-50.

Digital 88 *aka UA785*, 4-funct, blue fluor, 4-AA rep batt, 3.5x6.25", unusual and attractive case style, c1974, Malaysia, value $50-60.

Digital 88M 4-funct, mem, %, green fluor, 4-AA rep batt, 3.5x6.0", uncommon design, has unusual spring-loaded pull-out battery holder, same case as Award GT, Japan, value $55-65.

Solar 1 4-funct, mem, %, sq rt, yellow LCD, used large solar panel to power calculator and internal rechargeable batteries to retain a charge, 3.2x5.2x0.5", value $80-100.

3HPD 4-funct, mem, %, green fluor and paper printer, sealed batt, 2.75x5.5", one of the smallest printing/display calculators made in the 1970's, Japan, value $45-55.

5HPD 4-funct, mem, %, green fluor and paper printer, sealed batt, 3.25x9.0", 1981 price $89.95, Japan, value $25-35.

8MK-AD *aka EC30*, 4-funct, mem, %, sq rt, sgn chg, fluor, 4-C rep batt, 5.5x8.5", Japan, value $25-35.

10HPD 4-funct, mem, %, green fluor and paper printer, sealed batt, 4.25x9.0", Japan, value $25-35.

12HT *aka UA221*, sci-funct, green fluor, 4-AA rep batt, 3.0x6.0", looks like 90 or 91 model but larger, unusual Royal with "F" key to double usable entry keys, Japan, value $55-65.

80K *aka UA119*, 4-funct, %, green fluor, 3-AAA rep batt, 2.5x4.0", black color, Japan, value $25-35.

81CS 4-funct, mem, %, sq funct, recip, pi, green fluor, 2-AA rep batt, 3.0x6.0", thin, 1978 price $16.95, Japan, value $35-45.

81M *aka UA127*, 4-funct, mem, %, green fluor, 3-AAA rep batt, 2.5x4.0", black color, looks like 80K, 1978 price $11.50, Japan, value $25-35.

90K *aka UA120*, 4-funct, %, green fluor, 4-AAA rep batt, 2.75x4.5", black color, Japan, value $25-35.

90S *aka UA121*, 4-funct, %, sq rt, sgn chg, pi, green fluor, 4-AAA rep batt, 2.75x4.5", black color, looks like 90K, Japan, value $25-35.

91K *aka UA122*, 4-funct, %, mem, decimal slide switch green fluor, 4-AAA rep batt, 2.75x4.5", black color, looks like 90K, Japan, value $45-55.

91S *aka UA123*, 4-funct, %, sq rt, mem, decimal slide switch, green fluor, 4-AAA rep batt, 2.75x4.5", black color, looks like 90K, Japan, value $45-55.

99T *aka UA126*, sci-funct, green fluor, 4-AAA rep batt, 2.75x4.5", black color, looks like 90K, Japan, value $25-35.

1010 4-funct, mem, %, sgn chg, green fluor, 2-AA rep batt, 3.0x5.0", black color, looks like 90K, Japan, value $30-40.

Santron

12S 4-funct, 6 digit red LED, 9V rep batt, 2.5x4.75", Taiwan, value $25-35.
24M 4-funct, mem, %, sq funct, red LED, 9V rep batt, 2.9x5.0", Taiwan, value $35-45.

300SR sci-funct, 14 digit red LED, 3-AA rep batt, 3.2x6.0", black case, value $45-55.

400 4-funct educational calculator with clown face and red and green LEDs for eyes. After entering the equation and what you think is the answer (2+3=5 for example), you press the "?" key and a green LED verifies the right answer, a red LED will note if it's incorrect. 9V rep batt, Taiwan, value $35-45.

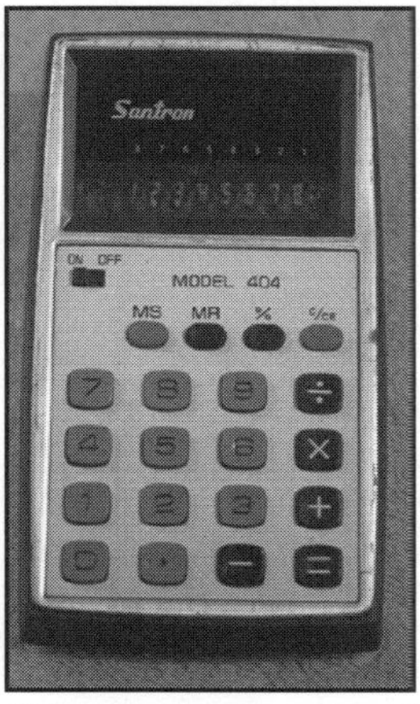

404 4-funct, mem, %, red LED, 2-AA rep batt, 3.0x5.0", Taiwan, value $35-45.

407 4-funct, mem, %, sgn chg, red LED, 9V rep batt, 3.0x5.2", Taiwan, value $25-35.

604 sci-funct, red LED, 9V rep batt, 3.0x5.0", uses RPN, Taiwan, value $40-50.

624 sci-funct, green fluor, 3.5x6.5", appears to be an attempt to compete with the most sophisticated of scientific calculators, Taiwan, value $40-50.

721 4-funct, mem, %, sgn chg, red LED, 9V rep batt, 3.0x5.0", has German instructions on back label, value $30-40.

725 sci-funct, green fluor, 3-AA rep batt, 3.0x6.0", Taiwan, value $40-50.

755 sci-funct, green fluor, 3-AA rep batt, 3.25x6.5", has German language markings on back, Taiwan, value $45-55.

Sanyo

Sanyo Electronics Company (Japan), is still in business but unlike Sharp and Casio, it no longer makes calculators. Sanyo's ICC models were among the first portable calculators in the world. These were solid precision-built machines with mainly metal cases. ICC apparently means Integrated Circuit Calculator. In the 1960's most electronic calculators used discrete components such as individual transistors and resistors and were the size of an IBM Selectric typewriter. The hand-held Sanyo ICC models were a real breakthrough. The ICC-0081 appears to have been Sanyo's first model.

CX-1032 4-funct, mem, %, sq rt, fluor, 2-AA rep batt, 3.0x5.0", one variation with white keys another with cream-colored keys, Japan, value $30-40.

CX-2007 4-funct, %, 6 digit blue fluor display with 12 digit calculating and readout ability, 4-AA rep batt, 3.25x5.25", Japan, value $45-55.

CX-8001 4-funct, constant, blue fluor, 4-AA rep batt, 3.5x6.0", similar to CX-8003A, c1973, Japan, value $35-45.

CX-8003A *aka Sacom Mini*, 4-funct, blue fluor, 4-AA rep batt, 3.5x6.0", white case, similar to CX-8001, Japan, value $40-50.

CX-8105 *aka Mini Calculator*, 4-funct, mem, %, sq rt, sgn chg, fluor, 4-AA rep batt, 3.5x6.25", hand strap, c1975, Japan, value $40-50.

CX-8136N 4-funct, mem, %, sq rt, sgn chg, green fluor, 2-AA rep batt, 3.0x5.0", Japan, value $35-45.

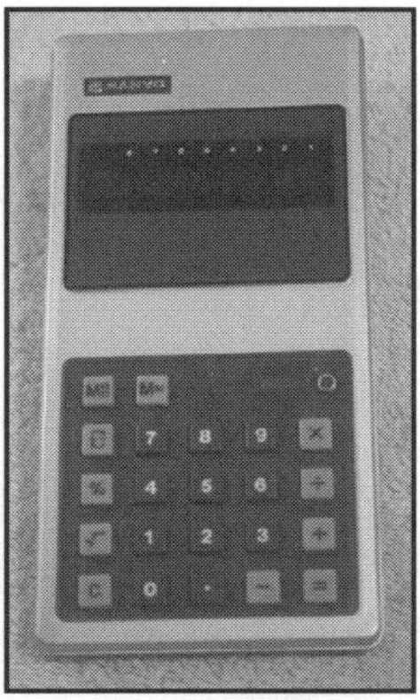

CX-8191 4-funct, mem, %, sq rt, red LED, 4-button rep batt, 3.0x6.0", thin (0.25") metal case, similar to Unisonic CB-14, Japan, value $45-55.

CZ-0111 *aka Scientific 84*, sci-funct, mem, exp, 4-AA rep batt, purple display, 3.5x6.5", Japan, value $40-50.

CZ-8101 sci-funct, fluor, sealed batt, c1974, value $45-55.

CZ-8112 sci-funct, LED, 9V rep batt, 1977 price $10, Japan, value $25-35.

CZ-8141 *aka Scientific Calculator*, sci-funct, green fluor, 2-AA rep batt, 3.0x5.25", Japan, value $40-50.

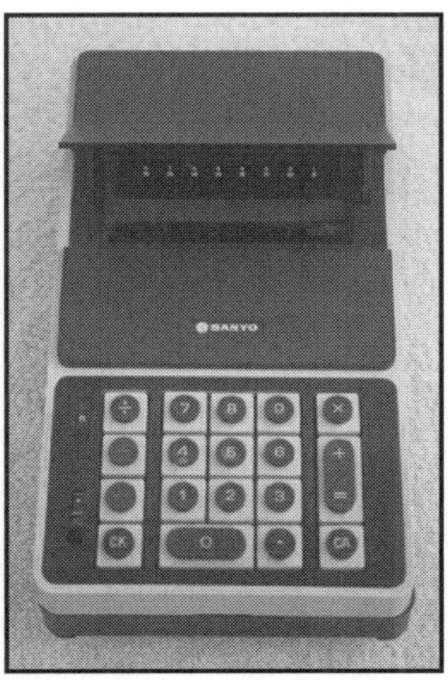

ICC-0081 4-funct, 8 digit tube with 16 digit calculating and readout ability, sealed batt, 5.5x9.75", very early model, probably first Sanyo portable calculator, flip-up lid over the display, early 1971 price $495, Japan, value $100-130.

ICC-82D 4-funct, 8 digit mini tube display with 16 digit calculating and readout capability, sealed batt, 5.5x8.25", battery meter, same as Dictaphone 1680, Japan, value $75-95.

ICC-083 4-funct, orange fluor, 4-D rep batt, 4.5x7.25", Japan, value $70-80.

ICC-802D 4-funct, orange fluor, sealed batt, 4.25x7.2", c1971, Japan, value $90-110.

ICC-804D 4-funct, red LED, sealed batt, 3.25x5.75", flip-up lid over display, heavy steel case, 804's are only known ICC model with LED displays. 1971 price $495, Japan, value $100-130.

ICC-804DE *aka Sacom mini E*, 4-funct, red LED, sealed batt, 3.25x5.75", flip-up lid over display, heavy steel case, like 804D but has several blue keypad buttons, Japan, 1971 price $465, value $100-130.

ICC-807D 4-funct, 8 digit fluor display with 16 digit calculating and readout ability, sealed batt, 3.5x6.0", very heavy, Japan, value $80-100.

ICC-808D 4-funct, 8 digit fluor display with 16 digit calculating and readout ability, sealed batt, 4.5x7.5", 4-D rep batt in very unique front panel battery holder, late 1972 price $115.95, Japan, value $70-80

ICC-809 4-funct, 8 digit fluor display with 16 digit calculating and readout ability, sealed batt, 4.0x8.0", horizontal shape, metal carrying handle, this is clearly a transistor radio case design adapted to use as a calculator, c1971-72, Japan, value $100-200.

ICC-810 4-funct, fluor, sealed batt, 3.5x6.0", Japan, value $40-50.

The first Calculator, Antique Science and Technology Collector's Show was held in 1995 in Dallas/Ft. Worth, Texas. Due to its popularity, the now annual event has doubled in size in just two years.

Satek

8M 4-funct, mem, red LED, 9V rep batt, 3.0x5.0", almost identical to the Unisonic 1542L which was made in Hong Kong, value $55-65.

SCM

See Smith Corona Marchant.

Sears

American department store chain which also sold through a general merchandise catalog. Unlike Montgomery Ward or Radio Shack, most Sears models appear to have been designed or re-designed exclusively for Sears - particularly the cases. Suppliers included Bowmar, Rockwell, and APF.

AC/DC 4-funct, %, LCD, sealed batt, 5.75x9.75", early use of LCD display, similar case style to Lloyd's 100, made by Rockwell, 1973 price $117.95, Mexico, value $45-55.

Digi-matic D-8 *aka Scientific Brain*, sci-funct, red LED, sealed batt, 3.0x5.25", same as Bowmar MX-100, made for Simpson/Sears, value $40-50.

Digi-matic T-8 *aka 41029*, 4-funct, red LED, 3-AA rep batt, 3.0x6.0", same case as 728.58821, made for Simpson/

Sears, Mexico, value $35-45.

Electronic Slide Rule *aka 801.58770*, financial funct, blue fluor, 4-AA rep batt, 3.5x6.25", probably made by Rockwell, has interesting case and key style, similar case to M8, 1974 price $168.95, Mexico, value $30-40.

Electronic Slide Rule II *aka 801.58780*, financial funct, blue fluor, 4-AA rep batt, 3.5x6.25", very similar to Electronic Slide Rule except with golden trim color and key markings slightly different, Mexico, value $40-50.

F85 *aka 711.58240*, 4-funct, mem, %, sq rt, fluor, 2-AA rep batt, 3.0x5.0", same case as APF Mark 65 except brown, Hong Kong, value $25-35.

M8 *aka 801.58870* 4-funct, mem, %, blue fluor, 4-AA rep batt, 3.5x6.25", probably made by Rockwell, has interesting case and key style, similar case to Universal Converter, 1973 price $108.95, Mexico, value $30-40.

Micro PD12 *aka 272.58040*, 4-funct, mem, % sq rt, sgn chg, fluor and paper printout, sealed batt, 4.0x7.0", Japan, value $35-45.

PPD-12 *aka 272.58020*, 4-funct, mem, %, sq rt, green fluor and paper printout, 4-C rep batt, 5.0x9.5", Japan, value $25-35.

Universal Converter *aka 801.58840*, 4-funct, has multiple measurement conversion funct, blue fluor, 4-AA rep batt, 3.5x6.25", probably made by Rockwell, has interesting case and key style, similar to M8, 1974 price $129, Mexico, value $30-40.

8 *aka 728.58862 and 728.58863*, 4-funct, %, red LED, sealed batt, 3.0x6.0", case slightly different from 58824, probably made by Bowmar, 1974 price $80, USA, value $20-30.

8m *aka 801.58240*, 4-funct, mem, %, red LED, 9V rep batt, 3.0x6.0", sleek black case, similar style to 801.58190, probably made by Rockwell, 1974 price $60, Mexico, value $20-30.

10m *aka 728.5825*, 4-funct, mem, %, sq rt, recip, sgn chg, red LED, sealed batt, 3.0x6.0", 1974 price $79.50, USA, value $20-30.

12PP *aka 272.58010*, 4-funct, mem, %, no display except for paper printout, 4-C rep batt, 4.75x8.5", Japan, value $25-30.

82 *aka 711.58151*, 4-funct, %, red LED, 9V rep, 2.5x5.0", similar case style to APF Mark 82, Hong Kong, value $25-35.

58824 4-funct, %, red LED, 3-AA rep, 3.0x6.0", similar case as 728.58821, similar to Bowmar Century Mark IV, USA, value $20-30.

728.5822 4-funct, %, red LED, 3-AA rep batt, 2.75x5.25", very unique "wood-grain" colored "roll-top" cover that slid underneath when calculator was in use, 1974 price $44.50, Mexico, value $35-45.

728.58821 4-funct, red LED, 3-AA rep batt, 3.0x6.0", similar case as 728.58850, probably made by Bowmar, 1973 price $58.95, Mexico, value $20-30.

728.58850 4-funct, constant, red LED, sealed batt, 3.0x6.0", same as Bowmar 905 except black, 1973 price $98.95, USA, value $20-30.

728.58862/3 *see Sears 8.*

728.58863 *See Sears 8.*

801.58190 4-funct, red LED, 9V rep batt, 3.0x5.25", sleek white case, similar to 8m, made by Rockwell, 1975 price $24.50, Mexico, value $30-40.

SEC

See Specialized Electronics Corporation.

Serd

German company.

Serd Bremen 4-funct, mem, %, sq funct, recip, paren, sgn chg, fluor, 2-AA rep batt, 3.25x5.5", Japan, value $40-50.

Sharp

Sharp Corp. of Japan is one of the few companies still in the calculator business. They made interesting desk-top calculators in the late 1960's before entering into the pocket calculator market. Their QT-8B model appears to be the first portable calculator to hit the market - but it was originally designed as an AC-only. Sharp's later EL-8 model was designed from the beginning as a portable, rechargeable model. (An AC-only model of the EL-8 was also available.)

CS-1120 4-funct, mem, %, sq rt, sgn chg, green fluor, sealed batt, 4.0x7.0", similar to EL-1106S, with built-in flip-up stand, Japan, value $45-55.

EL-8 4-funct, green tube, sealed batt, 4.0x6.5x2.5", very unusual styling, first Sharp designed from the beginning as a portable calculator, initially sold in early 1971 for $345 (may have sold in Japan in late 1970), Japan, value $70-90.

EL-8A 4-funct, green tube, AC only, 4.0x6.5x2.5", same as EL-8 except without rechargeable batteries, late 1971 price $185, Japan, value $80-100.

EL-8M 4-funct, mem, green tube, sealed batt, 4.0x7.25", similar case to EL-8 but longer due to addition of memory keys, Japan, value $80-100.

EL-102M 4-funct, mem, %, sq rt, red LED, 9V rep batt, 2.75x5.5", stylish case, Japan, value $30-35.

EL-102R 4-funct, %, sq rt, red LED, 9V rep batt, 2.75x5.5", stylish case, Japan, value $30-35.

EL-104 4-funct, %, sq rt, purple LED, 9V rep batt, 3.0x4.75", similar to EL-201, Japan, value $15-25.

EL-120 4-funct, green fluor, 3-AA rep batt, 6.75x2.5", horizontal, red case, has unique trigger-operated counting feature, Japan, value $45-55.

EL-122 4-funct, 6 digit green fluor display with 12 digit calculating and readout ability, 3-AA rep batt, 3.5x5.5", wedge shaped, c1975-76, Japan, value $40-50.

EL-201 4-funct, %, sq rt, green fluor, 2-AA rep batt, 3.0x4.75", looks like EL-104, 1976 price $9.75, Japan, value $15-25.

EL-201S 4-funct, %, sq rt, green fluor, 2-AA rep batt, 3.0x4.75", same as EL-201 but blue & white, looks like EL-104, Japan, value $15-25.

EL-210 4-funct, mem, %, sq rt, green fluor, 2-AA rep batt, 3.25x5.25", similar case and keypad to EL-215, Korea, value $25-35.

EL-215 4-funct, mem, %, sq rt, green fluor, 2-AA rep batt, 3.25x5.25", Korea, value $10-20.

EL-215S 4-funct, mem, %, sq rt, sgn chg, green fluor, 2-AA rep batt, 3.25x5.25", same as EL-215 but has sgn chg, Korea, value $10-20.

EL-500 sci-funct, green fluor, 2-AA rep batt, 3.0x5.5", Japan, value $20-30.

EL-500S sci-funct, green fluor, 2-AA rep batt, 3.0x5.5", same as EL-500 except lettering in gold instead of white, Japan, value $25-30.

EL-501 sci-funct, green fluor, 2-AA rep batt, 3.0x5.5", similar to EL-500, Japan, value $20-30.

EL-502 sci-funct, green fluor, 9V rep batt, 2.5x6.0", thin and stylish, Japan, value $30-40.

EL-801 4-funct, red LED, 4-AA rep batt, 3.0x4.0", unusual small boxy style, has pop-out battery holder, metal case, late 1972 price $129.95, Japan, value $55-65.

EL-805 4-funct, sgn chg, COS-LCD, 1-AA rep batt, 3.25x4.75", first use of the COS-LCD, flip-up display cover/shield, 1973 price $110, Japan, value $70-80.

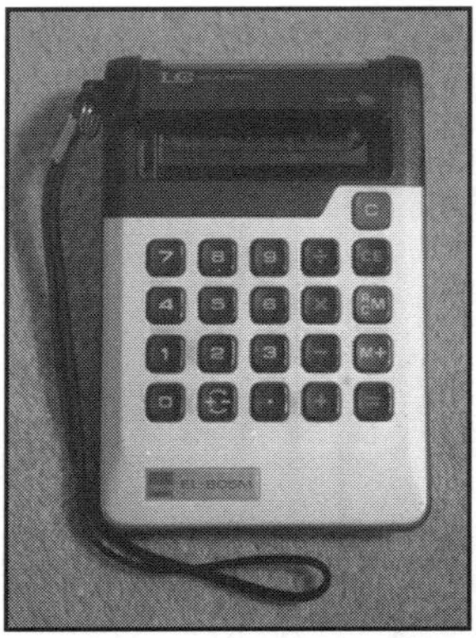

EL-805M 4-funct, mem, sgn chg, COS-LCD, 1-AA rep batt, 3.25x4.75", flip-up display cover/shield, c1973-74, Japan, value $60-70.

EL-808 4-funct, COS-LCD, 4-AA rep batt, 4.0x7.0", c1974, Japan, value $50-60.

EL-811 4-funct, mem, sgn chg, 8 digit green tube display with 16 digit calculating and readout ability, sealed batt, 4.0x6.75", late 1972 price $195, Japan, value $55-65.

EL-816 4-funct, mem, fluor, sealed batt, 4.25x6.75", silver metal front with black plastic around display, unique style, Japan, value $45-55.

EL-1063 4-funct, %, green fluor and paper printer, sealed batt, 4.0x7.0", Japan, value $35-45.

EL-1106S 4-funct, mem, %, sq rt, sgn chg, green fluor, sealed batt, 4.0x7.0", similar to CS-1120, with built-in flip-up stand, c1976, Japan, value $45-55.

EL-1163 4-funct, %, summing feature, green fluor and paper printer, sealed batt, 4.0x7.0", looks like EL-1063, 1977 price $99.95, Japan, value $35-45.

EL-1186 4-funct, mem, green fluor, 3.0x6.5", sealed batt, built-in printer, 4 slide switches, Japan, value $55-65.

EL-1621 4-funct, mem, %, 10 digit green fluor, 3.5x7.5", 3-AA rep batt, Korea, value $55-65.

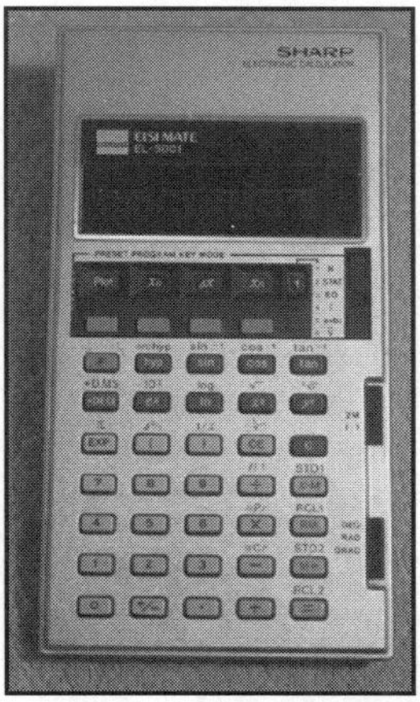

EL-5001 sci-funct, green fluor, 2-AA rep batt, 3.5x6.5", very unique with numerous extra programmed features and a keypad-located selectable menu, Japan, value $45-55.

EL-8002 4-funct, %, green fluor, 3-AA rep batt, 3.5x5.75", wedge-shaped, looks like EL-122, 1974 price $29.95, Japan, value $35-45.

EL-8005 4-funct, %, green fluor, 4-AA rep batt, 3.5x5.5", same as EL-8005S except has red and black colored case, very stylish, 1975 price $14.95, Japan, value $35-45.

EL-8005S 4-funct, %, green fluor, 4-AA rep batt, 3.5x5.5", same as EL-8005 except had white and blue colored case, very stylish, 1975 price $13.75, Japan or Korea, value $35-45.

EL-8008 4-funct, %, sgn chg, COS-LCD, 1-AA, 3.25x5.0" c1975, Japan, value $40-50.

EL-8009 4-funct, COS-LCD, button batt, 3.0x5.5" open, case is a folding "compact" style, 1976 price $40, value $55-65.

EL-8010 4-funct, %, sgn chg, COS LCD, button batt, 3.0x5.0", thin metal case in wallet, 1975 price $39.95, Japan, value $40-50.

EL-8011 4-funct, %, sq rt, green fluor, 4-AA rep batt, 3.25x5.5", blue & white stylish case, 1975 price $16.95, Japan, value $30-40.

EL-8015 4-funct, %, sgn chg, COS-LCD, sealed batt, 3.0x5.0", thin metal case in wallet, looks like EL-8010, Japan, value $40-50.

EL-8016 4-funct, %, green fluor, 2-AA rep batt, 3.0x5.0", looks like EL-215, Korea, value $15-25.

EL-8016R 4-funct, %, sq rt, green fluor, 2-AA rep batt, 3.0x5.0", looks like EL-8016, Japan, value $30-40.

EL-8018 4-funct, %, sq rt, sgn chg, green flour, has a feature called "Total Memory," green fluor, 2-AA rep batt, 3.0x5.5", Japan, value $20-30.

EL-8031S 4-funct, %, sq rt, green

fluor, 2-AA rep batt, 3.25x5.25", looks like EL-215, Korea, value $10-20.

EL-8051 4-funct, green fluor and paper printer, sealed batt, 4.0x7.0", looks like EL-1063, 1976 price $80, Korea, value $35-45.

EL-8100 4-funct, mem, %, sq rt, sgn chg, green fluor, 4-AA rep batt, 3.25x4.75", Japan, value $45-55.

EL-8100S 4-funct, sq, mem, green fluor, 4-AA rep batt, 3.25x4.75", carrying strap, Japan, value $45-55.

EL-8104 sci-funct, green fluor, 4-AA rep batt, 3.25x5.5", white case, unusual (for Sharp) case and keypad, Japan, value $40-50.

EL-8106 4-funct, mem, %, sgn chg, green fluor, 3-AA rep batt, 3.5x5.5", wedge-shaped, looks like EL-122, 1974 price $49.99, Korea, value $35-45.

EL-8110 4-funct, mem, %, sq rt, sgn chg, COS-LCD, button rep batt, 3.0x5.0", thin metal case in wallet, looks like EL-8010, c1975, Japan, value $40-50.

EL-8113 sci-funct, green fluor, 4-AA rep batt, 3.0x5.0", Japan, c1975, value $35-45.

EL-8114 4-funct, mem, %, sq rt, sgn chg, green fluor, 4-AA rep batt, 3.25x5.5", looks like EL-8011, 1975 price $19.95, Japan, value $30-40.

EL-8115S sci-funct, green fluor, 4-AA rep batt, 3.25x6.0", Japan, value $30-40.

EL-8116 4-funct, mem, %, sq rt, sgn chg, green fluor, 2-AA rep batt, 3.0x5.0", looks like EL-215, 1976 price $17, Korea, value $15-25.

EL-8117 4-funct, mem, %, sq rt, recip, sgn chg, green fluor, 2-AA rep batt, 3.0x5.0", Japan, value $25-35.

EL-8117K 4-funct, mem, %, sq rt, green fluor, 2-AA rep batt, 3.0x5.0", looks like EL-215, Korea, value $25-35.

EL-8118 partial sci-funct, green fluor, 2-AA rep batt, 3.25x5.5", Korea, value $30-40.

EL-8131 4-funct, mem, %, sq rt, green fluor, 2-AA rep batt, 3.25x5.25", looks like EL-215, Japan, value $10-20.

EL-8300 metric conversion funct, green fluor, 5-AA rep batt, 3.5x5.75", early conversion model, wrist strap, Japan, value $55-65.

PC-1802 sci-funct, green fluor, rep batt, Japan, value $40-50.

QT-8B *aka Micro Compet Cordless*, 4-funct, tube, sealed batt, 5.25x9.5", 1970 ad calls it the first portable calc, was based on older AC-only QT-8 calculator modified to hold rechargeable batteries, 3 pounds, used large charging cradle to recharge battery, July 1970 price $495, Japan, value $100-140.

VX-1118 4-funct, mem, %, sgn chg, 10 digit green fluor, sealed batt, 4.2x7.0", off-white colored case, Japan, value $50-60.

Sheen

004 4-funct, red LED, 9V rep batt, 2.5x4.5", looks like National Semiconductor 810, Hong Kong, value $45-55.

Silver Reed

European-market company. Also called Silver Seiko International. Apparently also sold typewriters.

8 4-funct, %, sq rt, sgn chg, pi, green fluor, 2-AA rep batt, 3.25x5.0", Japan, value $40-50.

8M 4-funct, sq rt, mem, green fluor, 4-AA rep batt, 3.5x5.0", wrist strap, Japan, value $45-55.

82 4-funct, mem, %, sgn chg, pi, sq funct, recip, fluor, 1-AA rep batt, 3.0x4.7", value $40-50.

SR 104 sci-funct, fluor, sealed batt, Japan, value $45-60.

Mini IV 4-funct, mem, %, sgn chg, red LED, 9V rep batt, 3.0x4.75", Japan, value $45-55.

Sinclair

British electronics company noted for its unique and innovative designs. Founder Sir Clive Sinclair is the British equivalent of Steve Jobs or Bill Gates. Sir Clive visited Texas Instruments in 1971 and returned to England with the newly developed LSI IC chip. He quickly developed several pocket calculators that were smaller than anything yet seen. Their first model sold was the Executive. Early models could be purchased assembled or as kits. Some who bought the tiny kits no doubt regretted their decision. Big soldering irons tend to damage delicate ICs and their wires! Sinclair went on to develop the popular Timex/Sinclair personal computers in the 1980's.

Cambridge 4-funct, purple LED, 4-AAA rep batt, 2.0x4.5", black and brown color versions, 1973 price $99.95, England, value $65-75.

Cambridge Memory 4-funct, mem, %, purple LED, 2-AA rep batt, 2.0x4.5", red and black color versions, looks like Cambridge, 1975 price $40, England, value $70-80.

Cambridge Scientific sci-funct, purple LED, 2-AAA rep batt, 2.0x4.5", white, looks like Cambridge, while the HP-35 used 5 ICs Sinclair was able to "shoehorn" all scientific functions onto a single chip, 1974, England, value $70-80.

Cambridge Programmable sci-funct and programmable, purple LED, 9V rep batt, 2.0x4.5", white, looks like Cambridge, bulge at back, 1978 price $34.95, England, value $75-80.

Enterprise Programmable sci-funct and programmable, purple LED, 9V rep batt, 2.5x5.5", c1977-78, England, value $90-100.

Executive 4-funct, red LED, 4-button rep batt, 2.25x5.5", very thin (0.4"), black case, very stylish, Sinclair's first calculator - 1972, England, value $90-100.

Executive Memory 4-funct, mem, red LED, 4-button rep batt, 2.25x5.5", very thin (0.4"), white case with black keypad, similar to Executive, c1973, England, value $70-80.

Oxford 100 4-funct, purple LED, 9V rep batt, 3.0x6.25", black case, similar to other Oxfords, c1975-76, England, value $70-80.

Oxford 150 4-funct, %, sq rt, purple LED, 9V rep batt, 3.0x6.25", black case, similar to other Oxfords, c1975-76, England, value $70-80.

Oxford 200 4-funct, mem, %, fluor, 9V rep batt, 3.0x6.25", black case, similar to other Oxfords, c1975-76, England, value $70-80.

Oxford 300 sci-funct, purple LED, 9V rep batt, 3.0x6.25", black case, similar to other Oxfords, c1975-76, England, value $70-80.

Oxford Universal 4-funct, mem, %, sq funct, recip, fluor, 9V rep batt, 3.0x6.25", similar to other Oxfords, c1975-76, England, value $70-80.

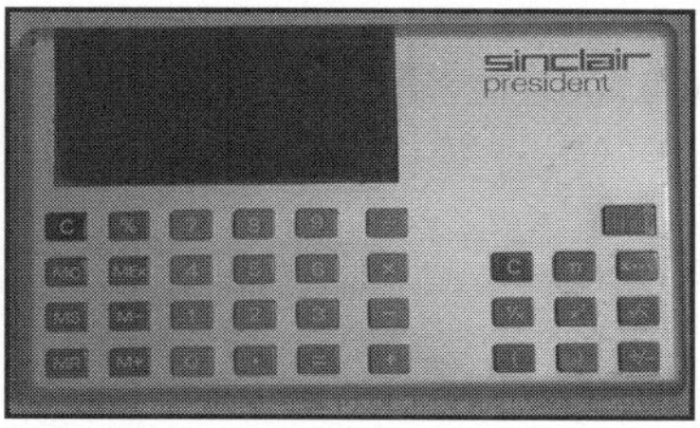

President 4-funct, mem, %, sq funct, recip, pi, sgn chg, paren, blue fluor, 2-AA rep batt, 6.5x3.75", horizontal, silver front, c1976-77, Hong Kong, value $70-80.

Scientific 4-funct, log and trig funct, purple LED, 4-AAA rep batt, 2.0x4.5", white, looks like Cambridge, 1974 price $119.95, England, value $70-80.

Sovereign 4-funct, mem, %, sq funct, recip, red LED, 2-button rep batt, 1.5x5.7x0.5", very thin, hefty weight due to its metal case, very elegant, 1976 price $100 in brush chrome, also available in black anodized finish and gold plate, three solid gold models were said to have been made, 1976 price $100 in chrome, England, value $100-140 chrome or black.

Wrist Calculator 4-funct, sq rt, mem, red LED, button-cell rep batt, this is not a calculator-watch. It is perhaps the world's only non-time, wrist-calculator and no doubt, the smallest LED calculator ever made. The idea was that you could wear a watch on one wrist and a calculator on the other. Amazingly it was available in kit form for the owner to build. An early ad noted it would take "three hours to build." 1977 price $19.95, England, value $100-200.

Singer-Friden

Singer is a well-known company specializing in sewing machines and related products. Friden of San Leandro California, was one of the main American producers of mechanical and electro-mechanical calculators. Around 1960 the two companies merged to become Singer-Friden. They produced some of the first Nixie® tube display electronic desk-top calculators, and also entered briefly into the pocket calculator market. Some models are labeled the Singer Company, Business Machines Division, others Singer-Friden. It appears that some of their pocket models were actually made by Commodore.

123 4-funct, red LED, 4-N rep batt, 3.0x4.0", same case as Commodore MM3, white color, c1973-74, Japan, value $40-50.

1008 4-funct, fluor, sealed batt, 5.0x7.0", 1973 price $325, value $55-65.

1207 sci-funct, exponents, red LED, sealed batt, almost identical to Commodore 4148R but with Singer-Friden logo, c1974, value $75-85.

1234 4-funct, mem, red LED, sealed batt, 3.0x4.0", same case as Commodore MM3M, white color, c1973-74, USA, value $50-60.

Sinoca

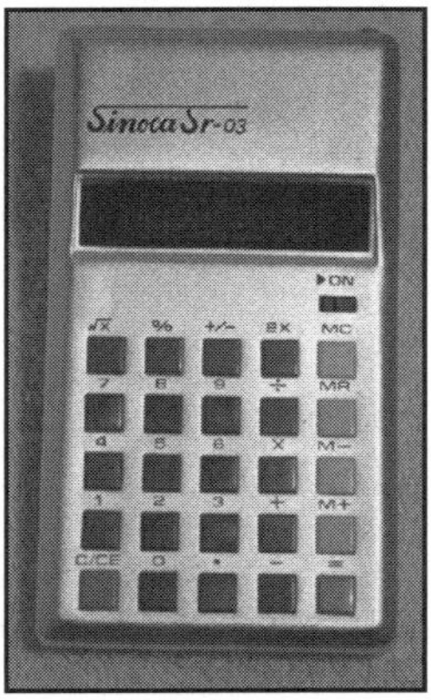

Sinoca Sr-03 4-funct, mem, %, sq rt, sgn chg, green fluor, 2-AA rep batt, 2.75x5.0", unusual with an all-metal, silver-colored case, Taiwan, value $40-50.

Smith Corona Marchant (SCM)

Smith Corona was a major typewriter company. Marchant of Oakland California was one of the oldest and largest manufacturers of mechanical and electro-mechanical calculators. They merged (sometime around 1960) to become SCM, continuing to produce complex electro-mechanical calculators and in the late 1960's large desk-top electronic calculators. In the early 1970's they sold some of the first "hand-held" electronic models.

Marchant 1 4-funct, orange tube display, sealed batt, 4.75x10.25", large and heavy early model, flip-up display cover, separate cover slides over keypad for closure, battery power meter, first sold in Spring 1971 for $495, USA, value $90-120.

Marchant 210 4-funct, mem, 12 digit blue fluor, sealed batt, 4.7x9.0", battery power meter, USA, value $80-90.

Marchant F80 4-funct, orange tube display, sealed batt, 4.75x10.25", looks similar to Marchant 1 except tan color not black, battery power meter, first sold in Spring 1971 for $495, USA, value $80-100.

Soundesign

8280 4-funct, fluor, 4-C rep batt, 4.5x7.75", Japan, value $35-45.

8300 *aka Mach II*, 4-funct, fluor, 4-C rep batt, 4.5x7.5", similar case to Morse Electrophonic Cal-801 and Mayfair 2W01B, 1973 price $99, Japan and Hong Kong, value $30-40.

8309 4-funct, mem, %, sgn chg, fluor, 4-C rep batt, 4.5x7.5", Japan, value $40-50.

8400 *aka Computer Mini*, 4-funct, sgn chg, tube display, sealed batt, 3.25x6.0", similar case to Kings Point 8413, Japan, value $45-55.

Sovrin

European-market company.

908 4-funct, mem, %, red LED, 9V rep batt, 2.75x5.25, Singapore, value $50-60.

Specialized Electronics Corporation (SEC)

SEC was located in Chicago, Illinois (USA) and in the 1970's produced extremely complex LED pocket calculators with navigational functions.

Nav-16 *aka Navatronic 16*, 4-funct and navigation-funct, red LED, sealed batt, 3.25x5.75", bright-dim switch to dim

LED's in cockpit at night, 14 LED indicator "bulbs" to display misc. functions such as air speed and altitude, USA, value $75-95.

Nav-1701t *aka Navatronic 1701t*, 4-funct and navigation-funct, red LED, sealed batt, 3.25x5.75", similar to NAV-16 but the 14 LED indicators are more protected in the case, USA, value $75-85.

Spectrum

The Spectrum name may have been the brand name of calculators sold by Chafitz Equipment Company, Rockville, Maryland (USA).

SP-70 sci-funct, 14 digit display, sealed batt, 3.5x6.75", similar case to models by Kings Point, 1974 price $129.95, value $45-55.

Sperry Remington Rand

American company with roots to early Burroughs and Remington adding machines. See Monroe-Litton, SCM, and Singer-Friden for other examples of calculator company mergers. Most of their portable calculators appear to have been designed and made by other companies. The 661 models, among the first pocket calculators on the market, used individual gas-filled tubes for each digit in the display.

661 4-funct, 6 digit tube with 12 digit calculating and display capability, 4-AA rep batt, 3.25x6.0", interesting style, c1972-73, 1973 price $80, Japan, value $45-55.

661-D 4-funct, 6 digit tube with 12 digit calculating and display capability, 4-AA rep batt, 3.25x6.0", different style from 661, also very unique, c1972, Japan, value $35-45.

663 2 different versions: version 1 - 4-funct, 6 digit tube with 12 digit calculating and display capability, 4-AA rep batt, 3.25x6.0", same case as 661-D; version 2 - 4-funct, 6 digit fluor with 12 digit calculating and display capability, 4-AA rep batt, 3.5x6.1", both from Japan with a value of $45-55.

665 4-funct, 6 digit fluor with 12 digit calculating and display capability, 4-AA rep batt, 3.25x5.25", Japan, value $40-50.

Obtaining information about the "Golden Age" of portable electronic calculators is very difficult since so little was documented at the time. The information in this book is gleaned from over 12 years of research. Should you be able to help with any additional data, please contact the authors at the addresses in the front section of the book.

667 4-funct, 6 digit fluor with 12 digit calculating and display capability, 2-AA rep batt, 3.0x5.25", Japan, value $40-50.

803C 4-funct, blue fluor, 5-AA rep batt, 4.5x7.25", same case as Casio 8U, Japan, value $35-45.

807B 4-funct, red LED, 4-AA rep batt, 3.0x6.0", case similar to 661 (not 661-D), very unusual red LED Sperry model and probably one of the first LED pocket calculators, Japan, c1972, value $85-95.

809SR 4-funct, sq rt, 8 digit fluor, 5-AA rep batt, 4.5x7.0", similar case to 1005-B, Japan, value $35-45.

811-GT 4-funct, fluor, 4-AA rep batt, 4.5x6.0", Japan, value $40-45.

819 4-funct, %, sq rt, fluor, 4-AA rep batt, 3.75x6.0", similar to 823-GT but has sq rt, Japan, value $35-45.

821-GT 4-funct, sq rt, fluor, 4-AA rep batt, 3.75x6.0", similar to 819 but lacks %, Japan, value $35-45.

On some of the early electronic calculators, a timing circuit turned the LED or fluorescent display off in order to save battery power. When pressed, a "D" key on those calculators turned the display back on.

823-GT 4-funct, %, fluor, 4-AA rep batt, 3.75x6.0", similar case to 831-GT and 833-GT, Japan, value $35-45.

831-GT 4-funct, mem, sq rt, fluor, 4-AA rep batt, 3.75x6.0", similar case to 823-GT and 833-GT, Japan, value $40-50.

833-GT 4-funct, mem, %, fluor 4-AA rep batt, 3.75x6.0", similar case to 823-GT and 831-GT, Japan, value $40-50.

1000 4-funct, sq rt, red LED, 2-AA rep batt, 2.5x4.0", very small, similar case to Casio Pocket Mini series, Japan, value $45-55.

1005-B 4-funct, 10 digit fluor, 5-AA rep batt, 4.5x7.0", similar case to

809SR but with 10 digit display, Japan, value $35-45.

CP-100 4-funct, mem, sq rt, red LED and horizontal paper printer, sealed batt, 4.25x7.75", same as Casio Mini-Printer, 1975 price $129.95, Japan, value $50-65.

SSR-8 partial sci-funct, fluor, 4-AA rep batt, 3.5x6.0", same case as Casio FX-10, Japan, value $40-50.

Spiegel

See Argyle.

Starshine Group

Starshine, Inc., Santa Barbara, California (USA).

RaceTrack Computer II *aka Computerized Performance Rating*, horse race handicapping calculator with no normal calculating functions, red LED, 9V rep batt, 2.75x5.0", case similar to Novus style, c1978, Hong Kong, value $15-25.

Summit

Summit was a marketing company aligned with Nuclear Controls and Electronics Corp, NCE, of Salt Lake City, Utah (USA). Summit was one of the first manufacturers of pocket calculators. Most of its early models have the classic TI Klixon keypad as do early Craig and Bowmar models. Unlike other pocket calculators, Summit models often have a knob to set the decimal place. Its first models sold in early 1972. In 1973-1974 dozens of companies entered the booming calculator market and prices plummeted. By the end of 1974 NCE/Summit was out of the calculator business. During its brief history NCE/Summit produced some of the most unique pocket calculators ever made.

E08 4-funct, orange fluor, 6-AA rep batt, 3.0x6.5, 1973 price $89, value $50-60.

Ko8 4-funct, decimal setting knob, red LED, sealed batt, 3.0x4.0", boxy shape, seen in white and black colors, USA, value $45-55.

Ko8M 4-funct, mem, %, decimal setting knob, red LED, sealed batt, 3.0x4.0", boxy shape, USA, value $55-65.

Ko9V 4-funct, red LED, sealed batt, 3.0x4.0" boxy shape, USA, value $45-55

K16 4-funct, red LED, sealed batt, 3.0x4.0", boxy shape, 1972 price $99.95, USA, value $45-55.

MB8 4-funct, red LED, sealed batt, 3.0x4.0", boxy shape, USA, value $55-65.

MCC *aka Metric Conversion Calculator*, 4-funct, mem, non-metric to metric conversions, %, red LED, sealed batt, two case versions depending on model year -- 1973 - 3.0x4.0", early boxy shape; 1974 - 3.0x5.0" later stylized shape, USA, value $55-65.

MR8 4-funct, mem, %, red LED, sealed batt, 3.0x4.0", boxy shape, USA, value $55-65.

SE88M 4-funct, mem, %, sq funct, recip, red LED, sealed batt, 3.0x4.0", original boxy shape, has some function buttons on case end, has at least 2 variations: black-colored case with square keys and white case with rectangular keys, 1973 price $99.95, USA, value $45-55.

SI-80 4-funct, %, sq funct, recip, red LED, two variations known - 9V rep or sealed batt, 3.0x5.0", slanted display case version, USA, value $45-55.

SI-90 sci-funct, red LED, sealed batt, 3.25x6.0", c1974, USA, value $50-60.

SL-8M 4-funct, mem, %, red LED, sealed batt, 2.7x4.75", slanted display case version, c1974, USA, value $45-55.

SL-8MR 4-funct, mem, %, red LED, sealed batt, 2.7x4.75", slanted display case version, 1975 price $35, USA, value $45-55.

SL-10 4-funct, mem, %, red LED, sealed batt, 2.7x4.75", slanted display case version, c1974, USA, value $55-65.

SM-8 4-funct, red LED, sealed batt, 2.0x3.25", other than the Sinclair wrist calculator the SM-8 may be the smallest LED-display calculator ever made, 1974 price $60, USA, value $85-95.

SM-20 4-funct, mem, %, red LED, 9V rep batt, 2.5x4.5", black case, smaller than the rest, same as American M-26, value $55-65.

SQR16M 4-funct, mem, sq rt, red LED, sealed batt, 3.0x4.0", USA, value $55-65.

Super Cal

Distributed by American Import Merchants Corp, New York (USA).

> *The "constant" function (or "K" button/switch) works similar to a memory. It allowed users to temporarily store a number they need to use numerous times in an equation. This was a common calculator feature before true memories came into widespread use.*

616 4-funct, 6 digit red LED, 9V rep batt, 3.0x5.0", uses RPN, Hong Kong, value $30-40.

Superlectron

Superlectron B.V., Vianen (Netherlands). Models mainly for the European market.

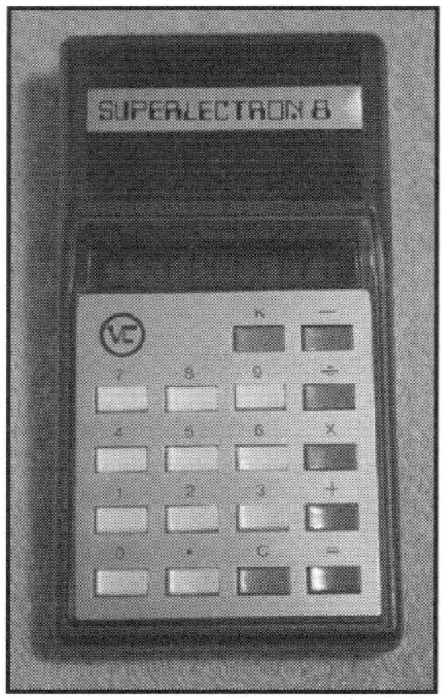

8 4-funct, red LED, 2 variations - one with 9V rep batt and 2.9x4.75", the other 3-AA rep batt and 3.0x5.5", either variation value $50-60.

8GT sci-funct, green fluor, 2-AA rep batt, 3.0x5.0", value $30-40.

SVM

Possible French company.

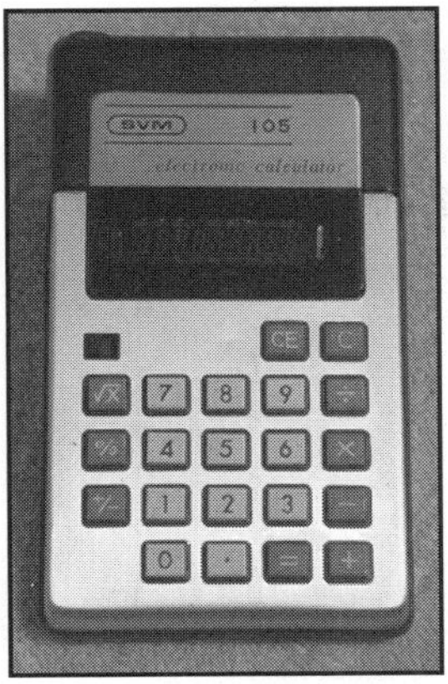

105 4-funct, %, sq rt, sgn chg, blue fluor, 2-AA rep batt, 3.0x5.0", Korea, value $35-45.

Tabulex

880 4-funct, red LED, 4-AA rep batt, unusual clear keys, 3.25x5.5", Hong Kong, value $45-55.

Delta 4-funct, %, sq rt, red LED, 2.25x4.75", 4-AAA rep batt, unusual clear keys, Hong Kong, value $45-55.

Tamaya

NC2 *aka Astro-Navigation Calculator*, partial sci-funct and navigational calculations, green fluor, 4-AA rep batt, 3.25x6.0", c1976, Japan, value $50-60.

Teal

Teal Industries, Inc., Carson, California (USA). Teal calculators have innovative designs which stand out from other brands. Teal models may have a link to Tokyo Electronics Applications Labs. See that additional listing.

110PD 4-funct, printer, fluor, sealed batt, 3.5x8.75", value $20-25.

806 4-funct, %, sq rt, green fluor, 2-AA rep batt, 3.25x5.0", Japan, value $25-35.

817 4-funct, mem, %, sgn chg, green fluor, 2-AA rep batt, 3.25x5.0", similar case to 806, Japan, value $25-35.

826 4-funct, mem, %, sq rt, green fluor, 2-AA rep batt, 3.25x5.0", similar case to 806, Japan, value $25-35.

SR82 sci-funct, mem, green fluor, 2-AA rep batt, 3.25x5.0", similar case to 806, Japan, value $30-40.

For a short time in the early 1970's, various manufacturers like Heathkit, M.I.T.S., Sinclair, and Daltone sold plans and kits of components for electronic hobbyists to build their own portable calculators. This saved some of the high labor costs involved in a fully-built model and added a layer of fun and pride for the owner.

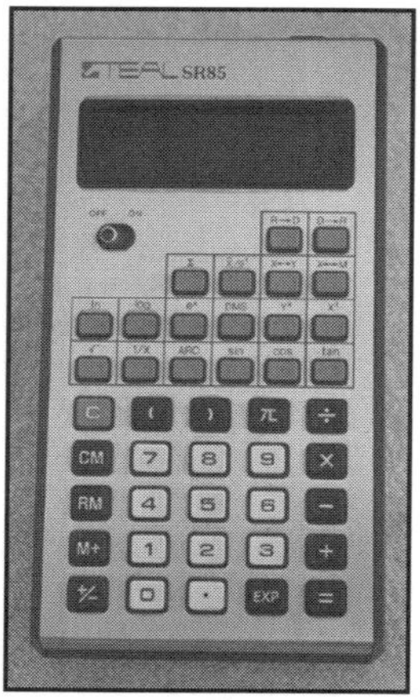

SR85 sci-funct, mem, green fluor, 3.25x6.0", Japan, value $35-45.

Tealtronic

Presumably a different company than "Teal" due to the nameplate and logo. Appears to have been a West Germany-based company.

TEM-28 4-funct, %, sq rt, fluor, value $35-45.

TEM-38 4-funct, mem, %, fluor, similar case to TEM-28, value $35-45.

TEM-48 4-funct, mem, %, sq funct, recip, fluor, value $45-55.

Tec

EC-201 4-funct, mem, %, sq rt, yellow LCD, solar panel power, 3.0x5.0" opened, very early solar unit with large (half the size of the calculator) solar panels, Japan, value $45-55.

Technico

European-market company.

In late 1972, manufacturers were beset with a shortage of LED displays. By mid-1973, LED's became more plentiful, but IC chips now became harder to get.

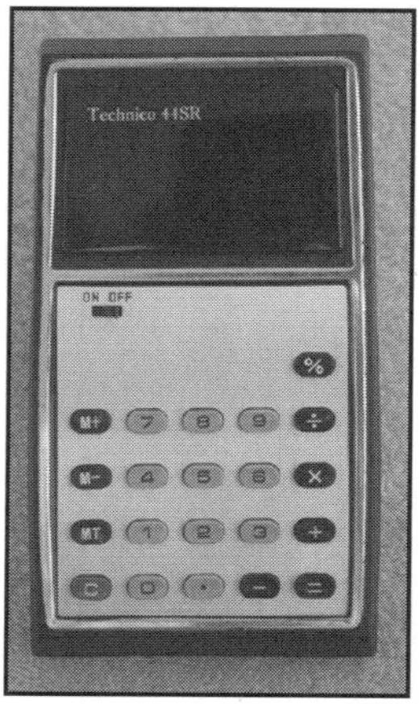

44SR 4-funct, mem, %, green fluor, 3-AA rep batt, 3.0x5.5", value $40-50.

55SR sci-funct, green fluor, 3-AA rep batt, 3.0x5.5", looks like 44SR, value $45-55.

Pocket Mini *aka 6SL*, 4-funct, mem, %, fluor, 9V rep batt, 2.5x4.0", value $40-50.

Texas Instruments

USA-based IC-chip maker which developed the first portable electronic calculator prototype in 1967 -- the Cal-Tech. TI actually holds the patent for the pocket calculator and TI scientists won many awards for this breakthrough. Originally they produced the ICs for calculator makers like Canon, Bowmar, and many others. TI also made the innovative "sticky-clicky" Klixon keypad used by most of these companies (used on Bowmar 901B and Craig 4501 for example). In June 1972 they decided to enter the field with their own calculators. Of the dozens of companies making pocket calculators in the early 1970's TI and HP are the only two US companies still in the business. Even they no longer actually manufacture calculators in the USA. In the 1980's TI opened a plant in Texas to make calculators specifically for Wal-Mart (due to a huge ad campaign promoting "Made in USA" products at Wal-Mart) but TI later closed the factory and now imports all models.

The TI-2500 (Datamath) is a must-have for all collectors. The country of manufacture listed may have changed over the course of the calculator's production run.

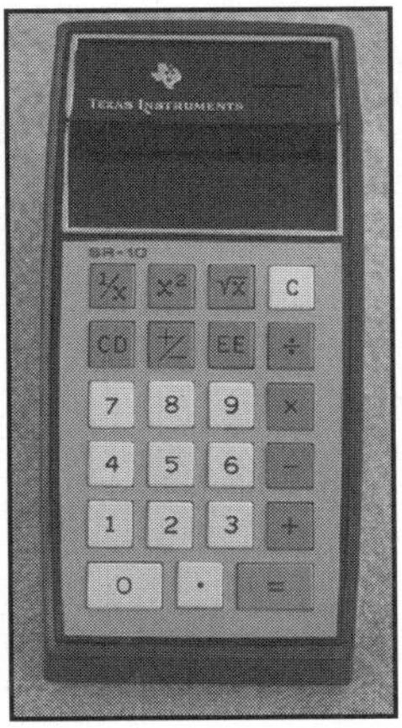

SR-10 4-funct, sq funct, recip, sgn chg, exp, red LED, sealed batt, 3.0x6.5", extreme wedge shape, another "classic" design, has 2 minor case variations - one with "SR-10" on keypad area, another with "SR-10" closer to display area, introduced in late 1972 at $149.95, USA, value $35-45.

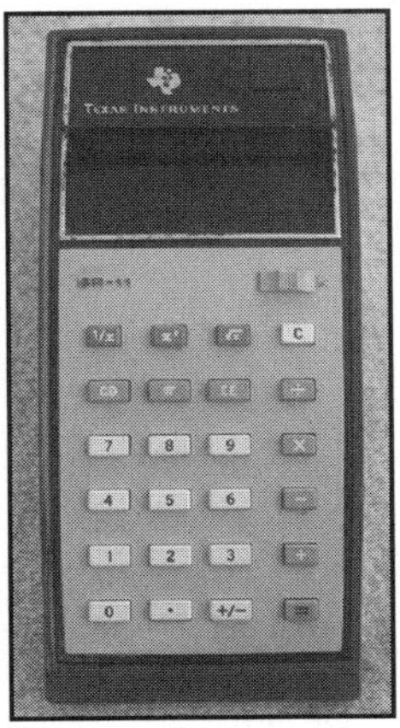

SR-11 4-funct, sq funct, pi, recip, sgn chg, exp, red LED, sealed batt, 3.0x6.5", extreme wedge shape similar to SR-10, keys are very small, 1974 price $66.50, USA, value $50-60.

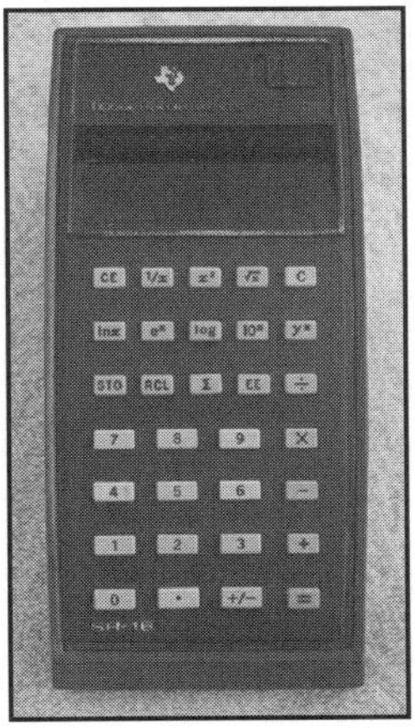

SR-16 4-funct, mem, log, sum, sq funct, recip, sgn chg, exp, red LED, sealed batt, 3.0x6.5", extreme wedge shape similar to SR-10, dark gray colored case, keys are very small, 1974 price $99.99, USA, value $50-60.

SR-16 II sci-funct, mem, red LED, sealed batt pack, 3.1x6.0", 1975 price $44.95, USA, value $30-40.

SR-22 4-funct, Hex/Octal, mem, red LED, AC model with an optional rechargeable batt pack, 6.5x9.0" and 2.75" thick, may be its largest "pocket calculator," SR-20 is a 110v only model using same case, 1973 price $350 plus $50 for battery pack, USA, value $85-95.

SR-40 sci-funct, red LED, sealed batt pack, 3.1x6.0", looks like SR-16 II, 1976 price $40, USA, value $20-30.

In 1972, calculators were so unique that upscale department stores set up special departments for them. Customers (usually male) would crowd these areas during lunch to punch up numbers on the sleek, new machines.

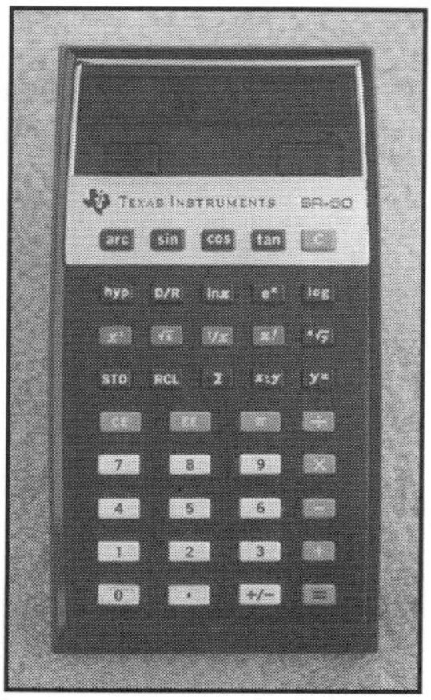

SR-50 sci-funct, red LED, sealed batt pack, 3.1x6.0", slightly fancier case with silver patch above keypad, considered a "classic TI," 1974 price $170, USA, value $35-45.

SR-50A sci-funct, red LED, sealed batt pack, 3.1x6.0", looks like SR-16 II, not as fancy a case as the SR-50, 1975 price $109.50, USA, value $20-30.

SR-51 sci and financial funct, red LED, sealed batt pack, 3.1x6.0", slightly fancier case with silver patch above keypad (similar to SR-50), c1975, USA, value $40-50.

SR-51A sci and financial funct (same as 51), red LED, sealed batt pack, 3.1x6.0", looks like SR-16 II, not as fancy case as the SR-51, 1975 price $109.50, USA, value $25-35.

SR-51-II sci and financial funct (same as SR-51), red LED, sealed batt pack, 3.1x6.0", looks like SR-16 II, 1976 price $80, USA, value $20-30.

SR-52 sci-funct, programmable, had a magnetic strip reader for storing and reading programs, red LED, sealed batt pack, 3.25x6.25", larger but looks like SR-16 II, 1976 price $229, USA, value $40-50.

SR-56 sci-funct, red LED, sealed batt pack, 3.1x6.0", looks like SR-16 II, 1976 price $83.50, USA, value $25-35.

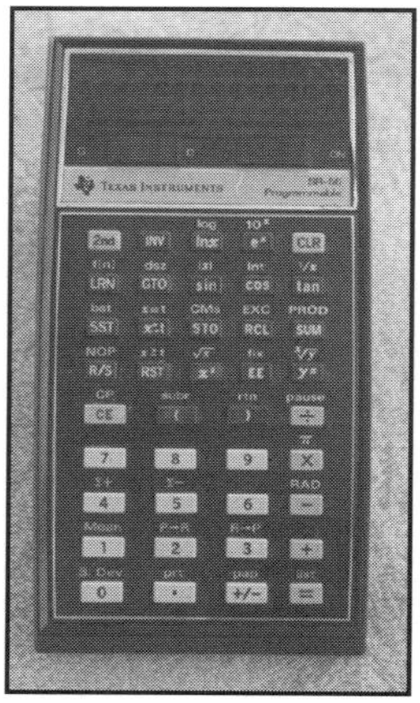

SR-56 Programmable sci-funct, programmable, red LED, sealed batt pack, 3.1x6.0", looks like SR-16 II, 1976 price $139., USA, value $25-35

T-1220 4-funct, red LED, 9V rep batt, 2.7x5.7", not TI-1220, box says custom model manufactured for True Value Hardware, USA, value $50-60.

T-1225 4-funct, mem, %, red LED, 9V rep batt, 2.7x5.7", looks like TI-1200, c1976-77, USA, value $20-30.

TI-20 *see Exactra 20.*

TI-30 sci-funct, red LED, 9V rep batt, 3.1x6.0", looks like SR-16 II, USA, probably the largest selling calculator of all time, 1976 price $24.95, USA, value $5-10.

TI-51-III sci and financial funct, red LED, sealed batt pack, 3.1x6.0", looks like SR-16 II, similar to SR-51-II but is programmable, 1976 price $80, USA, value $55-65.

TI-55 sci-funct, programmable, had financial funct, and had conversions for metric/imperial and temperature measurements, red LED, sealed batt pack, 3.1x6.0", looks like SR-16 II, USA, value $20-30.

TI-57 *aka TI Programmable 57*, sci-funct, programmable, red LED, sealed batt pack, looks like SR-16 II, 1977-78 price $79.95, USA, value $30-40.

TI-58 *aka TI Programmable 58*, sci-funct, programmable, had a magnetic strip reader for storing and reading programs, also had a replaceable memory module with built-in programs, red LED, sealed batt pack, 3.25x6.5", c1977, USA, value $40-50.

TI-58C *aka TI Programmable 58C*, sci-funct, programmable, had a magnetic strip reader for storing and reading programs, also had a replaceable memory module with built-in programs, red LED, sealed batt pack, 3.25x6.5", USA, value $40-50.

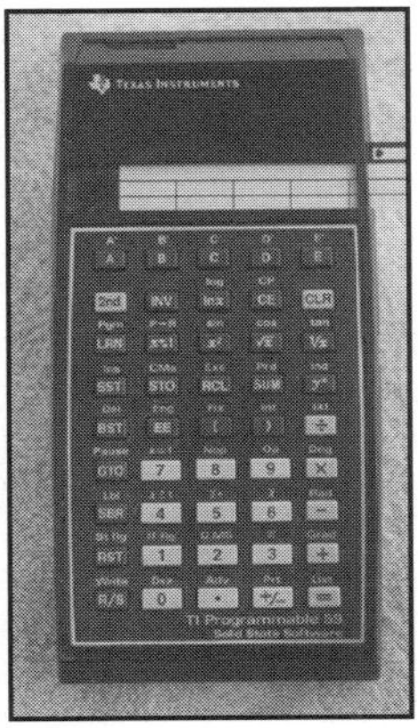

TI-59 *aka TI Programmable 59*, sci-funct, programmable, had a magnetic strip reader for storing and reading programs, also had a replaceable memory module with built-in programs, red LED, sealed batt pack, 3.25x6.5", 1977-78 price $299.95, USA, value $40-50.

TI-150 4-funct, orange fluor, 4-AA rep batt, 3.0x6.0", looks like TI-2550 but white not black and without memory keys, limited production run, USA, value $85-95.

TI-1000 4-funct, %, sgn chg, red LED, 9V rep batt, 3.0x5.7", 1978 price $9.77, USA, value $15-20.

TI-1025 4-funct, mem, %, sgn chg, blue fluor, 9V rep batt, 3.0x5.7", 1978 price $11.77, looks like TI-1000, USA, value $15-20.

TI-1050 4-funct, mem, %, sq rt, sgn chg, blue fluor, 9V rep batt, 3.0x5.7", 1977 price $12.95, USA, value $15-20.

TI-1200 4-funct, %, red LED, 9V rep batt, 2.7x5.7", 1975 price $14.88, USA, value $15-20.

TI-1205 4-funct, mem, %, red LED, 9V rep batt, 2.7x5.7", case like TI-1200 but with lighter colors, including beige case and orange/yellow faceplate, USA, value $35-45.

TI-1220 *See T-1220.*

TI-1225 *See T-1225.*

TI-1250 4-funct, mem, %, red LED, 9V rep batt, 2.7x5.7", looks like TI-1200, 1975 price $19.95, USA or Hong Kong, value $20-30.

TI-1265 4-funct, mem, %, sgn chg, unusual that it has a blue fluor display, 9V rep batt, looks like TI-1200, c1976-77, USA, value $25-35.

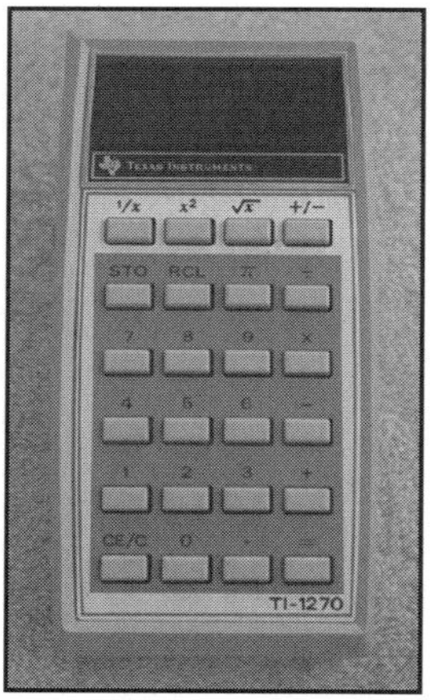

TI-1270 4-funct, mem, sq funct, recip, sgn chg, pi, red LED, 9V rep batt, 2.7x5.7", looks like TI-1200, USA, has orange-colored key plate, 1976 price $12.50, USA, value $25-35.

TI-1400 4-funct, %, sgn chg, red LED, 9V rep batt, 2.7x5.7", looks like TI-1200, c1976-77, USA, value $25-35.

TI-1450 4-funct, mem, %, sgn chg, red LED, 9V rep batt, 2.7x5.7", looks like TI-1200, 1976 price $16, USA, value $25-30.

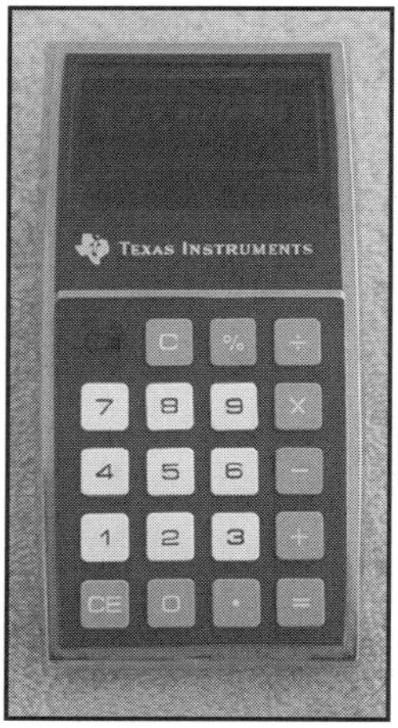

TI-1500 4-funct, %, red LED, sealed batt, 2.5x5.0", small and uncommon style, 1974 price $49.99, value $30-35.

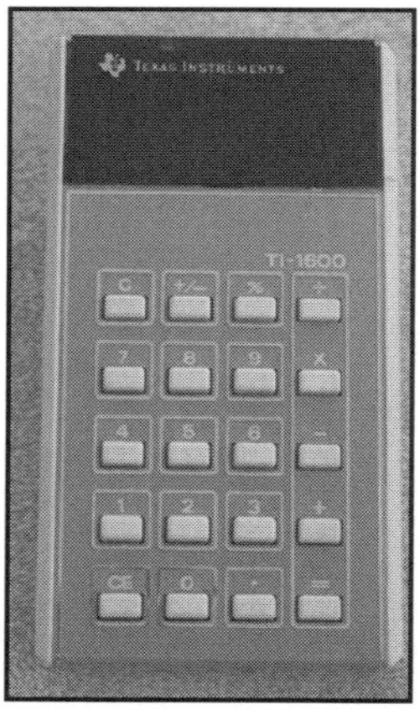

TI-1600 4-funct, %, sgn chg, blue fluor, sealed batt, 3.0x5.0", very flat model in blue and white, 1976 price $25, USA, value $25-35.

TI-1650 4-funct, mem, %, sgn chg, blue fluor, sealed batt, 3.0x5.0", very flat model, looks like TI-1600, 1976 price $24.95, USA, value $35-45.

TI-1680 4-funct, mem, %, sgn chg, has "replay" function, blue fluor, sealed batt, 3.0x5.0", very flat model, looks like TI-1600, 1977 price $29.95, USA, value $35-45.

TI-2500 *aka Datamath*, 4-funct, red LED, sealed batt, 3.0x5.5", first TI calculator (June 1972), at least 2 variations - one with the batteries "sealed" in the case and the other, a later version of the 2500, with batteries accessible through a "trap door," the TI-2500 first sold in the fall of 1972 for $149.95, engineers had tried to develop an LCD version of this calculator but were never able to solve all of the display's reliability and production problems, USA, value $25-35.

TI-2500B 4-funct, red LED, 4-AA batt, 3.0x5.5", same as TI-2500 except for use of disposable or rechargeable batteries, dark ivory color, USA, value $25-35.

TI-2500-II *aka Datamath II*, 4-funct, %, red LED, 2-AA rep batt, 3.0x5.5", same case style as TI-2500, USA, value $35-45.

The authors estimate over 2,500 different portable, LED/tube type calculators were designed, manufactured and sold around the world. If you know of any model not in this book, please contact us.

TI-2510 4-funct, red LED, 4-AA rep batt, 3.0x5.5", same case as TI-2500 except used only disposable batteries, dark ivory color, 1974 price $39.95, USA, value $25-35.

TI-2550 4-funct, mem, %, red LED, 4-AA rep batt, 3.0x6.5", similar to SR-10 wedge style, 1974 price $99.95, USA, value $30-40.

TI-2550 II 4-funct, mem, %, sq funct, recip, sgn chg, blue fluor, sealed batt pack, 3.1x6.0", unlike style of TI-2550, looks like SR-16 II, 1976 price $29.95, USA, value $30-40.

TI-2550 III 4-funct, mem, %, sq funct, recip, sgn chg, blue fluor, sealed batt pack, 3.1x6.0", looks like SR-16 II, same functions as TI-2550 II except it includes "RV" which exchanges the display with previous result or entry, 1976 price $34.95, USA, value $35-45.

TI-5025 4-funct, mem, %, fluor, sealed batt, paper tape printer, 3.5x7.0", 1979 price $84.99, USA, value $20-30.

TI-5050 4-funct, %, paper tape printer (no other display), sealed batt, 4.0x8.5", larger mini-desktop model, 1975 price $114.50, USA, value $30-40.

TI-5050M 4-funct, mem, %, paper tape printer (no other display), sealed batt, 4.0x8.5", larger mini-desktop model, 1976 price $94.95, USA, value $35-45.

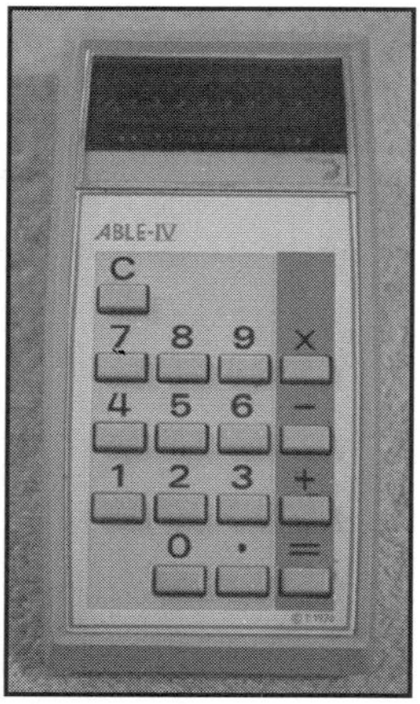

Able-IV 4-funct, %, red LED, 9V rep batt, 2.75x5.5", case like TI-1200 but has blue/yellow faceplate, USA, 1976, value $45-55.

Business Analyst *aka TI Business Analyst*, financial funct, red LED, 9V rep or sealed batt pack, 3.1x6.0", looks like SR-16 II, 1976 price $39.95, USA, value $15-20.

Business Analyst 1 *aka TI Business Analyst 1*, financial funct (same as Business Analyst), red LED, 9V rep or sealed batt pack, 3.1x6.0", looks like SR-16 II, has gold colored keypad cover, USA, value $20-30.

Concept 1 4-funct, %, red LED, 9V rep batt, similar to TI-1200 case, 2-tone colored faceplate, 2.7x5.7", USA, value $40-50.

Concept II 4-funct, mem, %, red LED, 9V rep batt, similar to TI-1250 case, 2-tone colored faceplate, 2.7x5.7", USA, value $40-50.

Exactra 19 *aka EX-19*, 4-funct, 6 digit red LED, 3-AA rep batt, 3.0x5.25", Exactras had a more stylish design than many other TIs, value $25-35.

Exactra 20 *aka TI-20 or EX-20*, 4-funct, floating decimal key, 6 digit red LED, 3-AA rep batt, 3.0x5.25", looks like Exactra 19, value $25-35.

Exactra 21 *aka EX-21*, 4-funct, 6 digit red LED, 3-AA rep batt, 3.0x5.25", looks like Exactra 19, value $30-35.

Exactra 22 *aka EX-22*, 4-funct, 6 digit red LED, 3-AA rep batt, 3.0x5.25", looks like Exactra 19, value $30-35.

Exactra 23 *aka EX-23*, 4-funct, %, 6 digit red LED, 3-AA rep batt, 3.0x5.25", looks like Exactra 19, value $30-35.

Lady 1200 4-funct, %, red LED, 9V rep batt, 2.7x5.7", looks like TI-1200, same case as TI-1200 but with pastel colored keyplate, c1975-76, USA, value $45-55.

Little Professor game calc, red LED, 9V rep, 3.0x4.75", yellow case. Several varieties of case styles were made over the years this model was produced, 1976 price $16.95, USA, value $10-15.

MBA financial funct, red LED, sealed batt pack, 3.1x6.0", looks like SR-16 II, brown color, 1978 price $55.95, USA, value $15-25.

Money Manager financial funct, red LED, sealed batt pack, 3.1x6.0", looks like SR-16 II, 1977 price $16.95, USA, value $20-30.

Mr. Challenger game calc, fluor, 9V rep batt, 3.5x6.0", USA, value $15-25.

Programmer 4-funct, mem, as well as programming functions in decimal, hex, and octal, red LED, 9V rep batt, 3.1x6.0", looks like SR-16 II, 1978 price $42.50, USA, value $20-30.

Spirit of 76 *aka 76*, 4-funct, %, red LED, 9V rep batt, 2.7x5.7", looks like TI-1200, multi-colored model in red, white and blue, designed to commemorate the USA's 200th birthday in 1976, 1976 price $6.95, USA, value $35-45.

Spelling B game calc, fluor, 9V rep, 3.5x6.2", USA, value $15-25.

Tax Planner *aka WG&G*, complex tax funct, red LED, 4-AA rep batt, 3.0x6.5", label says copyright 1983 Warren, Gorham & Lambert, appears to be a highly modified TI-59, value $65-75.

Wiz-A-Tron game calc, red LED, 9V rep batt, 3.5x5.0", USA, value $15-25.

Texatron

May have been made in the 1970's by Dismac Industrial, SA, a Brazilian Company.

In 1966, Tadashi Nakamura of Japan left his engineering job at Kobe Industries to launch Ise Electronics. He developed an innovative line of fluorescent-style, digital-readout tubes for calculators. His Digitron product line would become one of the leading display types for calculators in the world, utilizing their blue-green numerals on models made in Asia, the US and Europe.

Texatron 4-function, %, sq, blue fluor, sealed batt, 3.0x4.75", label is in Portuguese, c1974, Brazil, value $65-75.

Texet

880 *aka Executive*, 4-funct, mem, %, red LED, 9V rep batt, 2.75x5.25", cheap little model, same case as Nobility and Bohsei 3000, c1978, Hong Kong, value $15-20.

1500 4-funct, mem, %, LED, 9V rep batt, 3.0x5.25", value $35-45.

TKS 2002

Distributed in the USA by TKS Corporation, Los Angeles, California.

810N 4-funct, %, red LED, 3-AA rep batt, 3.25x5.0", bright gloss-white case, wrist strap, Korea, value $45-55.

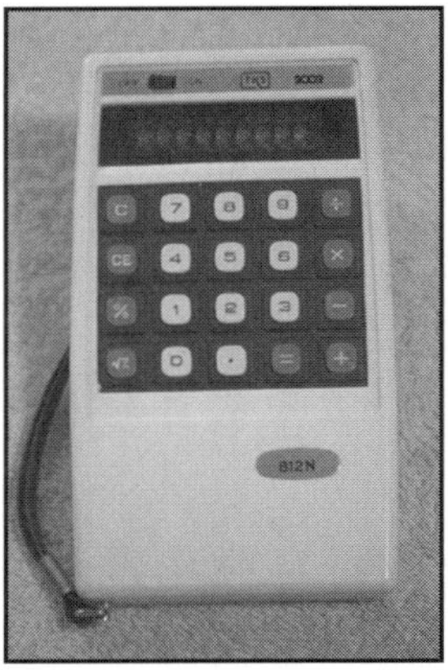

812N 4-funct, %, sq rt, red LED, 3-AA rep batt, 3.25x5.0", bright gloss-white case, wrist strap, Korea, value $45-55.

835MD 4-funct, mem, %, fluor, 3-AA rep batt, 3.25x5.75", Korea, value $25-30.

Tohotronic

Toho Tsusho Co. Ltd, (Japan). European-market company. Used Roger Fighter as brand.

Roger F-1 4-funct, %, sgn chg, green fluor, 2-AA rep batt, 3.0x5.5", Japan, value $55-65.

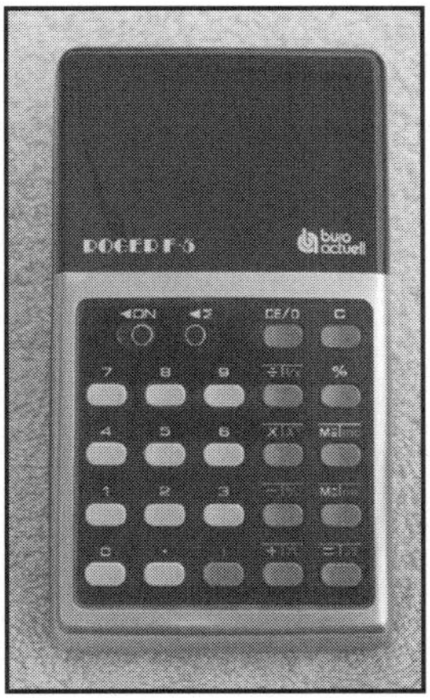

Roger F-5 4-funct, mem, %, sq funct, recip, sgn chg, pi, green fluor, 2-AA rep batt, 3.0x5.5", looks like F-1, has "buro actuell" on front, Japan, value $55-65.

Toko

Japanese Company.

> ***In late 1972, Hewlett-Packard sent letters to owners of the HP-35 advising of an error in an algorithm virtually nobody ever noticed. HP offered to correct the problem on returned calculators. They had virtually no takers -- no one wanted to part with their HP-35!***

Mini 8 4-funct, fluor, 4-AA rep batt, 3.5x6.0", Japan, value $25-30.

Tokyo Electronics Applications Labs

May be linked to Teal brand calculators.

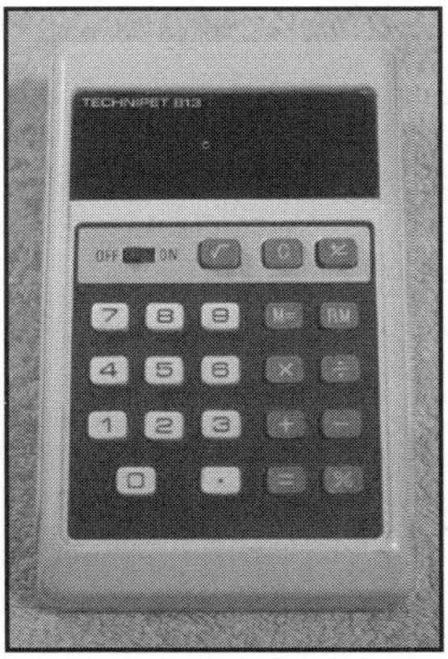

Technipet 813 4-funct, sq, green fluor, 4-AA rep batt, 3.5x5.5", Japan, c1972, value $65-75.

Toshiba

Tokyo Shibaura Electric Company (Japan). It seems that most Japanese electronic companies entered at least briefly into the pocket calculator market. Toshiba, Panasonic, Sanyo and many others soon dropped out. In contrast, Casio and Sharp continue to compete with HP and TI.

BC-603L 4-funct, sq rt, sgn chg, blue fluor, 4-AA rep batt, 3.2x6.0", Japan, value $45-55.

BC-0801B 4-funct, green fluor, sealed batt, 4.0x6.5", c1971-72, Japan, value $60-70.

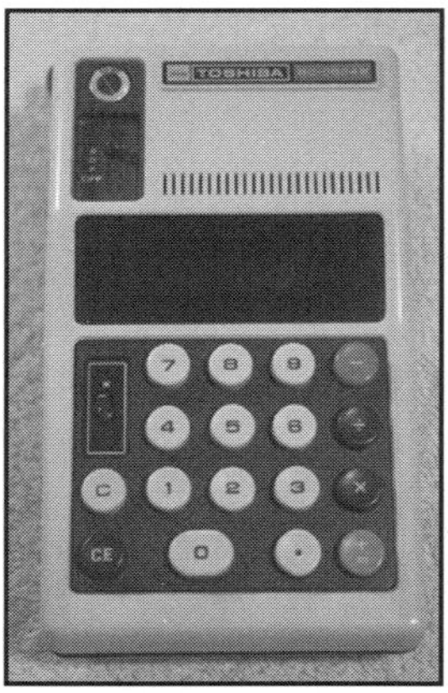

BC-0804B 4-funct, green fluor, 4-AA rep batt, 4.0x7.0", batt indicator, wrist strap, round buttons like early Sanyo, c1972, Japan, value $50-60.

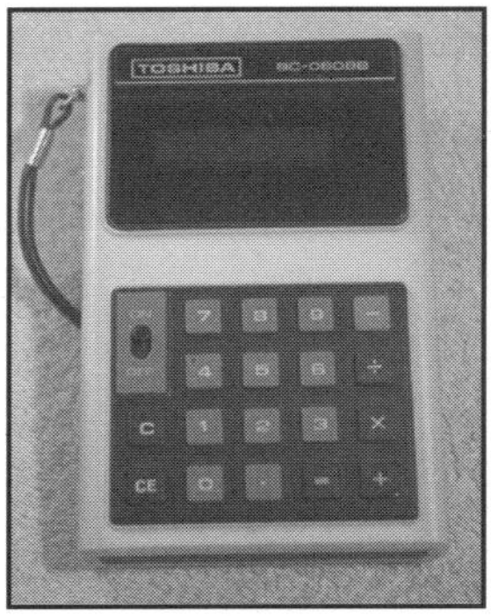

BC-0808B 4-funct, blue fluor, 4-AA rep batt, 3.75x5.75", wrist strap, Japan, value $40-50.

BC-815 4-funct, mem, %, sq rt, blue fluor, 4-AA rep batt, 3.25x7.0", c1975, Japan, value $25-35.

BC-819 4-funct, %, sq, mem, blue fluor, 2-AA rep batt, 3.25x5.5", Japan, value $35-45.

BC-1010BJ black jack game and calculator, 4-funct, sq rt, paren, fluor, 2-AA rep batt, 3.25x6.0", orange color case, Japan, value $20-30.

BC-1015 4-funct, mem, %, blue fluor, 2-D rep batt, 6.0x6.5", horizontal, Taiwan, value $25-30.

BC-8013 4-funct, %, sq rt, blue fluor, 2-AA rep batt, 3.25x5.25", c1975-76, Japan, value $25-35.

BC-8016 4-funct, %, sq rt, blue fluor, 1-AA rep batt, 3.25x5.0", Japan, value $25-35.

In 1971, Commodore noted in a news article that they would only sell calculators that were "Made in the U.S.A." The intent was to counter concerns of the Japanese holding too large a portion of the market. Their first series of calculators was called "Minuteman", after the Revolutionary War militiaman who was ready to fight on a minute's notice. However, within a short time, Commodore was back to making many of their models in Japan.

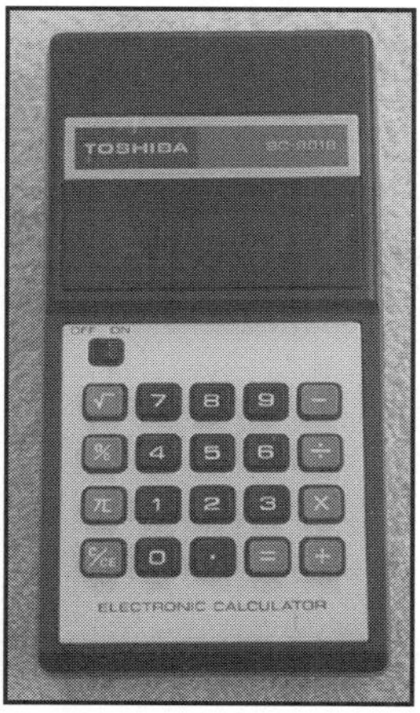

BC-8018 4-funct, %, sq rt, pi, blue fluor, 2-AA rep batt, 3.0x5.25", Japan, value $20-30.

BC-8018B 4-funct, %, sq rt, pi, blue fluor, 2-AA rep batt, 3.0x5.25", looks like BC-8018, Taiwan, value $20-30.

BC-8111 4-funct, mem, %, sq rt, pi, blue fluor, 2-AA rep batt, 3.0x5.5", looks like BC-8018B, Taiwan, value $25-35.

BC-8111B 4-funct, mem, %, sq rt, pi, blue fluor, 2-AA rep batt, 3.0x5.5", looks like BC-8111, Taiwan, value $25-35.

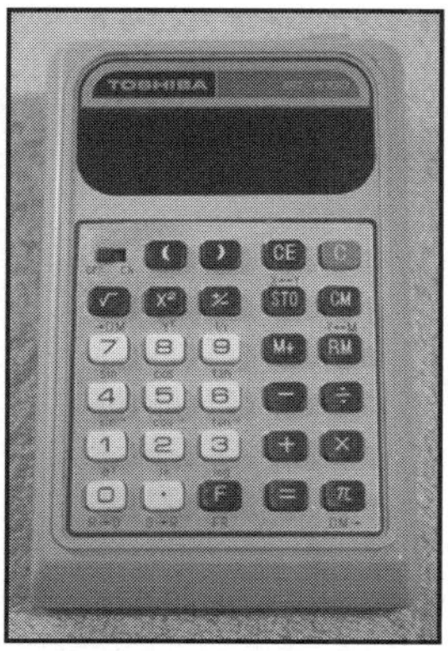

SC-6100 sci-funct, mem, green fluor, 4-AA rep batt, 3.5x5.5", early Toshiba with sci-funct, Japan, value $65-75.

SC-7100 sci-funct, mem, 10 digit green fluor, Japan, value $65-75.

Tricom

Tricom 4-funct, sq rt, green fluor, 2-AA rep batt, 3.0x5.0", orange two-tone case, Japan, value $35-45.

Triumph

European-market company, Associated with Adler and Royal.

60 4-funct, 6 digit green fluor, 4-AA rep batt pack, 4.0x6.0", Japan, value $40-50.

80C 4-funct, %, green fluor, 4-AAA rep batt, 3.0x4.75", value $40-50.

81S 4-funct, mem, %, sq rt, sgn chg, pi, green fluor, 4-AAA rep batt, 3.0x4.75", same case as Adler 81S, Japan, value $45-55.

82M 4-funct, metric conversions, green fluor, 4-AAA rep batt, 3.0x4.75", c1974, same case as Adler 82M, Japan, value $50-60.

HP hand-held calculators have never lacked in popularity. This prompted user groups to band together to share new ways of programming and utilizing the calculators. To this day, there are still several large groups in the US and England whose members meet on a regular basis.

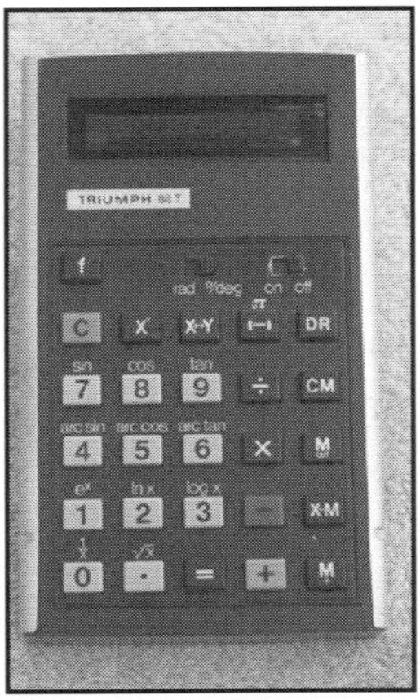

88T *aka EC25*, sci-funct, green fluor, 4-AA rep batt, looks like various Adler models, 3.0x4.75", value $50-60.

Lady *aka EC-20L*, 4-funct, green fluor, 3-AAA rep batt, 2.5x3.75", unusual maroon and gold case, value $65-75.

Sir 4-funct, green fluor, 3-AAA rep batt, 2.5x3.75", same case styling as Lady, value $65-75.

Tryom

Tryom, Cleveland, Ohio (USA).

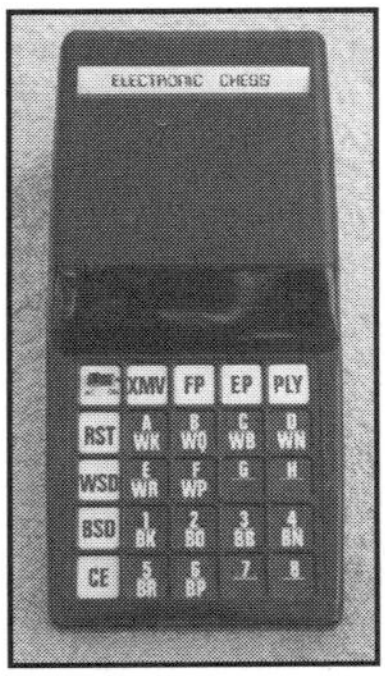

CC-7000 *aka Electronic Chess Game*, chess movement functions, 3.0x6.5", uses Litronix case with membrane key-pad, 9V rep batt, USA, value $15-20.

TSI (Telesensory Systems Inc.)

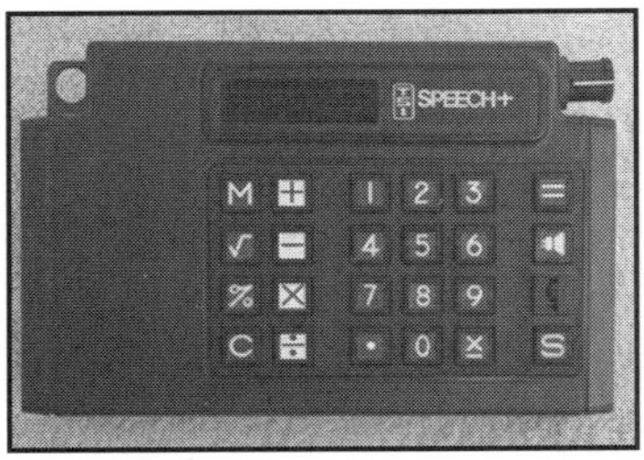

Speech+ 4-funct, mem, %, sq rt, red LED, sealed batt, 4.75x7.25", horizontal, calculator for the blind, sounding numbers thanks to advanced sound synthesis chip from Hewlett-Packard, brown color, c1975, USA, value $50-60.

Student Speech+ 4-funct, mem, %, sq rt, red LED, sealed batt, 4.75x7.0", horizontal, calculator for the blind, very similar case to Speech+ except in blue color, has "APH" logo on front, USA, value $60-80.

T Research

897D 4-funct, mem, red LED, 9V rep batt, 3.0x5.5", apparently sold in Italy but made in USA, label says "Fabbricato Negli Stati Uniti," value $55-75.

UDM

See Universal Data Machine.

UIT

Apparently an Italian company. No additional information.

22SP sci-funct, red LED, 4-AAA rep batt, 2.0x4.5", very similar case to Sinclair models (e.g. Sinclair Cambridge), value $55-65.

Unico

European-market company.

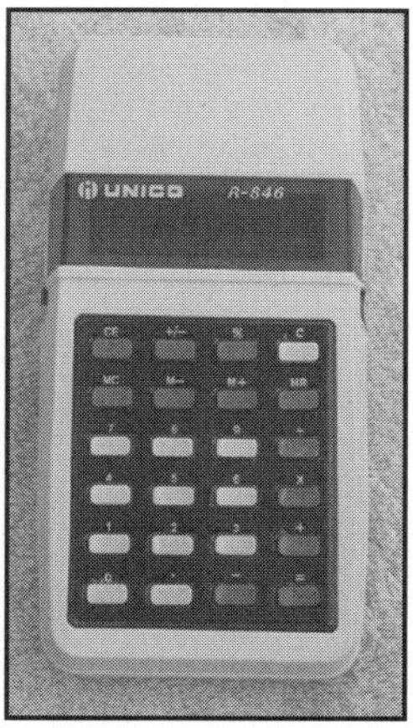

R-846 4-funct, mem, %, sgn chg, red LED, 9V rep batt, 2.75x5.5", Singapore, value $20-25.

Unicom

Once independent calculator maker started by USA integrated circuit maker American Microsystems, Inc. (AMI). They were purchased by Rockwell International in 1972. "Unicom" brand name was soon phased out in favor of "Rockwell."

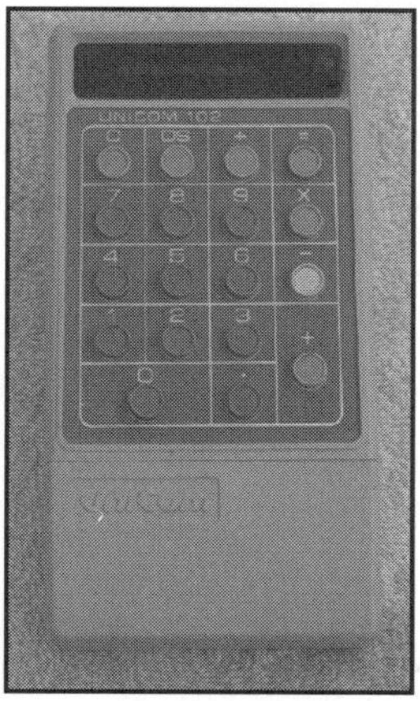

102 4-funct, red LED display, 9V rep batt, 3.0x6.0", 1973 price $59.95, Mexico, value $30-40.

103 4-funct, mem, red LED display, 9V rep or sealed batt, 3.0x6.0", similar case to 102, c1973, Mexico, value $35-45.

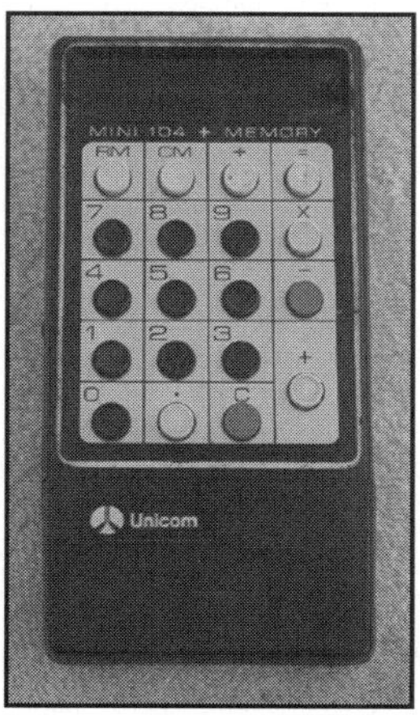

104+ 4-funct, mem, red LED display, 9V rep, 3.0x6.0", similar case to 103

only in black, Mexico, value $40-50.

201 4-funct, mem, %, tube display, 4-AA rep batt, 3.5x6.5" similar case to 202/SR, 1973 price $99.95, Mexico, value $60-70.

202/SR *aka Slide Rule*, sci-funct, tube display, 4-AA rep or sealed batt, 3.5x6.5", Mexico, value $35-45.

802 4-funct, red LED, rep batt, 6.25x3.25", horizontal, stylish design, value $40-50.

Unifive Industries

Label states made in the USA by Unifive Industries Corp, Marietta, Georgia.

301 *aka The Magic Slate*, 4-funct, mem, red LED, sealed batt, 3.0x5.25", very thick (1.5"), similar to early Bowmar, value $85-95.

Unimark

European-market company but appears to be connected to Interpur of Orlando, Florida (USA) based on label on back of calculator.

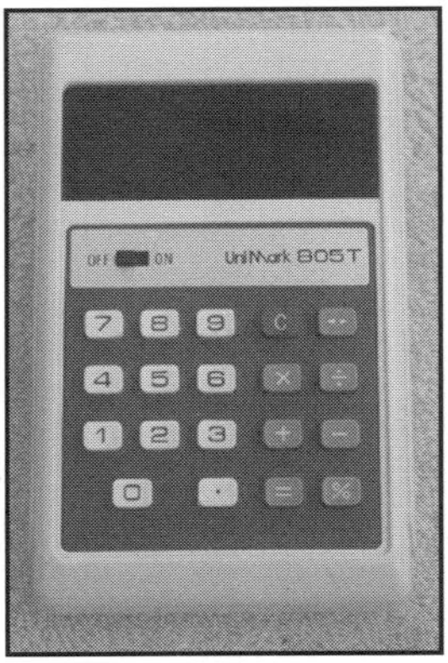

805T 4-funct, %, green fluor, 4-AA rep batt, 3.5x5.5", similar case to Prinztronic 88P and Karstadt MR40, Japan, value $45-55.

813T 4-funct, mem, %, sq rt, sgn chg, green fluor, 4-AA rep batt, 3.5x5.5", interesting white case, Japan, value $45-55.

Unisonic

Unisonic was and is a major marketer of calculators. In the 1970's they produced a huge array of LED and fluorescent display pocket calculator models, perhaps more styles than any other manufacturer. Many have all metal or partially-metal cases. Some Unisonics like the tiny 911's are quite attractive. Individual Unisonic models often have several revisions of a body style - sometimes minor, sometimes not - usually indicated by a letter at the end of a number, such as 811-A and 811-C.

8PPMD 4-funct, mem, %, fluor and paper printer, 4.0x7.5", Hong Kong, value $25-35.

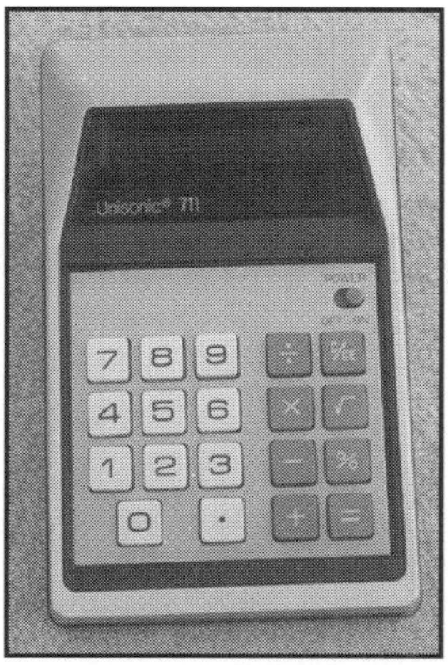

711-E 4-funct, %, sq rt, green fluor, 4-AAA rep batt, 3.0x5.0", Japan, value $10-20.

728 4-funct, sq funct, sgn chg, green fluor, 4-AA rep batt, 3.5x6.0", Japan, value $10-20.

730 4-funct, %, sq rt, sgn chg, green fluor, 4-AAA rep batt, 3.0x5.0", looks like 711-E, Japan, value $10-20.

733 4-funct, %, sq rt, sgn chg, pi, green fluor, 4-AA rep batt, 3.5x6.0", looks like 728, Japan, value $10-20.

737 *aka Slide Rulette*, 4-funct, mem, %, green fluor, 4-AA, 3.5x5.25", Japan, value $20-25.

738 *aka Slide Rulette*, 4-funct, mem, %, sgn chg, green fluor, 4-AA, 3.5x5.25", looks like 737, Japan, value $20-25.

739SQ 4-funct, %, sq funct, recip, sgn chg, green fluor, 4-AA rep batt, 3.5x6.0", looks like 728, Japan, value $10-20.

740-B 4-funct, mem, %, sq rt, sgn chg, green fluor, 4-AA rep batt, 3.5x6.0", looks like 728, Japan, value $10-20.

740-D 4-funct, mem, %, sgn chg, green fluor, 4-AA rep batt, 3.5x6.0", looks like 728, Japan, value $10-20.

790R-C 4-funct, mem, %, sq rt, sgn chg, green fluor, 4-AA rep batt, 3.5x6.0", looks like 728, Japan, value $10-20.

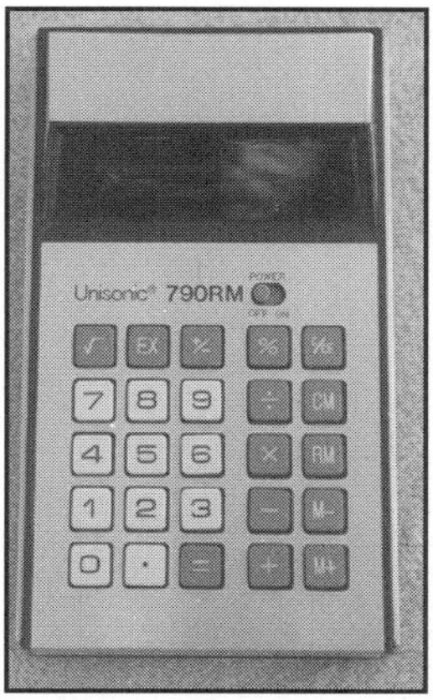

790RM-1 4-funct, mem, %, sq rt, sgn chg, green fluor, 4-AA rep batt, 3.5x6.0", looks like 728, Taiwan, value $10-20.

796-B sci-funct, green fluor, 4-AA rep batt, 3.5x6.0", looks like 728, Japan, value $10-20.

811-A 4-funct, %, green fluor, 4-AAA rep batt, 3.0x5.0", looks like 711-E, Japan, value $10-20.

811-C 4-funct, %, sgn chg, red LED, 4-AAA rep batt, 3.0x5.0", looks like 711-E, Hong Kong, value $10-20.

811L 4-funct, %, sgn chg, red LED, 4-AAA rep batt, 3.0x5.0", looks like 711-E, Japan, value $10-20.

811L-B 4-funct, %, red LED, 4-AAA rep batt, 3.0x5.0", looks like 711-E, Japan, value $10-20.

830-A 4-funct, %, sq rt, sgn chg, green fluor, 4-AAA rep batt, 3.0x5.0", looks like 711-E, Japan, value $10-20.

839 SQ 4-funct, mem, %, sq rt, 10 digit display, 4-AA rep batt, 3.5x6.0", Japan, value $20-30.

840-C 4-funct, mem, %, sgn chg, green fluor, 4-AAA rep batt, 3.0x5.0", looks like 711-E, Japan, value $10-20.

840-E 4-funct, mem, %, sq rt, sgn chg, green fluor, 4-AAA rep batt, 3.0x5.0", looks like 711-E, Japan, value $10-20.

849-A 4-funct, mem, %, sq funct, recip, sgn chg, pi, green fluor, 4-AAA rep batt, 3.0x5.0", looks like 711-E, Japan, value $10-20.

850 4-funct, mem, %, sq funct, recip, sgn chg, green fluor, sealed batt, 3.0x5.5", thin aluminum case, comes with a wallet, Taiwan, value $25-35.

888 *aka Slide Rulette*, 4-funct, %, green fluor, 4-AA, 3.5x5.25", looks like 737, a second case style variation has a "K" switch and two of the keys are a different color and size, 1975 price $40, Japan, value $20-25.

890 4-funct, %, green fluor, 4-AA rep batt, 3.5x6.0", looks like 728, Japan, value $15-26.

890-A 4-funct, %, green fluor, 4-AA rep batt, 3.5x6.0", looks like 728, Japan, value $10-20.

890-C 4-funct, %, green fluor, sealed batt, 3.5x6.0", Japan, value $15-25.

911-C 4-funct, %, sq rt, green fluor, 3-AAA rep batt, 2.5x3.75", Japan, value $15-25.

911L-A 4-funct, %, red LED, 3-AAA rep batt, 2.5x3.75", looks like 911-C, Japan, value $15-25.

911L-B 4-funct, %, sq rt, red LED, 3-AAA rep batt, 2.5x3.75", looks like 911-C, Japan, value $15-25.

911L-C 4-funct, %, sq rt, red LED, 3-AAA rep batt, 2.5x3.75", looks like 911-C, Japan, value $15-25.

931-B 4-funct, %, sq rt, green fluor, 3-AAA rep batt, 2.5x3.75", looks like 911-C, Japan, value $15-25.

931-C 4-funct, %, sq rt, green fluor, 3-AAA rep batt, 2.5x3.75", looks like 911-C, slightly larger case than 931-B, Japan, value $15-25.

940 4-funct, mem, %, green fluor, 3-AAA rep batt, 2.5x3.75", looks like 911-C, 1978 price $10.97, Japan or Taiwan, value $15-25.

940-A 4-funct, mem, %, green fluor, 3-AAA rep batt, 2.5x3.75", looks like 911-C, Japan, value $15-25.

940-B 4-funct, mem, %, green fluor, 3-AAA rep batt, 2.5x3.75", looks like 911-C, more keys than 940 and 940-A, Taiwan, value $15-25.

940-C 4-funct, mem, %, sq rt, green fluor, 3-AAA rep batt, 2.5x3.75", looks like 911-C, Taiwan, value $15-25.

1011-A 4-funct, %, green fluor, 4-AAA rep batt, 3.25x5.5", looks like 728, Taiwan, value $10-20.

1034-D 4-funct, %, sq funct, recip, pi, sgn chg, green fluor, 4-AAA rep batt, 3.25x5.5", looks like 728, Japan, value $10-20.

1040-A 4-funct, mem, %, sgn chg, green fluor, 4-AAA rep batt, 3.25x5.5", looks like 728, Japan or Taiwan, value $10-20.

1040-C 4-funct, mem, %, sq rt, sgn chg, green fluor, 4-AAA rep batt, 3.25x5.5", keys shaped different than 1040-A, looks like 728, Japan, value $10-20.

1040-1 4-funct, mem, %, sgn chg, green fluor, 4-AAA rep batt, 3.25x5.5", same as 1040-A except has GPM key, Taiwan, value $10-20.

1048-A 4-funct, mem, %, sq funct, recip, paren, sgn chg, green fluor, 4-AAA rep batt, 3.25x5.5", looks like 728, Japan, value $10-20.

1049-A 4-funct, mem, %, sq funct, recip, pi, sgn chg, green fluor, 4-AAA rep batt, 3.25x5.5", looks like 728, Japan, value $10-20.

1099-A sci-funct, green fluor, 4-AAA rep batt, 3.25x5.5", looks like 728, Japan, value $10-20.

1111-A 4-funct, %, sq rt, green fluor, 3-AAA rep batt, 3.75x4.75", Japan, value $10-20.

1196 sci-funct, green fluor, 3-AA rep batt, 2.75x4.75", value $25-35.

1212 *aka Slide Rulette*, 4-funct, green fluor, 4-AA, 3.5x5.25", looks like 737, 1974 price $43.95, Japan, value $15-25.

1299R-A sci-funct, green fluor, 4-AA rep batt, 3.5x6.0", looks like 728, Japan, value $10-20.

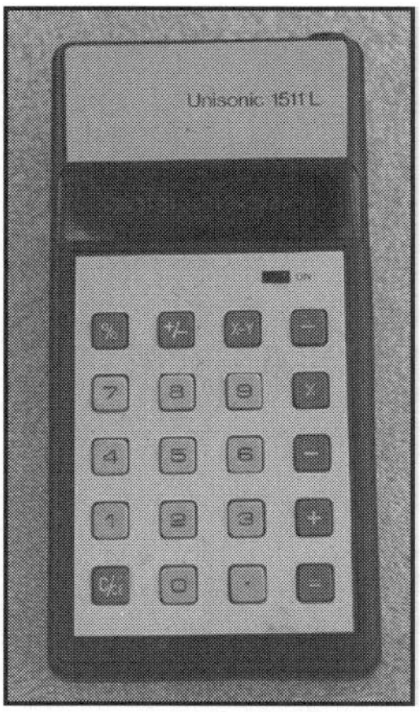

1511L 4-funct, %, sgn chg, red LED, 2-AA rep batt, 3.0x6.0", Hong Kong, value $20-30.

1540D 4-funct, mem, %, sq rt, sgn chg, green fluor, 2-AA rep batt, 3.0x6.0", looks like 1511L. Hong Kong, value $20-30.

1540L 4-funct, mem, %, sq rt, sgn chg, red LED, 2-AA rep batt, 3.0x6.0", looks like 1511L, Hong Kong, value $20-30.

1541L 4-funct, mem, %, red LED, 9V rep batt, 3.0x5.25", c1978, Hong Kong, value $20-30.

1542L 4-funct, mem, %, sq rt, recip, pi, red LED, 9V rep batt, 3.0x5.25", c1978, Hong Kong, value $20-30.

1548 4-funct, mem, %, sq funct, recip, paren, sgn chg, red LED, 2-AA rep batt, 3.0x6.0", looks like 1511L, Hong Kong, value $25-35.

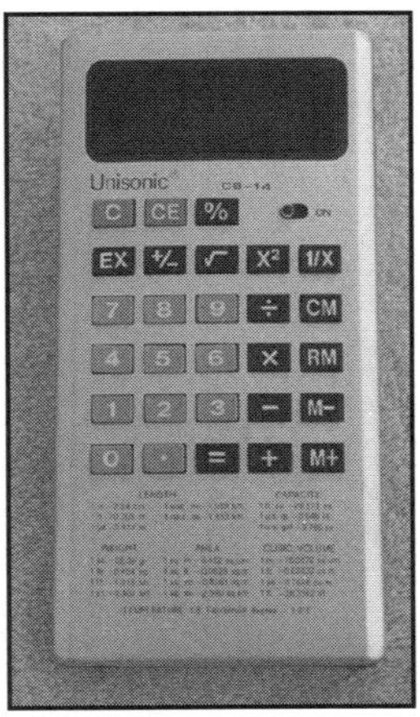

CB-14 2 different versions, version 1: 4-funct, mem, %, sq rt, sgn chg; version 2: 4-funct, mem, %, sq funct, sgn chg, recip; both have green fluor, 3-AAA rep batt, 3.0x5.5", Taiwan, value $25-35.

XL-101 4-funct, mem, %, 10 digit fluor, 2-D rep batt, 6.0x6.5", Taiwan, value $15-20.

XL-112 4-funct, mem, %, sgn chg, 10 digit green fluor and paper printer, sealed batt, 3.75x7.5", Taiwan, value $25-35.

XL-115 4-funct, mem, %, sgn chg, green fluor and paper printer, sealed batt, 5.0x9.0", Japan, value $25-35.

Casino 7 4-funct and blackjack game, green fluor, 4-AAA rep batt, 3.25x5.25", Taiwan, value $20-30.

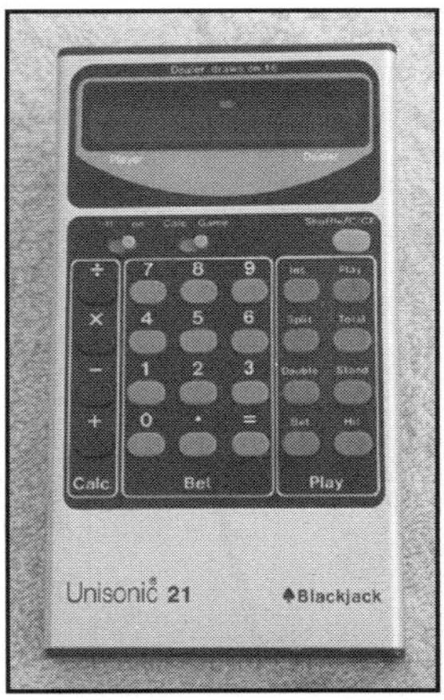

Unisonic 21 *aka 21-P1*, 4-funct and "Jimmy the Greek" blackjack game, green fluor, 3-AAA rep batt, 3.0x5.25", 1977 price $30, Taiwan, value $15-25.

Unitrex

Eiko Business Machine, (Japan).

8PPMD 4-funct, mem, %, fluor and paper printer, 4.0x7.5", same case as Unisonic XL-111, Hong Kong, value $25-35.

80F *aka Handy Mini 80F*, financial-funct, red LED, 3-AA rep batt, 3.0x5.75", wrist strap, all-metal case, early business model, Japan, value $60-70.

80KF 4-funct, 8 digit green tube, 4-AA rep batt, 3.5x6.5", early model, big keys, Japan, value $60-70.

90SC sci-funct, mem, red LED, 9V rep batt, 2.75x5.5", similar case to 902RM, Hong Kong, value $45-55.

91PM 4-funct, mem, %, red LED, 9V rep batt, 2.75x5.5", similar case to 902RM, Hong Kong, value $30-40.

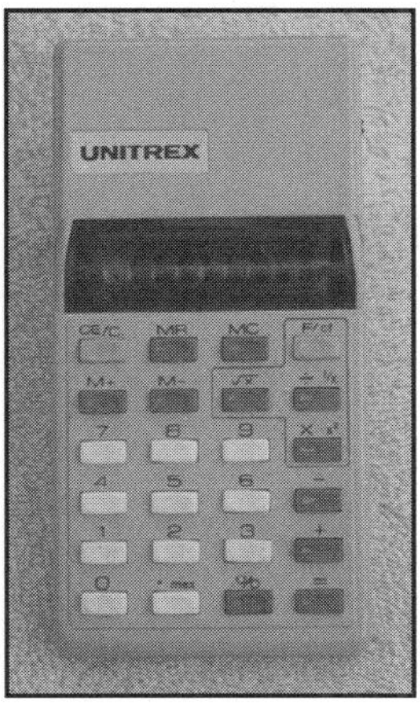

95SL 4-funct, mem, %, sq funct, recip, red LED, 9V rep batt, 2.75x5.25", similar case style to Radofin 1610 and Radio Shack EC-221, Hong Kong, value $35-45.

800D 4-funct, %, fluor, 4-AA rep batt, 6.5x6.0", horizontal, Japan, value $20-30.

800K 4-funct, fluor, 4-AA rep batt, 6.5x6.0", horizontal, looks like 800D, Japan, value $20-30.

800KD 4-funct, fluor, 4-AA rep batt, 6.5x6.0", horizontal, looks like 800D, Japan, value $20-30.

801D 4-funct, %, green fluor, 2-AA rep batt, 3.25x6.0", similar case to 801R, Japan, value $40-50.

801K 4-funct, fluor, 4-AA rep batt, 6.5x6.0", looks like 800D, horizontal, Japan, value $20-3

801R 4-funct, mem, %, sq rt, pi, sgn chg, green fluor, 2-AA rep batt, 3.25x6.0", similar case to 801D, Japan, value $40-50.

801MR 4-funct, mem, %, sq rt, green fluor, 3-AA rep batt, 3.0x5.5", wrist strap, Japan, value $40-50.

803MP 4-funct, mem, %, sq rt, pi, sgn chg, fluor, sealed batt, 4.25x6.25, Korea, value $35-45.

901M 4-funct, mem, %, fluor, 2-AA rep batt, 3.25x5.5", one model has white keypad, another has black keypad, Korea, value $40-50.

901MR 4-funct, mem, %, sq rt, sgn chg, fluor, 2-AA rep batt, 3.25x5.5", Korea, value $30-40.

901PM 4-funct, mem, %, sq rt, sgn chg, pi, fluor, 2-AA rep batt, 3.25x5.5", Korea, value $40-50.

901R 4-funct, %, sq rt, sgn chg, fluor, 2-AA rep batt, 3.25x5.5", Korea, value $30-40.

901SR sci-funct, %, fluor, 2-AA rep batt, 3.25x5.5", early model with "f" function key and deg/rad slide switch, Korea, value $50-60.

902AS sci-funct, green fluor, 2-AA rep batt, 3.25x7.0", nice quality scientific model, 1976 price $29, Hong Kong, value $45-55.

902RM 4-funct, mem, %, sq rt, fluor, 2-AA rep batt, 2.75x5.5", similar case to 91PM, Hong Kong, value $30-40.

902SL 4-funct, mem, %, sq rt, fluor, 2-AA rep batt, 2.75x5.5", similar case to 91PM, Hong Kong, value $30-40.

902SN sci-funct, fluor, 2-AA rep batt, 3.25x5.5", Korea, value $30-40.

1000 4-funct, mem, %, red LED, 9V rep batt, 2.75x5.25", cheap little model, same case as Nobility 3000, Bohsei 3000, and Tronica 3000, Hong Kong, value $10-15.

1000M 4-funct, mem, %, 10 digit blue fluor, 2-D rep batt, 6x6.5", same case as Royal D-120, Taiwan, value $20-30.

1203 4-funct, mem, %, 12 digit green fluor, 5-AA rep batt, 5.5x8.0", Korea, value $30-40.

CB8SL 4-funct, mem, %, sq funct, recip, red LED, 6-AAA, 3.25x6.0", fits into wallet case with "ears" on ends of case, Hong Kong, value $30-40.

Executron 817D sci-funct, fluor, 2-AA rep batt, 3.5x5.75", similar case as Brother 863, distributed by Unitrex of Canada, Korea, value $40-50.

Micro 6 4-funct, mem, red LED, 9V rep batt, 2.75x5.0", small black "cute" model, similar case to Mini 8, Japan, value $35-45.

Mini 8 4-funct, red LED, 9V rep batt, 2.75x5.0", small white "cute" model, similar case to Mini Handy 80M and 80R, 1975 price $20, Japan, value $35-45.

Mini Calculator 4-funct, mem, %, sgn chg, red LED, 9V rep batt, 2.5x4.5", miniature copy of a Rockwell style calculator, Hong Kong, 1973 price $90, value $35-45.

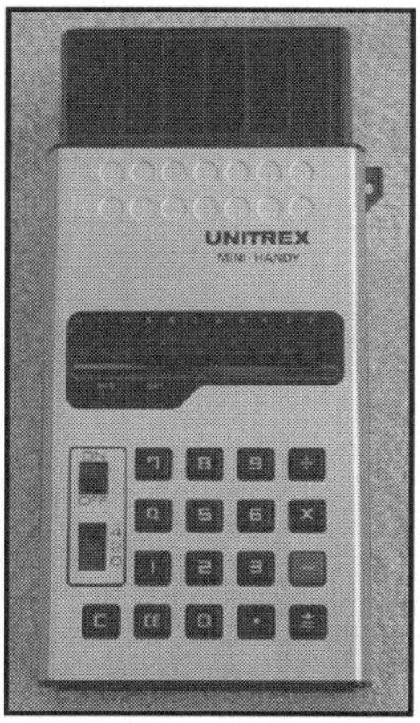

Mini Handy 4-funct, 12 digit red LED display, 4-N or 4-AA rep batt, 3.0x5.75", 1973 price $49.95, very unusual in that it has 2 different sized battery clips which allows owner to use either AA or small sized N batteries, Japan, value $70-80.

Mini Handy 80M 4-funct, mem, %, red LED, 9V rep batt, 2.75x5.0", small "cute" model, similar case to Mini 8, Japan, value $35-45.

Mini Handy 80R 4-funct, %, sq rt, sgn chg, red LED, 9V rep batt, 2.75x5.0", small white "cute" model, similar case to Mini 8, Japan, value $35-45.

Mini Handy 80SR sci-funct, red LED, 3-AA rep batt, 3.2x6.0", black color,

Japan, value $40-50.

Universal

See note regarding Xonex.

202 4-funct, mem, %, red LED display, 9V rep batt, 2.75x4.5", value $20-25.

303 4-funct, mem, %, sq rt, sgn chg, tube display, 2-AA rep batt, 2.75x4.5", metal face plate, value $35-45.

Universal Data Machine (UDM)

A Chicago-based company that briefly made pocket calculators in the USA during 1972. They made sturdy products similar to the first Bowmar or Craig pocket models.

9V9 4-funct, red LED display, 9V rep batt, 3.0x6.0", bright white case, Klixon keypad, late 1972 price $69.99, USA, value $75-95.

TKB 0001 4-funct, red LED display, sealed batt, 3.0x5.25", late 1972 price $99.95, USA, value $55-65.

Uranus

Calculator Watch 4-funct, red LED, button rep batt, very uncommon styling, round case with button shaped keys along edge, c1976, value $300-400.

U-Tac

??? 4-funct, tube display, batt indicator, 4-C rep batt, 5.25x9.5", Japan, value $20-30.

Vanguard

Cahue Industrial of Spain. Cahue also mde radios and televisions in their Spanish factories.

X-802 4-funct, %, red LED, 4-AA rep batt, 3.5x6.5", one of the only models known from this country, wedge design shape, Spain, value $75-95.

Ventron

VT-600 4-funct, green fluor, 3-AA rep batt, 3.75x6.25", very thick (1.5") two-tone case, slide switch to show 12 digit answer on 6 digit display, Japan, value $55-65.

> *One of the most unique calculator personalities is Britain's Sir Clive Sinclair, founder of the Sinclair calculator line. A slightly-eccentric, engineer-entrepreneur known for his skills at packaging a lot of electronics in a very small package, Sir Clive has been at the forefront of miniature, portable televisions as well as the earliest of inexpensive home computers (Sinclair ZX-81 and Timex-Sinclair). His pocket calculators were among the best designed and smallest ever made. Sinclair products were also usually built by his own factories (as opposed to overseas).*

VT-1200C *aka Metric Conversion*, 4-funct, 12 digit red LED, 4-AA rep batt, 4.0x6.75", has metric conversion functions using a slide switch to set units, Japan, value $55-65.

??? *version 1* 4-funct, mem, green tube display, 4-AA rep batt, 6.5x3.25" horizontal, Japan, value $15-20.

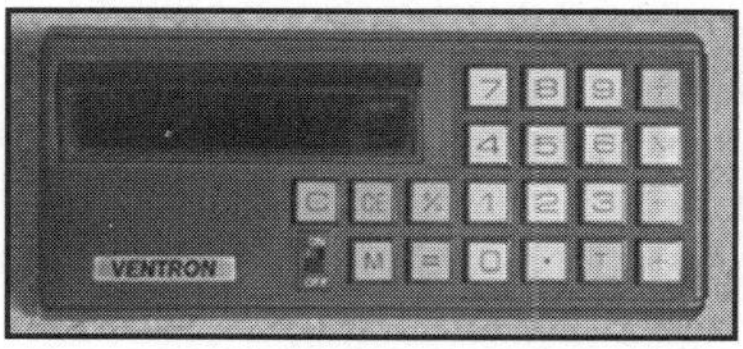

??? *version 2* 4-funct, mem, %, sealed batt, 6.5x3.0" horizontal, Japan, value $15-20.

Verax

874 4-funct, %, sgn chg, fluor, 3.25x5.5", value $40-50.

Vic

Apparently a Mexican company since all text on the label is in Spanish and the calculator states "Hecho en Mexico" meaning "Made in Mexico."

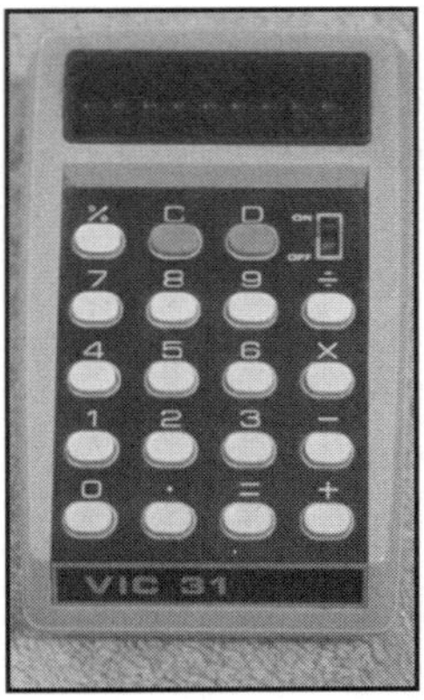

31 4-funct, red LED, 9V rep batt, 2.5x4.0" nice white case, purple cover over display, similar to Mongomery Ward P90, c1974, Mexico, value $75-85.

Victor Comptometer

Large office machine company that entered the portable calculator business, without long-lasting success. Mechanical calculators by Comptometer date back to the 1800's. Victor electro-mechanical adding machines were quite popular up to the late 1960's when electronic calculators made them obsolete. "MEC" meant "Miniature Electronic Calculator."

1 *aka MEC/1 or 80-1420*, 4-funct, %, tube display, sealed batt, 4.0x8.0", 1972 price $279, USA, value $50-60.

2 *aka MEC/2 or 80-1421*, 4-funct, mem, %, tube display, sealed batt, 4.0x8.0", same case as models 1 and 226, 1972 price $319, USA, value $45-55.

85 *aka Tallymate*, 4-funct, tube display, 6-AA rep batt, 3.5x9.0", Victor-green case, batt indicator, overflow and negative indicator LEDs, a classic, 1973 price $119, Japan, value $60-75.

95 4-funct, red LED display, 4-AA rep batt, 3.0x6.75", Canada, same case as General EZ2000 and Radio Shack EC-225, probably made by General Instruments, value $60-70.

104R 4-funct, mem, %, sq funct, recip, sgn chg, pi, fluor, 3-AA rep batt, 3.25x6.25", value $40-50.

106 sci-funct, mem, green tube display, 4-AA rep batt, 3.75x7.25", Japan, value $45-55.

223 *aka MEC/223*, 4-funct, mem, %, 12 digit tube display, sealed batt, 4.0x8.0", c1973, USA, value $55-65.

225 *aka MEC/225*, 4-funct, mem, %, 12 digit tube display, sealed batt, 4.0x8.0", c1973, USA, value $50-60.

226 *aka MEC/226*, 4-funct, mem, %, tube display, sealed batt, 4.0x8.0", same case and functions as 225 but with a 13 digit display, Japan, value $50-60.

Vista

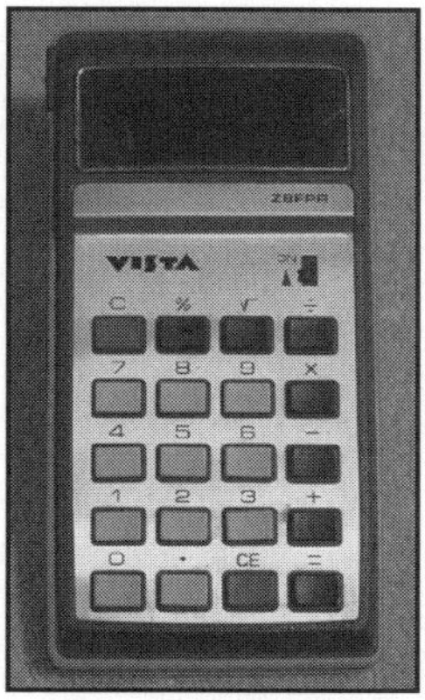

Z8FPR 4-funct, %, sq rt, green tube, 2-AA rep batt, 3.0x5.5", same case as Craig 4521, Japan, value $40-50.

Z48M 4-funct, mem, %, sgn chg, red LED, 2-AA rep batt, 2.5x3.75", gold tone, Japan, value $35-45.

Z48P 4-funct, %, purple LED, 4 N rep batt, 2.25x3.25", gold tone, Japan, value $35-45.

Z48AA 4-funct, %, sq rt, sgn chg, pi, red LED, 2-AA rep batt, 2.5x3.75", gold tone, Japan, value $35-45.

Vito

Swiss calculator maker.

Elektron 2000 4-funct, red LED, 2-9V rep batt, 2.5x5.75", c1973, unusual case style, only model known so far from Vito, Switzerland, value $100-125.

Voesa

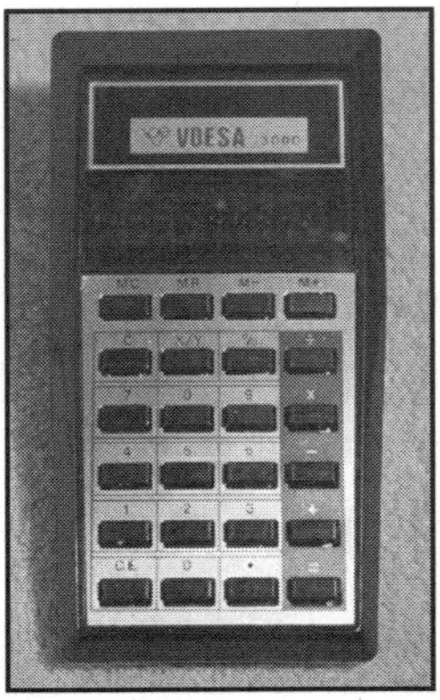

3000 4-funct, mem, %, red LED, 9V rep batt, 2.75x5.25", same case as Bohsei 3000, Hong Kong, value $10-15.

Western Auto

American store chain that sold hardware and auto parts.

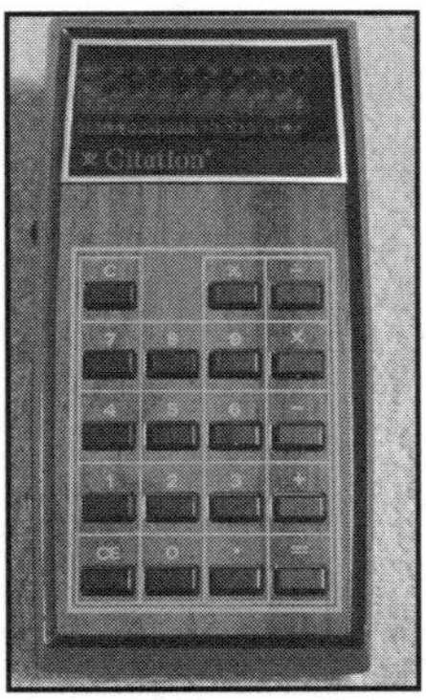

Citation *(version 1) aka 66-4986-7*, 4-funct, %, red LED, 9V rep batt, 2.75x5.5", same as Electronic Wizard except box shows different nameplate, made by Texas Instruments, same case as TI-1200 except with wood-grain colored face plate, price on box showed $10.99, USA, value $35-45.

Citation *(version 2 - no 2nd model number seen)*, 4-funct, mem, %, sgn chg, fluor, 9V rep batt, 2.75x5.5", made by Texas Instruments, same case as TI-1025 except with wood-grain colored face plate, c1977, USA, value $35-45.

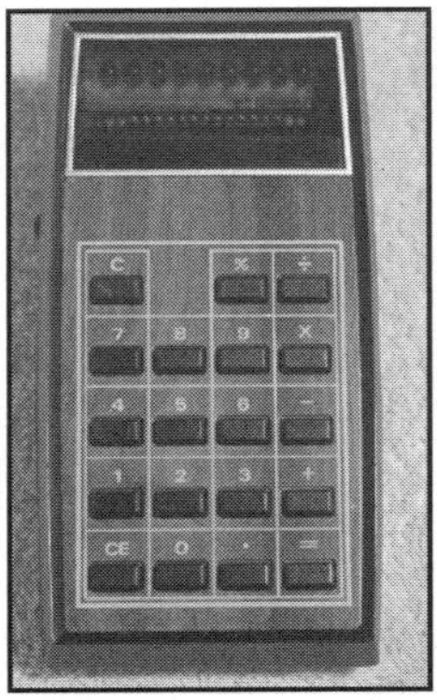

Electronic Wizard *(version 1) aka M4986 and 66-4986-7*, 4-funct, %, red LED, 9V rep batt, 2.75x5.5", same as Citation (version 1) except box shows different nameplate, made by Texas Instruments, same case as TI-1200 except with wood-grain colored face plate, USA, value $35-45.

Electronic Wizard *(version 2) aka TXI 4993A47*, 4-funct, %, red LED, 3-AA rep batt, similar case to TI Exactra 23 except with wood-grain colored face plate, USA, value $40-50.

XAM

Brand name of calculators sold by the Korvettes Department Store chain in New York City, New York (USA).

867 4-funct, mem, %, sq rt, green tube display, 9V rep batt, 3.0x5.25", black color, c1975-76, Taiwan, value $20-30.

877 4-funct, mem, %, red LED, 9V rep batt, c1975-76, Taiwan, value $20-30.

Xonex

Unclear situation: Xonex box found with Universal 303 calculator inside and appearing to be an original fit. It appears that "Universal 303" is the model name and "Xonex" is company. However, There is no Xonex on the calculator, with Universal appearing to be the company name. See Universal for information on the calculator.

Yashica

Yashica Co, Ltd. of Japan.

Pickey 4-funct, green fluor, sealed batt, 4.0x6.0", older and attractive style, comes with a slipcase mimicking a book jacket, Japan, value $70-80.

Long-time technicians of the older electro-mechanical business machines would complain about proliferation of the electronic calculators noting that the semiconductors within the calculators were inherently fragile and likely to break down. They noted that after the usual one-year guarantee, the newer electronic calculators were prone to failure and expensive repairs. Fortunately, they were wrong. Most calculators are still functioning perfectly, even after 20 years!

•

Some collectors remove the rechargeable batteries from their calculators. The nicad batteries have a tendency to leak acid with age and may damage the internal components if left unchecked. The usual method is to cut the connected wires as close as possible to the battery and remove the battery. If doing this yourself, be sure to be very careful and don't get battery acid on your skin or your clothes. Dispose of the old battery properly.

Novelty Calculators

Unlike ordinary calculators, novelty calculators include some feature which has nothing to do with calculation. This often made the calculator more fun to use. Some were specifically made as promotional or advertising items, others were made for children. Most were made after 1980 and have LCD displays. Novelty calculators with LED or Fluorescent displays were generally made in the 1970's or early 1980's and are much more difficult to find.

Calculator-Rulers

By the late 1970's LCD calculators flourished and soon were made small enough to incorporate into a ruler. Some calculator-rulers are still made today. Many of the calculator measurements for this book were taken with calculator-rulers!

ASJ RC-805 4-funct, mem, LCD, button rep batt, 2.0x12.0", also has built-in digital clock, value $35-45..

Avon ruler *aka Supersmart*, 4-funct, sq rt, mem, LCD, button rep batt, 2.5x6.5", has 6" ruler, fits into pencil-set with holes made to fit into binder, value $15-25.

Canon Ruler-8 4-funct, mem, LCD, button rep batt , 1.25x8.0", contains a 6" ruler, very early LCD model, Japan, value $50-60.

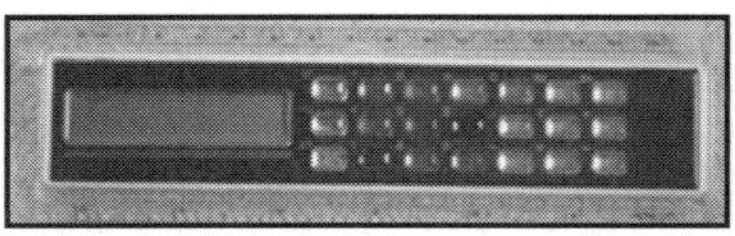

Jewel-Ruler 4-funct, mem, LCD, button rep batt , 2.0x6.0", buttons are colorful fake jewels Taiwan, value $35-45.

LeClaire 10012 4-funct, mem, LCD, button rep batt , 2.0x12", Taiwan, value $25-35

Sharp EL-5804 sci-funct, mem, LCD, button rep batt, 1.75x7.0", 15-cm ruler on back, was used as part of the uniform on Battlestar Galactica TV series, Japan, value $55-65.

Credit Card Size Novelty Calculators

Most of these are about the size of a credit card and only about 1/8" thick. On some, the data entry buttons are shaped like objects, for example pills or teeth. They often say NEW Products Line or Design Factory Tokyo on the back.

BMW 4-funct, sq rt, mem, LCD, solar, 2.25x3.75", Hong Kong, value $20-30.

Computer *(small display)* 4-funct, sq rt, mem, LCD, solar, 2.25x3.75", China, value $20-30.

Computer *(large display)* 4-funct, sq rt, mem, LCD, solar, 2.25x3.75", Hong Kong, value $20-30.

Hello Kitty 4-funct, sq rt, mem, LCD, button rep batt, 2.0x3.5", Taiwan, value $10-15.

House 4-funct, sq rt, mem, LCD, solar, 2.25x3.75", China, value $20-30.

Jet Plane 4-funct, sq rt, mem, LCD, solar, 2.25x3.75", Hong Kong, value $20-30.

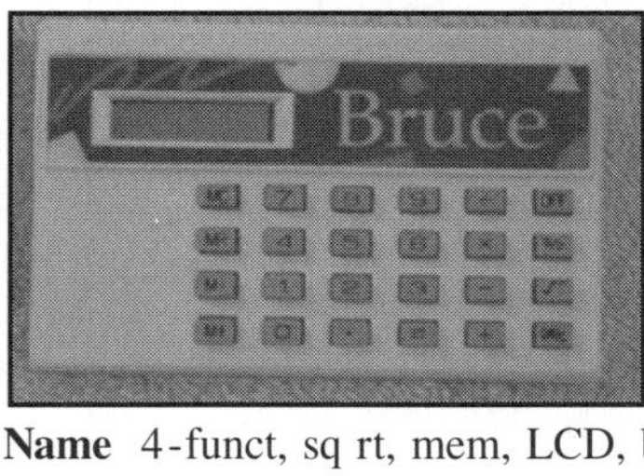

Name 4-funct, sq rt, mem, LCD, button rep batt, 2.0x3.5", has boy's or girl's first name on face, Taiwan, value $5-10.

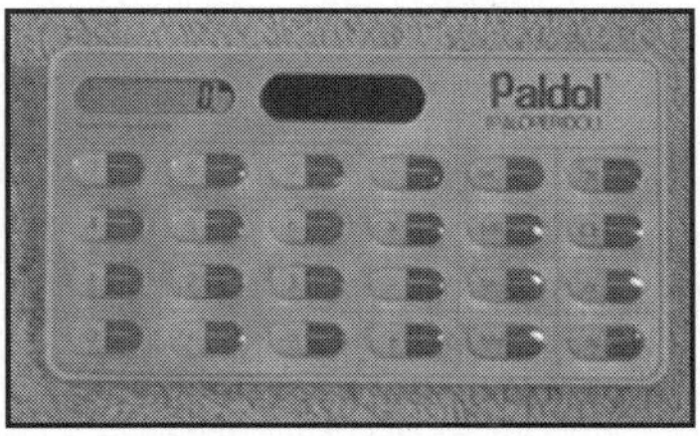

Pill 4-funct, sq rt, mem, LCD, solar, 2.25x3.75", Hong Kong, value $20-30.

Telephone 4-funct, sq rt, mem, LCD, solar, 2.25x3.75", Hong Kong, value $20-30.

Tooth 4-funct, sq rt, mem, LCD, solar, 2.25x3.75", Hong Kong, value $20-30.

Truck 4-funct, sq rt, mem, LCD, solar, 2.25x3.75", china, value $20-30.

Fake Jewelry Calculators

These have data entry buttons shaped like faceted gem-stones or pearls. Some of these are still sold and remain quite popular.

Gem Touch 4-funct, LCD, button rep batt, 2.0x3.25", China, value $20-30.

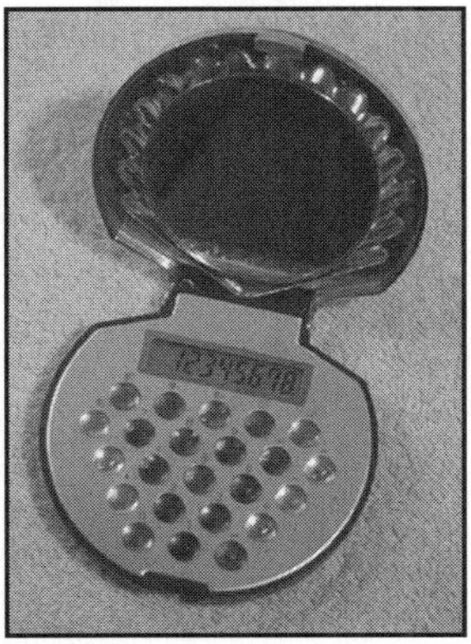

Gold Shell 4-funct, LCD, button rep batt, 3.0x4.0", opens like a compact with mirror inside and multicolor fake jewel buttons, Taiwan, value $45-55.

Heart 4-funct, LCD, button rep batt, 4x4", entire calc is heart-shaped as are the fake jewel buttons, Taiwan, value $45-55.

Jewel Box 4-funct, LCD, button rep batt, 3.5x5.0", fake gemstone buttons, storage compartment, China, value $35-45.

Plexiglass type 1 , 4-funct, LCD, button rep batt, 3.5x5.0", buttons are clear like diamonds except the on/off button is green like a sapphire, Taiwan, value $35-40.

Plexiglass type 2 same as type 1 but says "GIA" on front, value $25-30.

Plexiglass type 3 4-funct, LCD, button rep batt, 3.5x5.0", buttons are different color fake gemstones, China, value $35-45.

Rectangle Pearl, 4-funct, LCD, button rep batt, 4.0x5.0", gold and silver fake pearl buttons, Taiwan, value $25-35.

Round Pearl Shell 4-funct, LCD, button rep batt, 3" round, buttons are fake pink pearls, opens with mirror inside, Taiwan, value $30-40.

Figural Calculators

These are calculators shaped like other objects. Figural telephones and radios have been popular for many years. When non-collectors view a calculator collection the figural calculators always seem to steal the show! To a non-collector a crayon-calculator is far more interesting than a rare 1971 LED pocket calculator.

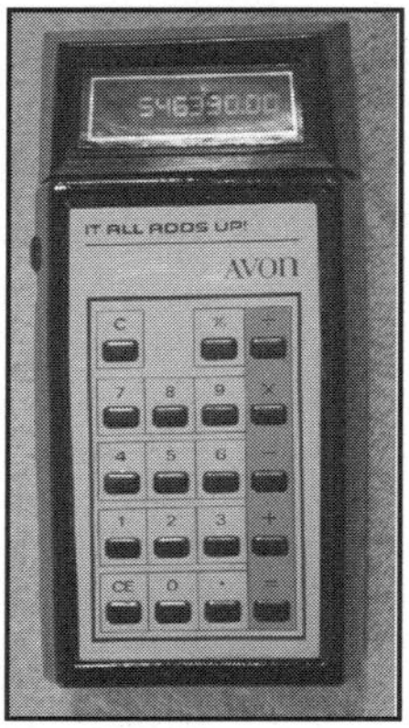

Avon Bottle this is actually a bottle shaped like a calculator and not a working calculator, a strange concept indeed, value $15-20.

Cash Register 4-funct, %, LCD, solar, 5.0x6.5", bell rings when cash drawer opens, too nice to give to your kids, China, value $35-45.

Cash Register *aka calculator 8000*, 4-funct, LCD, 2-AA rep batt, 6x7", Keypad similar to National Semiconductor 750, Hong Kong, value $35-45.

Compact *aka make-up kit*, 4-funct, mem, LCD, solar, 2.5x3.5", colored fake make-up trays are really data entry keys, of course it has a mirror, for the woman who has everything! by Design Factory, Tokyo, value $35-55.

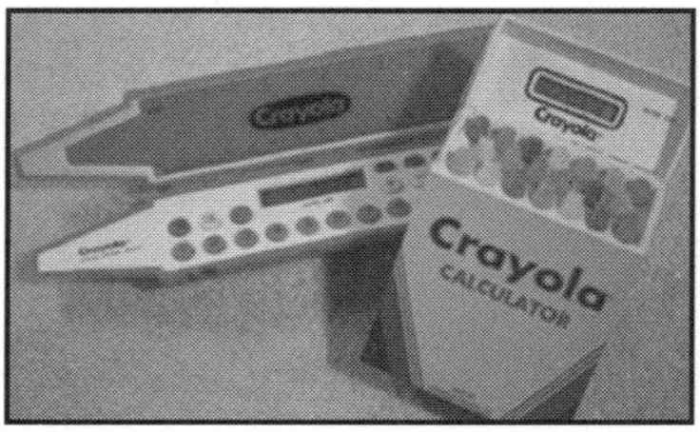

Crayon *aka Large Crayola*, 4-funct, %, sq, mem, LCD, sealed batt, 2.0x8.5", folds open to reveal calc and ruler, China, value $10-20.

Crayon *aka Small Crayola*, 4-funct, %, LCD, sealed batt, small keypad rolls out like the Calcuchrome film-roll calculator, China, value $30-40.

Crayon Box 4-funct, %, LCD, sealed batt, 3.25x4.75", buttons are fake crayon tips seen when box is opened, China, 1995, value $10-20.

Director 4-funct, sq rt, mem, LCD, 2.0x2.5", sealed batt, folds shut like the thing directors use when they say "take 5!" very "Hollywood," value $30-40.

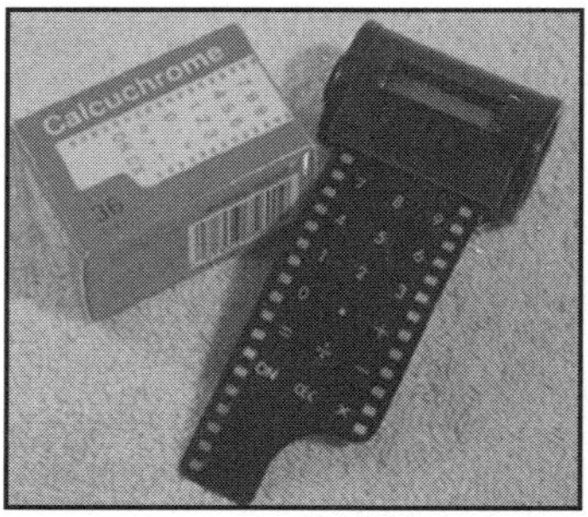

Film Roll *aka Calcuchrome* 4-funct, LCD, sealed batt, 1.0x2.0", key pad is imbedded in film, box says "calculate before 12/2000", funny but probably true since you'd have to nuke it to change batteries! China 1991, value $25-35.

Floppy Disk 4-funct, sq rt, mem, LCD, solar, 3.5x3.5", looks so much like the real thing that it comes with warning not to insert it into a computer! metal cover slides open to reveal display and solar cell, China, value $5-15.

Match Book 4-funct, %, mem, LCD, button-cell rep batt, 2.0x2.0", looks like the real thing but folds open to reveal a calculator, perfect for the bar-hopping nerd, China, value $15-25.

Money *aka small $100 bill*, 4-funct, sq rt, mem, LCD, solar, 2.0x4.5", not legal tender!, value $35-45.

Money *aka large $100 bill*, 4-funct, sq rt, mem, LCD, solar, 2.5x6.0" built-in mini phone-directory, stamped VOID so you won't be tempted to spend it!, China, value $45-55.

Pen *aka Penculator*, 4-funct, LCD, sealed batt, 1.0x5.0", small keypad rolls out like the Calcuchrome film-roll calculator, China, value $35-45.

Phone *aka desk phone*, 4-funct, sq rt, mem, LCD, button rep batt, 3.0x4.0", hand-set has digital clock in ear-piece, very odd, Taiwan, value $35-45.

Phone *aka cordless phone*, 4-funct, sq rt, LCD, sealed batt, 2.0x7.5", antenna is a pen, back slides open to reveal ruler and other desk accessories, value $20-40.

Phone *aka flip-phone*, 4-funct, mem, LCD, solar, 2.0x4.0", weighted to feel like the real thing, complete with pull-up antenna, sure to impress your friends! value $35-55.

Phone Directory 4-funct, sq rt, mem, LCD, solar, 4.0x6.0", just like the thing that sat by the phone in the 1950's but this one's got a solar calculator, very retro! Taiwan, value $25-45.

Piano 4-funct, mem, sq rt, LCD 2-AA rep batt, 5.0x7.0", built in clock, the only known calculator you can play the blues on!, Taiwan, value $45-55.

Picture Frame 4-funct, sq rt, mem, LCD, solar, 3.75x5.5", your favorite 3.0x4.0" photo can be viewed through the crystal-clear key pad, China, value $20-40.

Pin Ball Machine *aka flipper pool*, 4-funct, sq rt, mem, LCD, solar, 3.5x7,5", one of the most interesting calculators ever made, 1991, value $35-55.

Pink Cadillac 4-funct, sq rt, mem, LCD, button-cell rep batt, 3.0x5.0", open the trunk and find a working calculator, way cool!, value $45-55.

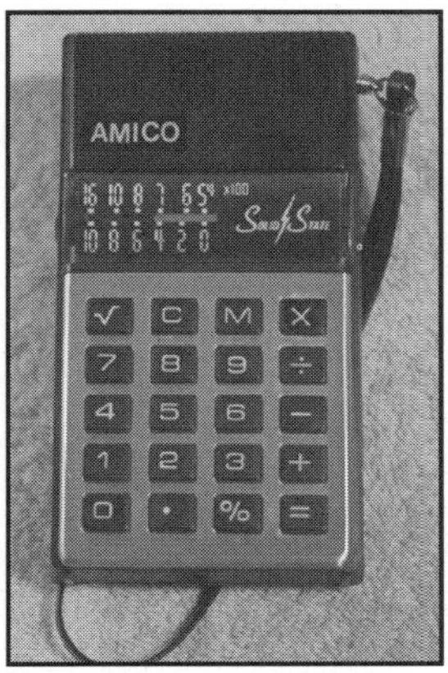

Radio This is actually a novelty radio shaped like a calculator complete with data entry buttons, back says British Design Registration number 982930, Hong Kong, value $35-45.

Tank 4-funct, LCD, button rep batt,

3.5x5.0", toy tank with built-in credit card size calc, Mattel Inc., 1989, China, value $35-45.

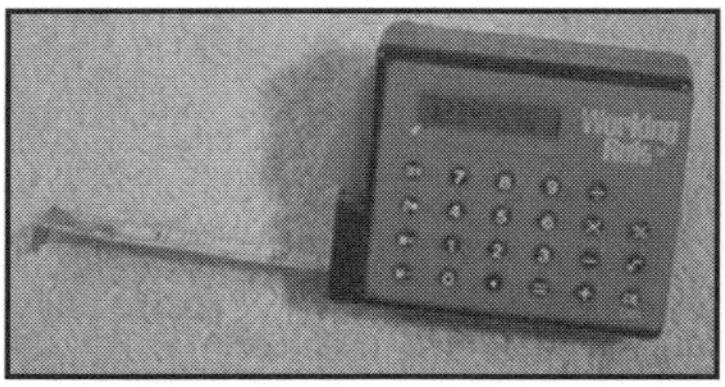

Tape Measure *aka working rule*, 4-funct, sq rt, mem, LCD, sealed batt, real 12-foot tape measure, Taiwan, value $20-40.

Keychain Calculators

The scientists who 25 years ago invented the first hand-held calculator would be blown away by these tiny things. They probably don't last long if kept in your back pocket!

Flip-Open 4-funct, sq rt, LCD, button-cell rep batt, 1.0x2.25", China, value $15-25.

Oval 4-funct, LCD, button-cell rep batt, 1.0x2.25", China, value $15-25.

Sports-Oriented Calculators

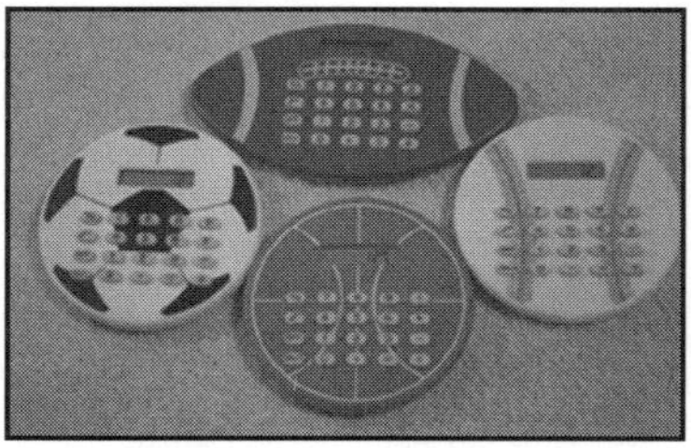

Baseball 4-funct, sq, LCD, sealed batt, 3" circle, China, value $15-20.

Baseball Field 4-funct, mem, sq, %, wedged-shape pen is a baseball bat, sealed batt. Taiwan, value $30-40.

Baseball-Ruler 4-funct, sq, mem, LCD, solar and rep button batt, ruler folds up like Anaheim Angels logo, value $15-20.

Basketball *aka Michael Jordan*, 4-funct, mem, %, LCD, sealed batt, 1.5x5.0", sold in set with plastic Michael Jordan watch, China, value $15-25.

Billiards 4-funct, mem sq, %, keys are billiard balls on pool table, solar, 4.75x7.0", pen holder in one pocket, Taiwan, value $35-45.

Football *(oval)* 4-funct, sq, LCD, sealed batt, 2.5x4.5 oval shape, China, value $15-20.

Football 4-funct, sq, LCD, sealed batt, 3" circle, China, value $15-20.

Football field 4-funct, mem, LCD, sealed batt, 4.75x7.0", keys are little footballs, Taiwan, value $35-45.

Football Helmet 4-funct, %, mem, LCD, solar, 3 pens inside, several models with different team helmet decals on top, China, value $15-20.

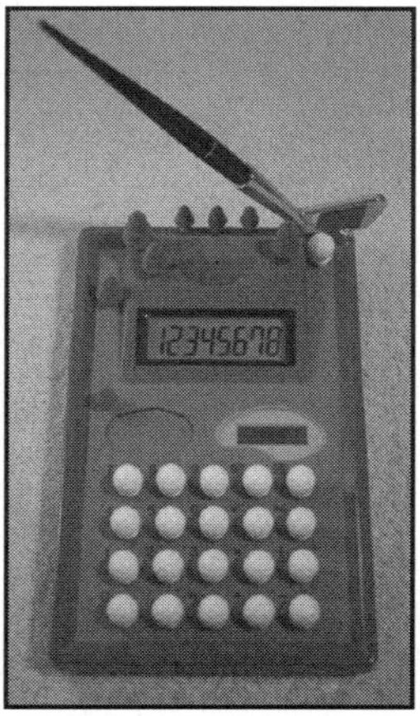

Golf 4-funct, mem, sq, LCD, 4.75x 7.5", solar, keys are golf balls, 8 small trees, gold club pen holder, Taiwan, value $30-40.

Golf-Master 4-funct, %, mem, bizarre shape, LCD, sealed batt, complete with real golf tee, Taiwan, value $45-55.

Soccer Ball 4-funct, sq, LCD, sealed batt, 3" circle, China, value $15-20.

Soccer field 4-funct, mem, LCD, sealed batt, 4.75x7.0", keys are little soccer balls, Taiwan, value $35-45.

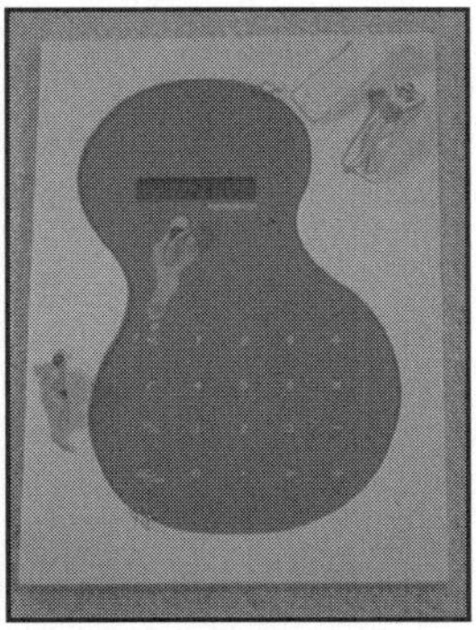

Swimming Pool 4-funct, sq, %, LCD, button rep batt, 4.5x6.5", keypad is in pool, swimmer in pool and 3-D sunbathers sit around pool, China, value $60-75.

Toy Calculators
(Early models: LED or Fluorescent Display type)

Since many of these are over 20 years old and were used by kids, some are in very poor condition. Models in near-new condition are worth more than the values given below. Note: Some LED models are not actually calculators but rather quiz games used to teach math. They often have only 2 LED's to indicate right or wrong answers. This type may be mentioned in the main list of this book (see National Semiconductor-Quiz Kid, TI-Little Professor, Mattel-JR Ewing, TI-Mr. Challenger, TI-Wiz-A-Tron, Santron-Clown.)

Barbie 4-funct, 6-digit blue fluor, 4-AA rep batt, 7.5x7.5", made by Omron for Alco, similar to Mickey Math, 1980, Japan, value $75-100.

Mickey Math *aka Omron* 18, 4-funct, 6-digit blue fluor, 4-AA rep batt, 7.5x7.5", made by Omron for Alco, everyone loves this calculator! Japan, value $75-100.

Mickey Mouse *aka 4610*, 4-funct, red LED, 9-V rep batt, 4.0x7.0", wrist strap, one of the most beautiful LED calculators ever made, Concept 2000, Hong Kong, value $75-95.

Mickey Mouse School *aka Unisonic SH 2013*, math quiz, 2-LED's 9-V rep batt, Hong Kong, value $35-45.

Professor Mathics 4-funct, red LED, 9-V rep batt, 4x5", carrying strap, Hong Kong, value $45-55.

Toy Calculators
(Slide-open type)

These calculators usually turn on automatically when opened. Some models also play a song such as "happy birth-

day" when opened. Although they are children's toys they do function as real electronic calculators.

Bear reading book 4-funct, sq, %, LCD, sealed batt, 2.5x3.5", slide up to turn on, China, value $20-30,

Cat 4-funct, sq, %, LCD, sealed batt, 2.0x4.5", plays the song "Yesterday," Japan, value $20-25.

Child 4-funct, sq, %, LCD, sealed batt, 2.0x4.5", Hong Kong, value $20-25.

Clown 4-funct, sq, %, LCD, sealed batt, 2.0x4.5", Hong Kong, value $20-25.

Dog with bone 4-funct, sq, %, 2.5x3.5", slide up to turn on, LCD, sealed batt, China, value $20-30,

Little mermaid 4-funct, sq, %, LCD, sealed batt, 2.0x4.5", made specially for the Disney Store by Hope Ind. Inc., China, value $20-25.

Martian, 4-funct, sq, %, LCD, sealed batt, 2.0x4.5", China, value $20-25.

Mouse 4-funct, sq, %, LCD, sealed batt, 2.0x4.5", plays "Yesterday," Hong Kong, value $20-25.

Pooh Bear 4-funct, sq, %, LCD, sealed batt, 2.0x4.5", like Little Mermaid was made specially for the Disney store by Hope Ind. Inc., China, value $20-25.

Santa 4-funct, sq, %, 2.5x3.5", slide up to turn on, LCD, sealed batt, China, value $20-30.

Train *aka Thomas the Tank Engine*, 4-funct, sq, %, LCD, sealed batt, Play Tech, 1992, China, value $20-25.

Toy Calculators
(Fold-Open type)

These models fold open to reveal a keypad on bottom and LCD display on top. An animal-figure decorates the lid.

Cat *aka Hello Kitty*, 4-funct, sq, mem, LCD, sealed batt, 2.25x3.5", China, value $15-20.

Dog *aka Pochacco*, 4-funct, sq, mem, LCD, sealed batt, 2.25x3.5", China, value $15-20.

Frog *aka KeroKeroKeroppi*, 4-funct, sq, mem, LCD, sealed batt, 2.25x3.5", China, value $15-20.

Toy Calculators
(Other types)

Calculator Book *aka My first calculator book*, 4-funct, LCD, sealed batt, 2.0x3.5", by McClanahan book company, 1991, Hong Kong, value $15-25.

Fun' N Calc *aka Radio Shack 23-582*, 4-funct, LCD, 2-AA rep batt, 4.0x6.0", very cute, China, value $20-25.

Fun' N Numbers *aka Radio Shack EC 2029*, 4-funct LCD, 1-AA rep batt, 4.0x6.5", very colorful, China, value $20-25.

Junior Calculator *aka modern kids*, 4-funct, sq rt, mem, LCD, 3.5x6.0", plays notes when buttons pressed, China, value $25-35.

Lego Calculator 4-funct, LCD, comes with Lego blocks, the only calculator you can build things on! value $25-35.

Little Professor 4-funct, LCD 9V rep batt, 3x5", made by TI to replace their popular LED Little Professor (see TI), USA, value $10-20.

Math To Go 4-funct, math games, LCD, 2-AA rep batt, 3.0x8.0", large handle, made by TI in 1989, value $25-45.

Mystery Box 4-funct, sq rt, mem, LCD, sealed batt, 3.25x3.5", by the time you figure out how to open this calculator you could have done the math with a pencil and paper! made by Enterprex, value $35-45.

My First Buddy's 4-funct, sq rt, mem, LCD, solar, 4.0x6.0", built-in handle, 1988 by Buddy L. Corp, China, value $35-45.

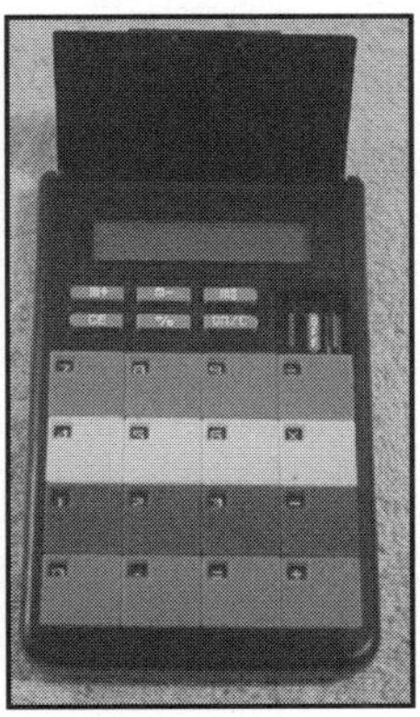

Puzzle 4-funct, mem, LCD, button rep batt, 3.0x5.0", yes, you can actually slide the key covers around and play the puzzle! No doubt this would quickly destroy the calculator! Taiwan, value $45-55.

Space-N-Counter 4-funct, mem, LCD, button-cell rep batt, 2.5x4.5", 1982 by General Consumer Electronics, as the clever name implies this is an early LCD game but also a calculator, perfect for the nerd who has everything! Hong Kong, value $45-55.

Star Trekulator *aka ST 101A*, 4-funct, sq rt, green fluor, 4-AA rep batt, 5.0x9.0", complete with strange flashing LEDs and sound effects, a must for space travel, c1977, Taiwan, value $75-100.

Other Novelty Calculators

Wedge *aka Spettro*, 4-funct, mem, LCD, sealed batt, 4.0x4.0", built-in pen, Taiwan, unique design, Taiwan, value $35-45.

Water-powered calculator 4-funct, sq rt, mem, LCD, 5.0x5.0", one of the most bizarre calculators ever made! Water is added to cylinders to generate power, value $45-55.

The Hewlett-Packard HP-35 Computer Calculator

Description

The HP-35 is a 35-key, pocket-sized scientific and engineering calculator. It performs logarithmic, trigonometric, and mathematical functions with single keystrokes and eliminates the need to refer to log or trig tables. It displays up to 10 significant decimal digits and automatically positions the decimal point throughout its 200-decade calculating range (10^{-99} to 10^{99}).
It combines the portability and convenience of the slide rule with the problem-solving power of a desk-top scientific calculator. However, it provides answers in a fraction of the time required for slide rule calculation.

Single Keystroke Functions

A series of specific functions or formulas are pre-programmed into the HP-35 to provide its unique capability for performing trigonometric and exponential functions with single keystrokes. This feature makes it unnecessary to refer to tables for the values of these functions:

Arithmetic: Add, subtract, multiply, divide and square root.

Trigonometric: Sin x, Cos x, Tan x, Arc Sin x, Arc Cos x, Arc Tan x.

Logarithmic: Log_{10} x, Log_e x, and e^x.

Other functions: x^y, 1/x, π and data storage and positioning keys.

$269.90

IT IS FANTASTIC!!

Description	Product / Accessory Number	Unit Price
☐ **HP-35 Scientific Pocket Calculator** Including four operational registers; one storage register; trigonometric, logarithmic, exponential and other pre-programmed single keystroke functions; dynamic range 10^{-99} to 10^{99}	HP - 35	$295.00
☐ **Standard Accessories** (One each supplied with each HP-35 purchased. Additional orders for accessories are priced as indicated.)		
☐ Battery Pack(s)	82001A	5.95
☐ Battery Charger(s) / AC Adapter(s)	82002A	13.95
☐ Travel Safety Case(s)	82003A	4.00
☐ Soft Carrying Case(s)	82005A	6.00
☐ Self(s) of Four (4) Personalizing Labels	7120-2946	.50
☐ Operating Manual(s)	00034-90008	1.50
☐ **Optional Accessories**		
☐ Battery Holder(s) w/Battrry Pack(s)	82004A	18.00
☐ Hard Leather Field Case(s)	82006A	19.50
☐ Security Cradle(s)	82007A	24.50

The ad says "IT IS FANTASTIC!" and that was no exaggeration. Hewlett-Packard's first pocket model and the world's first pocket scientific calculator, the HP-35, first sold for $395 in January, 1972. It was so incredibly popular that the price did not drop below $300 until 1974. The HP-35 was loved by scientists and engineers around the world and it's a must-have for any collector.

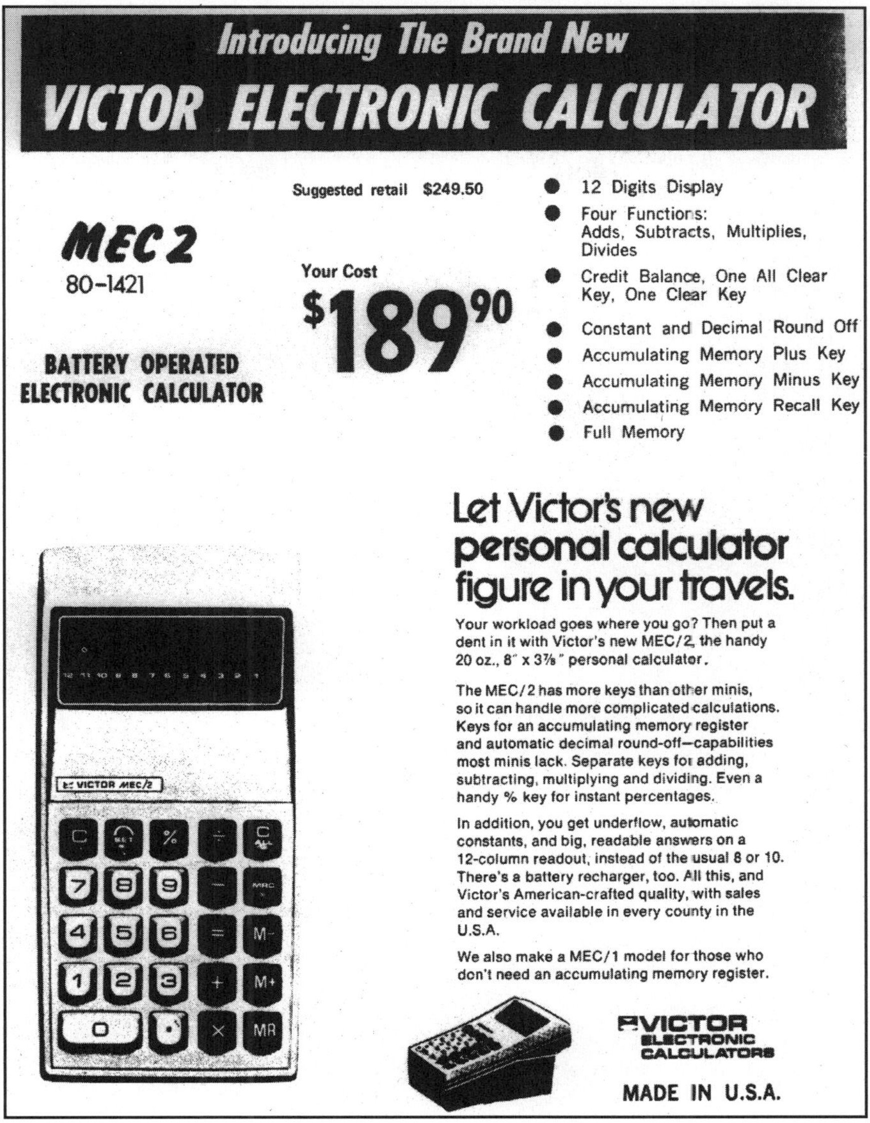

The Victor MEC 2 was introduced in 1972 for about $319 but the price quickly fell to under $200. That's still about $600 (in 1997 inflation-adjusted dollars) for a basic four-function calculator.

At 19 ounces in weight without its six batteries, the Victor Tallymate would fit only a very large pocket! This 1973 ad points out that Victor had joined forces with Comptometer, a company that had produced mechanical calculators since the late 1800's.

The MX40 Bowmar Brain

A Four Function, hand held
rechargeable Electronic Calculator
in handsome decorative colors
red and yellow

The MX40 Features:

- 8 Digit Display
- Full Floating Decimal
- Manual Constant
- Vinyl carrying pouch
- Adapter/ Charger

$69.90
YOUR COST FROM US

Detailed Specifications:

Functions:	Clear, clear entry, +=, −=, X, ÷, K
Capacity:	8 digits in, 16 out with underflow
Decimal:	Full Floating Decimal
Display:	Light Emitting Diode, 8 digits with indicator bit
Indicators:	Minus Sign, Overflow, Low Battery, Over Entry
Powers;	NiCad Battery, Rechargeable System, 3 hrs continuous operating time 7 hrs recharge period
Size:	5 1/2"x 3"x 1 1/2"
Weight:	9 oz.
Accessories:	Adapter/ Charger, Vinyl Carrying Pouch, Instruction Manual
Warranty:	1 Year parts and labor.

The MX60 Bowmar Brain

The MX60 Features:

- Replaceable battery operation
- % Key for automatic mark-ups & discounts
- 8 Digit Display
- Full Floating Decimal
- Omni-Constant (The constant with a brain, operable in all five functions)
- Vinyl carrying pounch and AC Adapter

A Five Function
Battery Operated Hand-held
Electronic Calculator
with % key

$77.90
YOUR COST FROM US

Detailed Specifications:

Functions:	Clear/ clear entry, + , −, X, ÷ , %, =
Capacity:	8 digits in/ 8 out
Decimal:	Full Floating Decimal
Display:	Light Emitting Diode, 8 digits plus indicator bit
Indicators:	Minus Sign, Overflow, Low Battery,
Power:	3 Alkaline AA Cells, 10 hrs. continuous use or AC with adapter
Size:	5 1/2"x 3"x 1 1/2"
Weight:	9 oz.
Accessories:	AC Adapter, Vinyl Carrying Pouch, Instruction Manual
Warranty:	1 year parts and labor.

The Bowmar Brain was the best selling line of calculators in the early 1970's. The term was so common, to many consumers "Bowmar Brain" was synonymous with pocket calculators.

Today's global corporate giant Unisys (then called Sperry) can trace its roots back to the first ENIAC computer as well as the early 1970's calculators above. The company includes merged parts of Remington Rand and Burroughs, both major mechanical calculating machine makers of the early 20th Century. Sperry-Remington brand calculators were sold by a small division and most were actually made by Casio.

Introduced in 1973, HP's second pocket calculator, the HP-80, rocked the financial world. The ad's claim, "The most revolutionary financial device of our time" was not marketing hype, but fact. Bankers and finance people could hardly believe what this little machine could do.

Lloyd's Accumatic Portable 100, one of the world's first liquid crystal calculators. The ad is circa 1972 and even has a section explaining what liquid crystal is. The display was large and well illuminated.

During the 1970's, JS&A was the leading mass marketer of portable calculators in the world. The company started on the road to success by selling the Craig 4501 model from a very small, "home-office" type of operation and grew to a multi-million dollar company. Twenty-five years later, JS&A still survives as a dynamic international marketing company with a variety of consumer items. Yet, they still pay tribute to their early days of selling calculators. This ad is circa 1973.

An ad for the Sinclair Scientific calculator. Note the photo of the slide rule and the illustration for it being pocket size. There's even a section entitled "Farewell Old Friend," referring to the now outdated slide rule. When was the last time you've seen one in use?

Unfair

An unfair comparison between the Texas Instruments 2500 and the ICP 530 calculator.

You be the judge. After reading this article you decide if we've treated Texas Instruments unfairly. Shown above are the 2500 and 530 in a side by side comparison. The reason you see the digits on the 530 and not on the TI unit is that the plastic overhang above the display shields the digits. On the ICP 530 the digits are clearly visible when viewed directly above or on an angle for desktop use.

Hats off to Texas Instruments! This remarkable company was the pioneer in the development of the integrated circuit whose miniaturization and low cost made consumer calculator ownership a reality.

But there's more. After becoming America's leading integrated circuit manufacturer, TI then introduced their own line of hand-held calculators and became America's number one brand name.

And when you become the standard of the industry you are always subject to comparison. It's the price of leadership.

What we are about to prove is how a new memory calculator far exceeds the capabilities and performance of the Texas Instruments TI-2500, yet costs practically the same.

FIRST THE PRICE

The TI-2500 by Texas Instruments costs $69.95.

The ICP 530 by International Consumer Products costs $79.95.

The respective display sizes of the ICP 530 (on top) and the TI 2500.

NOW THE COMPARISON

The ICP 530 has a fully addressable chain memory. This means that the ICP 530 can store answers to chain calculations in a memory bank and later recall them. The TI-2500 has no memory. The ICP 530 has an automatic add-on percentage system. For example to find out 5% of $50 enter $50; then press the times key, the number 5 and the percent key. The answer of $2.50 appears. To subtract the $2.50 from your original $50 all you do is press the minus key. (An answer of $47.50 will appear.) Or to add the $2.50, press the plus key. ($52.50 will appear.) The TI-2500 has no percentage system.

The ICP 530 has a sign change feature. (You can change a positive number to a negative number or a negative number to a positive number by pressing one key.) The TI-2500 has no sign change feature.

Now let's talk constants. The ICP 530 has an automatic constant on five functions—addition, subtraction, multiplication, division and percentage. The TI calculator has a switch-activated constant on two functions.

The ICP 530 has an LED display with digits large enough to read from practically across the room. The TI-2500 has the standard LED display.

The ICP 530 comes with regular batteries. However, it has an easily accessible battery compartment that permits you to put in either rechargeable or standard batteries. The TI-2500 has rechargeable batteries, but to change them you must send your unit to a factory service location.

The ICP 530 has click action keys that let you know when you've entered a digit. So does the TI-2500.

Both units have a one year warranty backed by substantial companies. ICP is a subsidiary of Arlen Realty, a multi-million dollar public company. Both companies provide excellent service-by-mail facilities, and both units come complete with instructions, AC adapter/charger, and carrying case.

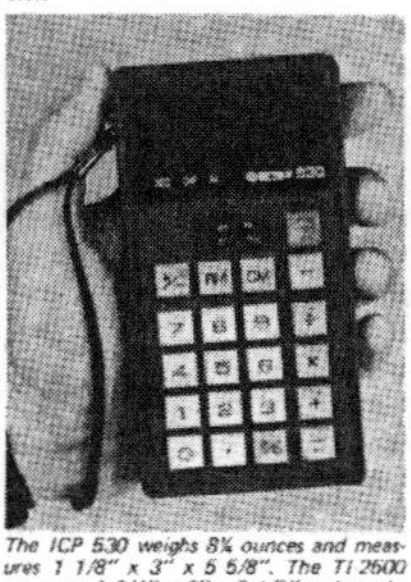

The ICP 530 weighs 8¼ ounces and measures 1 1/8" x 3" x 5 5/8". The TI 2500 measures 1 3/4" x 3" x 5 1/2" and weighs 10 ounces. Both have excellent styling.

The battery compartment on the ICP 530 is easily accessible for rechargeable or standard battery replacement.

We call our comparison unfair because the TI-2500 was introduced in 1972 and the ICP 530 was introduced in 1974. Calculator technology has changed quite a bit in two years. The integrated circuitry for the memory calculator and the large display used on the 530 were not even on the drawing boards when the 2500 was introduced. An unfair comparison? Maybe. But one thing is clear. The ICP 530 is a better calculator than the TI-2500—and to think Texas Instruments made it all possible.

A NEW WAY TO BUY

The best way to buy a calculator is to first use it. JS&A's concept of a two week trial period gives you the opportunity to use the ICP 530 in your home or office under your everyday conditions—not showroom conditions. After two weeks of actual use, you decide whether or not you want to keep it. If you decide to keep your unit, you have the first-hand knowledge that the 530 fits your requirements and the peace of mind in knowing that you've made the right choice. If you decide to return it, there's no obligation and you'll receive a prompt and courteous refund. In fact, we go one step further. To practically eliminate any inconvenience to our customers we will pick up your unit in most states, at our expense, right at your door. JS&A customers are the most pampered in the nation. They have come to expect good service, honest value and the opportunity to be the first to purchase the really exciting new products of our decade. Order your ICP 530 at no obligation today.

Credit Card Buyers—Call (800) 323 5886 if you wish to phone in your order.

ILLINOIS RESIDENTS CALL (312) 498 6900

ORDER FORM

Please rush me .... ICP 530 memory calculator(s) @ $82.45 each ($79.95 plus $2.50 postage and handling), and please include standard batteries, AC adapter/charger, carrying case, instruction booklet and one year warranty. I understand that I may return my purchase within two weeks if I am not absolutely satisfied.

☐ Enclosed is my check for $________

Illinois residents add 5% sales tax.

Mail orders to: JS&A National Sales Group 4200 Dundee Rd., Northbrook, Ill. 60062

☐ Please charge my Master Charge, (also include four numbers above name) Bank Americard, Diners Club, or American Express (be sure there are 13 digits) credit card account

NO. ________ EXP ________

SIGNATURE ________

NAME ________

COMPANY ________

ADDRESS ________

CITY ________ STATE ________

ZIP ________ PHONE ________

The JS&A National Sales Group is one of the leading national distributors of electronic calculators and other consumer and business related electronic products. Despite our size we insist upon complete customer service and satisfaction. Our descriptions must be accurate, our products must represent good value and you must be completely satisfied. You deal with people (not computers) and you receive answers to your letters and prompt refunds if you so request. The names of our customers are kept confidential and not sold for mailing lists. Our insistence on the highest standards of customer service is your assurance of complete satisfaction.

JS&A NATIONAL SALES GROUP

4200 Dundee Road, Northbrook, Illinois 60062 (312) 498 6900

Unfair? This is a great comparison ad from about 1974 with a look at TI's first calculator. Note the comparison photo of the digital read-outs and the small, eye-straining size of the LEDs used in the TI calculator.

SLIDE RULE

Introducing the NEW Lloyd's Accumatic electronic slide rule–the first real alternative to the Hewlett Packard HP-35.

Hats off to Hewlett Packard! This remarkable company managed to hold its very own market position for almost two years selling its $300 to $400 slide rule calculators directly to the consumer.

But good old American competition has produced what we feel to be a better alternative than Hewlett Packard's famous HP-35. And it costs considerably less! It's called the Lloyd's Accumatic electronic slide rule.

MORE FEATURES THAN THE HP-35

The Lloyd's Accumatic has features that the Hewlett Packard's HP-35 does not have. For example, it has a fully addressable memory which permits you to store calculations for later use or recall. It automatically squares a number and simultaneously adds it to memory—ideal for statistical applications. It gives you answers in radians or degrees—a great help to civil and electrical engineers. The Accumatic also has the common antilogarithm 10^x which the HP-35 does not have.

ADDRESSABLE MEMORY VS SCIENTIFIC NOTATION

The Lloyd's Accumatic has more features than the HP 35 with the exception of scientific notation. When the Accumatic was designed, Lloyd's engineers considered a fully addressable memory to be of greater value to engineers than scientific notation which they felt was a luxury similar to power seats on an automobile. Scientific notation on a calculator is not really necessary in most engineering and math applications especially when given memory as an alternative.

WRAP-AROUND DECIMAL

When using the four basic functions, the Accumatic has what is called "wrap-around decimal." When the answer in whole numbers is greater than eight, the decimal will move eight places to the left of its actual position and an overflow indicator will light up. To continue your calculations, simply clear the indicator light, note the number of places your decimal moved to the left, and continue to calculate. The calculations can therefore be carried on infinitely without the necessity of scientific notation.

TO PERFORM A SCIENTIFIC FUNCTION

To use the functions indicated above the keys, you first depress the F key and then the corresponding function key. For example, to determine the sin of 30° you enter 30 on the display, press the F key and then the number 1. Your answer of 0.5 is then automatically displayed.

DUAL ERROR CORRECTION

Another handy feature is the Accumatic's new double error correction capability. To clear an error before pressing the equal or scientific function key, you simply press the "C" key and you erase your last entry without erasing the entire calculation. But let us say that you enter the number 4325 when you meant 4321. Simply press the "F" key twice and the clear key, and the display will read 432. Then enter the correct number 1 so your display reads 4321. In short, you have your choice of correcting everything on your display or just the last digit entered.

UNFAIR TO COMPARE

It might be unfair to compare the HP-35 with the Lloyd's Accumatic. After all, the HP-35 is over two years old, and calculator technology has developed a great deal since then. What took five separate integrated circuits two years ago now takes just one in the Accumatic. The new larger florescent green display available on the Accumatic wasn't available when the LED display was first used in the HP-35. An unfair comparison? Maybe. But one thing is clear—the Lloyd's Accumatic represents today's most advanced feature package at a most reasonable price.

Small, compact and ready to use. The Lloyd's Accumatic is only 7/8" thin and easily fits in coat pocket or briefcase.

A COMPLETE ELECTRONIC PACKAGE

The Lloyd's Accumatic is a compact mini calculator that easily fits in your coat pocket or briefcase. Its handy size of 7/8" x 3 1/4" x 5 3/4" and its light 12 ounce weight make it the ideal unit to use at work or during travel. The Accumatic has a large eight digit easy-to-read florescent green display which can be viewed easily for desk top use, and it features automatic constants on all four basic functions. The Accumatic comes complete with AC adapter/charger, 4 rechargeable alkaline batteries, handsome travel case and an explicit 56 page instruction booklet with specific examples on how to use the calculator.

NATIONAL INTRODUCTORY PRICE:

$199.95

SUG. RETAIL: $229.95

The Lloyd's Accumatic has more features than the Hewlett Packard HP-35 plus a large florescent display.

ONE YEAR WARRANTY

The Lloyd's electronic slide rule is manufactured by Rockwell International exclusively for Lloyd's Electronics who backs their unit with 3 national service-by-mail locations in New Jersey, Illinois, and California and with an unconditional one year warranty. Although the Accumatic is built to last, it is good to know that the manufacturer is service-conscience—a very important consideration when you purchase any calculator.

A NEW WAY TO BUY

The best way to buy a calculator is to first use it. JS&A's concept of a two week trial period gives you the opportunity to use the Lloyd's Accumatic in your home or office under your everyday conditions—not showroom conditions. After two weeks of actual use, you decide whether or not you want to keep it. If you decide to keep your unit, you have the first-hand knowledge that the Accumatic fits your requirements and the peace of mind in knowing that you've made the right choice. If you decide to return it, there's no obligation and you'll receive a prompt and courteous refund. In fact, we go one step further. To practically eliminate any inconvenience to our customers we will pick up your unit in most states, at our expense, right at your door. JS&A customers are the most pampered in the nation. They have come to expect good service, honest value and the opportunity to be the first to purchase the really exciting new products of our decade. Order your Lloyd's Accumatic at no obligation today.

Credit Card Buyers—Call (800) 323-5886
if you wish to phone in your order.

Illinois Residents call (312) 498-6900

ORDER FORM

Please send me _____ Lloyd's Accumatic electronic slide rule(s) complete with AC adapter/charger, four alkaline rechargeable batteries, travel case, 56 page instruction booklet and one year unconditional warranty. I also understand that I may return my Accumatic within two weeks for a prompt refund if I am not absolutely satisfied.

Enclosed is my check for $ _______

Include $2.50 postage and handling for each unit ordered. Illinois residents add 5% sales tax.

Mail orders to JS&A National Sales Group
4200 Dundee Rd., Northbrook, Ill. 60062

☐ Please charge my Master Charge, (also include four numbers above name) Bank Americard, Diners Club, or American Express (be sure there are 13 digits) credit card account

NO. ______ EXP ______

SIGNATURE ______

NAME ______

COMPANY ______

ADDRESS ______

CITY ______ STATE ______

ZIP ______ PHONE ______

The JS&A National Sales Group is one of the leading national distributors of electronic calculators and other consumer and business related electronic products. Despite our size we insist upon complete customer service and satisfaction. Our descriptions must be accurate, our products must represent good value and you must be completely satisfied. You deal with people (not computers) and you receive answers to your letters and prompt refunds if you so request. The names of our customers are kept confidential and not sold for mailing lists. Our insistence on the highest standards of customer service is your assurance of complete satisfaction.

JS&A NATIONAL SALES GROUP
4200 Dundee Road, Northbrook, Illinois 60062 (312) 498-6900

A circa 1973 ad for Lloyd's Accumatic electronic slide rule
Note the comparison to a then current HP model. No matter how JS&A and Lloyds tried to sway buyers with a cheaper price, the HP-35 would continue to be in high demand and live on in the hearts of engineers and scientists almost like a "first true love."

At Left:
Here it is, a photo of the Sinclair Executive! The minimalist approach shows product and eliminates the clutter of endless copy about various features. A true "art" ad for the day.

Below:
Another circa 1973 super value ad featuring the JCE Mark II.

No matter what you pay for it, a calculator is worthless if it isn't with you when you need it.

And it won't be with you if it's too bulky, too thick, too heavy to carry around in your pocket. Many "pocket" models weigh a half a pound or more.

That's why we're proud to present the world's smallest, lightest and thinnest electronic calculator: the Sinclair Executive.

No longer than your pocket pen, the Sinclair Executive is only 3/8" thick and weighs a mere 2½ ounces. It slips into your shirt pocket without sag or bulge.

Exclusive five-year guarantee:

There is no other calculator like it. Its unique, wafer-thin design results from an ingenious British development in miniaturized circuitry. And it's made to British standards of workmanship: so carefully crafted that we guarantee it not for the usual year but for a full *five* years of service. If any defects arise in normal use during the first 5 years, the unit will be replaced or repaired, free of charge, if returned to place of purchase.

What will the Sinclair Executive do for you?

All the usual calculations, and more. Add, subtract, multiply and divide, rounding off your answers to 2, 4, or 6 decimal places or allowing the decimal point to float. Perform chain or mixed calculations. Multiply or divide by a constant, over and over again. Work out percentages, interest rates, taxes, compound interest...in fact, once you own it, you'll keep discovering new uses.

Price includes soft wallet, batteries and instructions. The Sinclair Executive is now available at fine stores including:

B. Altman & Co. · Abercrombie & Fitch · Foley's · Famous Barr Co. · G. Fox & Co. Inc. · Gus Mayer · Hammacher Schlemmer · The Hecht Co. · Jacobson Stores, Inc. · Kaufman Dept. Stores · Lord & Taylor · Marshall Field & Co. · The May Co. Neiman-Marcus Co. · The M. O'Neil Co. · Park Plaza Gift Shop · Saks Fifth Avenue · Sakowitz. · Strauss-Hirshberg Co.

Σ SIGMA DISTRIBUTORS
ELECTRONIC CALCULATORS

1433 MOTOR ST.
SUITE 303
DALLAS, TEXAS 75207
214 638-5481

sinclair

Was this the "Infinity" of calculators? Judging from the content, the Sinclair Executive is being pitched to a distinct business market. With Neiman-Marcus and Saks being included in the list of retail outlets, this item is definitely an exclusive one. There is also no mention of cost in this ad.

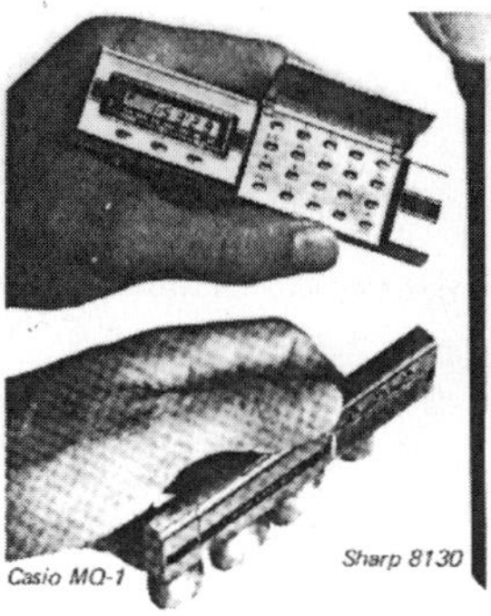

Casio MQ-1 Sharp 8130

The New Calculator Revolution

Calculators are getting flatter, smaller and more convenient. Here is a report on the latest trends.

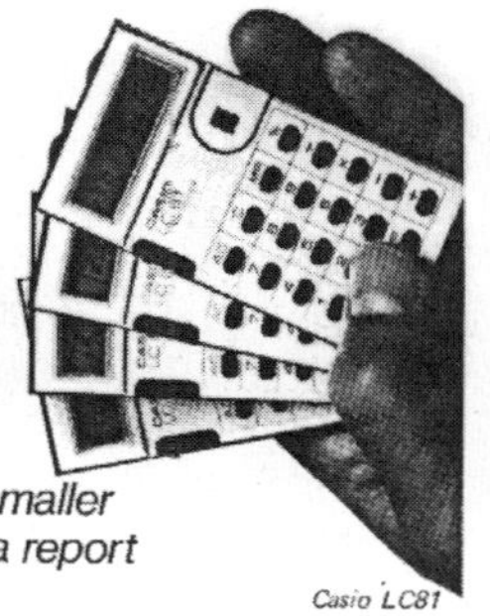

Casio LC81

Calculators are changing. All but gone is the LED display—those small red digits that you've always associated with calculators. Replacing the LED display are liquid crystal digits—larger, easier to read and requiring a mere fraction of the power the older LED displays required.

THE SIZE BREAKTHROUGH

Advancing technology has also been able to reduce nearly all the previously complex components onto a single integrated circuit, so calculators are now thinner, smaller and thus easier to carry with you all the time.

The first fatality of the new crop of calculators has been the calculator watch which was developed as a better way to keep a calculator handy. The new generation of calculators are inexpensive and can almost be carried in your wallet, so the calculator watch is now more a gimmick than a positive contribution to technology.

THE BATTERY LIFE BREAKTHROUGH

The other new breakthrough feature is long battery life. The new liquid crystal displays use much less power than the LED's. The batteries are therefore smaller, easily replaceable, and last years without replacement. The savings in batteries alone now justify the purchase of a new calculator.

Just about everybody who needs a calculator already has one. But with the latest breakthroughs in calculator technology, a whole new market has developed. Convenience, savings and the opportunity to give a unique gift has again brought increased sales to the few calculator manufacturers left.

JS&A was the first company to introduce and mass market the first pocket calculator in 1971, literally creating a new industry. During the past six years we have introduced every major calculator breakthrough. After reviewing hundreds of units during the past few months, the three products described below were carefully selected by JS&A as the best examples of the new calculator technology.

The Sharp 8130 is thinner than two quarters, emits a tone when you touch the keyboard, and shuts itself off automatically.

THE CASIO MINI COMPUTER

The Casio LC81 is smaller than a business card and so small that you can actually hide it in your hand. In spite of its size, you can still press the keys without your finger overlapping onto the next key. The unit features a full memory and percentage key, so it's perfect for both business and personal use. The size of the two ounce Casio LC81 is only 5/16" x 1 5/8" x 3" and comes complete with batteries and carrying case.

THE SHARP 8130

Thinner than two quarters and as light and flat as you could imagine, the Sharp 8130 is unquestionably the world's thinnest calculator. To enhance its thinness, Sharp engineers have eliminated the conventional keyboard. Instead, a flat sheet of vinyl imprinted with numbers covers the keyboard and emits a tone each time you touch a key position. You get the positive feel that you've entered a digit without having to glance at the display. The tone can be shut off by simply pressing the tone key if you don't want to disturb anyone. In addition to the standard functions, the unit also features square root, percentage and memory. The two ounce unit comes complete with a notebook, carrying case and batteries.

THE CASIO MQ-1 AND MQ-2

In addition to size and battery advantages, more and more functions can be incorporated into calculators. The new Casio MQ-1 is a very small lighter-sized unit with a digital watch, a stopwatch and a calculator all built in. The advanced model, the MQ-2, also has a small alarm. The practical uses are numerous. You can have your unit buzz you when your parking meter time expires. You can remind yourself to take your pills, move your lawn sprinklers or prepare for appointments. You can use it as a pocket travel alarm. You can use it instead of your watch to tell the time. You can time sporting events and travel times or use it as you would any stopwatch accurate to within 1/10th of a second. And since you can program four different alarm settings, you can use it for a combination of many different applications.

The unit is also a perpetual calendar which even adjusts for leap years. You can figure the number of days between two different dates so you can do everything from amortization tables to biorhythm calculations. And you don't need an engineering degree to figure it out. A simple four-function eight-digit calculator and five other function buttons are all you use, and it takes just a few minutes to learn how to use them. The new Casio unit combines every practical application of new calculator technology into one single 1¼ ounce unit only 3/8" x 1¼" x 4 3/8".

THE SERVICE BREAKTHROUGH

Both Sharp and Casio are world-wide leaders in calculator production. They are solid companies with their own service-by-mail organizations. There's the other breakthrough. The new crop of calculators are practically service free. With all the electronics condensed on a single integrated circuit and with the new advanced technology, there is very little that can go wrong. Each calculator is backed by a limited one year warranty.

WHY BUY THEM FROM JS&A

There are good reasons to buy directly from JS&A. First, you pay no postage and handling charges. Not only does this save you money, but you are never penalized if you decide to return your unit. Secondly, we pay all applicable sales tax—again a savings. Thirdly, you have a long trial period—thirty full days. You get the opportunity to see how easy it is to use the keyboard and how convenient it is to carry in your pocket before you decide to keep your calculator.

To order your calculators, specify the model and submit a check for the amount indicated below. Do not add sales tax or postage and handling charges. Credit card buyers may call our toll-free number below.

Join the new calculator revolution. Order a new generation calculator at no obligation, today.

Casio LC 81 Mini Calculator $29.95
Sharp 8130 Thin Calculator 34.95
Casio MQ-1 Calculator/Clock 59.95
Casio MQ-2 Calculator/Clock/Alarm . . . 69.95

JS&A NATIONAL SALES GROUP

Dept. AI One JS&A Plaza
Northbrook, Ill. 60062 (312) 564-9000
CALL TOLL-FREE. . . . 800 323-6400
In Illinois call . . . . (312) 498-6900

©JS&A Group, Inc.,1977

This 1977 ad touts how the current technology enables calculators to be made flatter and smaller. Prices have also come down to "an amazing" $69 and under.

At Left:
Unitrex has a "peanut sized" calculator. This 1974 ad pitches such a small item as a second calculator or one for use by school children. The market for pocket calculator use has broadened significantly with the increased technology.

Below:
This circa 1974 ad shows a new price breaker for memory calculators. At $39.95, costs have decreased significantly from earlier models.

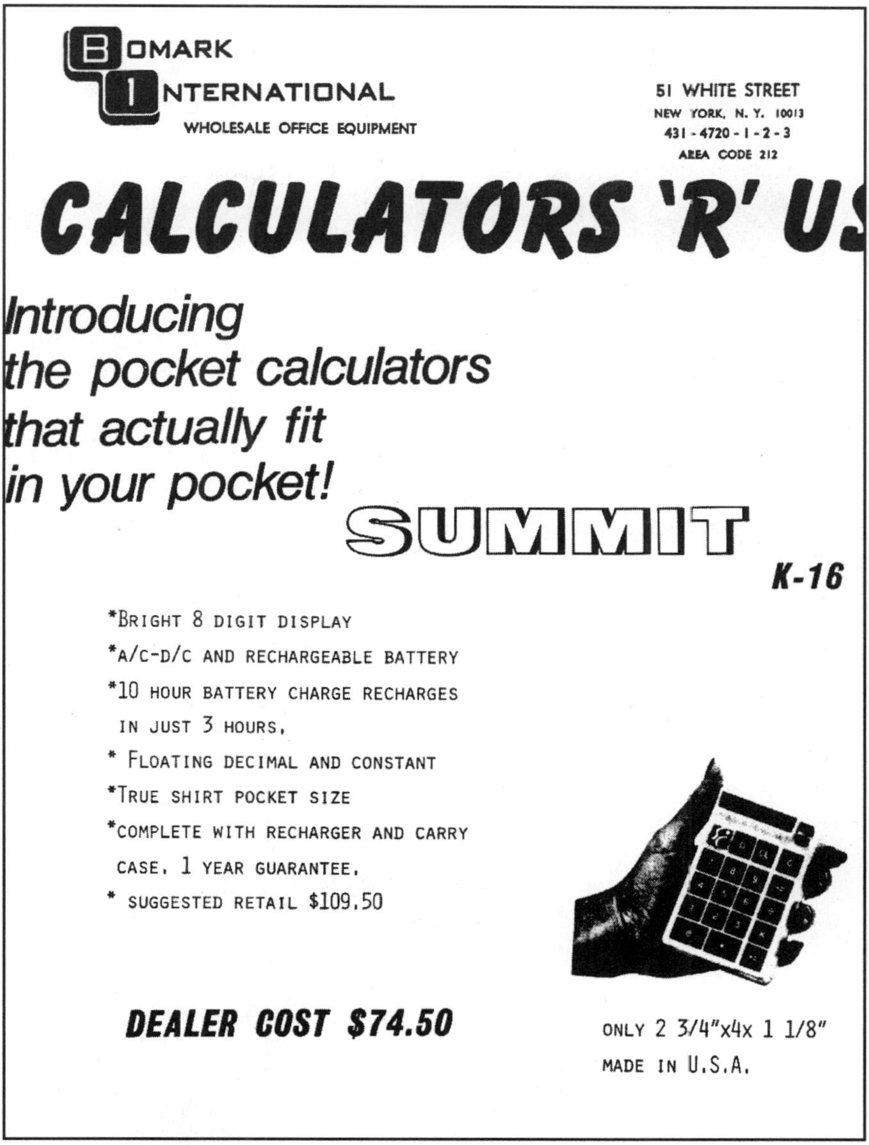

Calculators 'R' Us -- The "Great Calculator War" is in full throttle!
Today, you can actually purchase them at toy stores.

the End

A new memory calculator breakthrough means the end of the AC adapter, rechargeable battery and small display and the introduction of a new memory system.

$59.95

NATIONAL INTRODUCTORY PRICE
Sug. Retail $79.95

The world's first ambient light liquid crystal memory pocket calculator—the DataKing 800 manufactured by Rockwell International, can operate for one year on the same set of disposable batteries.

If you've been waiting for the world's most advanced memory calculator—your timing is perfect.

Powered by two inexpensive 9 volt batteries, the 800 will last almost one year on the same set of batteries or ten times longer than even the lowest drain pocket calculators. But there are several other very exciting new feature breakthroughs.

RECHARGEABLE VS DISPOSABLE BATTERIES

It all boils down to convenience vs savings. Rechargeable batteries cost roughly $3.00 per year to power the average pocket calculator. That isn't very expensive. But the calculator owner who wishes to recharge his batteries is always at the mercy of his AC adapter/charger. And the adapter 1) is always subject to malfunction, 2) is often heavier than the calculator and 3) requires AC power to drive it.

If you've ever been on an airplane when your calculator pooped out or if you have been unable to use your calculator because your AC adapter didn't work, you can appreciate the convenience of the disposable battery. But disposable batteries are more expensive—an average of about $4 to $7 to operate the average calculator per year.

The DataKing 800 costs roughly $1.00 per year to operate using readily available 9 volt batteries. Therefore no AC adapter is required nor is one provided.

BIG DISPLAYS VS SMALL DISPLAYS

The display is the biggest consumer of battery power in a calculator. The bigger the display, the more power required to light it. Sunlight can easily overpower the display's light-emitting elements making legibility impossible.

The DataKing 800 has a large easy-to-read liquid crystal display. When small electrodes, arranged to form digits, are charged by microcurrents of electricity, the liquid crystal turns opaque. The resulting numbers must then be illuminated by a light source to provide the contrast needed to read the display. The 800 employs a light-gathering prism that eliminates any need for an internal lighting system and consequently uses a mere fraction of the power required by other conventional calculators. And the brighter the room light, the easier it is to read—even in sunlight.

NEW CLICK-THRUST KEYBOARD

The DataKing 800 has taken the full-thrust keyboard feel and added a click to provide the world's first "click-thrust" keyboard. Not only do you get a very positive data entry feel, but your chance of false entry is greatly minimized by the unique widely-spaced keys.

NEW ACCESS MEMORY SYSTEM

Memory on a calculator is such an important feature that units without it are practically outdated. Memory permits you to store individual numbers or answers to calculations in a memory bank and then recall the total of those numbers directly onto your display without erasing the total in your memory.

The DataKing 800 has the new access memory. You can now take any number on your display and divide or multiply your memory total by that number—all while retaining that same number on your display. No other calculator has this feature. For example, to add a number to memory, press "M" and the plus key. To divide a number into memory, press "M" and the divide key.

MANY OTHER FEATURES

Now that we've told you all about those revolutionary features, here are some additional qualities that make the DataKing the nation's unquestioned memory leader.

1) Easiest to use Even if the 800 is your first pocket calculator, you'll find it a snap to learn. The algebraic logic (you perform the functions as you think) makes it easy to perform chain calculations. The automatic constants on all six functions require no separate switch to turn on, and there's a separate memory-plus and memory-minus entry system.

COMPARED TO TEXAS INSTRUMENTS

America's leading brand-name calculator is Texas Instruments. TI recently announced their new TI 2550 memory unit for $99.95. That same calculator is now outdated by the introduction of the 800. The TI 2550 uses rechargeable batteries and has a small display and the older chain memory system. Compare price, features, performance and dependability, and you can easily see why the DataKing is America's greatest memory calculator value.

2) The best percentage system To add 5% to a $50 purchase, simply enter $50, then press the plus key, the 5 key and then the percent key. The percentage amount of $2.50 is displayed. Then press the equal key—$52.50 is displayed. In short, you perform percentage problems exactly as you think for both addition, subtraction, multiplication and division.

3) The finest display The large 8-digit liquid crystal display with floating decimal has negative balance and overflow indicators. You can also clear any overflow condition and continue your calculations.

4) Shock resistant The calculator enclosure also eliminates the need for a carrying case and provides a high degree of shock resistance. The display and prism are recessed and thus protected by its rugged high impact resistant case even when accidentally dropped.

5) Handsome styling Rarely do you find so many outstanding features in a highly-styled calculator. The DataKing 800 measures only 1½" x 3½" x 6" and weighs only 10½ ounces. Other features include a clear entry system for memory or mistaken entries, zero suppression, and a full floating decimal.

You are no doubt familiar with Rockwell International and their approach to quality. The DataKing 800 is no exception. Although the 800 was designed to be service-free, your unit is backed by a one year warranty and DataKing's national service-by-mail facility. DataKing, Inc. is a well financed and established company and a leading consumer electronics firm—further assurance that your modest investment is fully protected.

JS&A is so convinced that the 800 is the best memory unit you can buy that we are making the following offer: try the DataKing 800 for a full month. Compare it with every other calculator on the market for features, value, keyboard—whatever. If you are not absolutely convinced that it is the finest calculator value ever offered, return it anytime within that month for a prompt and courteous refund. Truly an unprecedented offer.

EXCHANGE YOUR PRESENT UNIT

Want to exchange your old, outdated calculator for the DataKing 800 without losing too much money? We've got a way. After you are absolutely satisfied with your DataKing 800, send us your outdated unit. JS&A will then send it to a deserving school, non-profit organization, or charitable institution who in turn will send you a letter of appreciation and a certificate acknowledging your contribution. Then use that contribution as a legitimate deduction on your income tax return. You'll be helping somebody in need while justifying the purchase of the latest calculator technology.

TO ORDER BY MAIL

Each unit is supplied with batteries, warranty card and a thorough instruction booklet. To order the 800 simply send your check for $62.45 ($59.95 plus $2.50 postage and handling Illinois residents add $3.00 sales tax) with your name, address, city, state, and zip code to the address shown below. If you wish to charge the 800 to your Master Charge, BankAmericard, Diners Club, or American Express credit card account, call our toll-free number or send us a brief note listing all numbers on your credit card, expiration date, signature and telephone number. Pick up the phone and order your DataKing 800 at no obligation today.

CREDIT CARD BUYERS CALL

(800) 323-5880

IN ILLINOIS CALL (312) 498-6900
Lines open until 11pm (C.S.T.)

JS&A
NATIONAL SALES GROUP
4200 Dundee Rd.
Northbrook, Illinois 60062

This was one of the earliest uses of Liquid Crystal Displays (LCD) in a portable calculator. However, Data King 800's display unit was not very dependable and not easily manufacturable. Rockwell had made one big production run of this calculator and returned to the more reliable LED displays for its other models. The ad is from early 1974.